LOCOMOTIVE Portfolios

OLIVER BULLEID'S LOCOMOTIVES

OLIVER BULLEID'S LOCOMOTIVES

Their Design and Development

COLIN BOOCOCK

First published in Great Britain in 2020 by
Pen and Sword Transport
An imprint of
Pen & Sword Books Ltd
Yorkshire - Philadelphia

Copyright © Colin Boocock, 2020

ISBN 978 1 52674 923 9

The right of Colin Boocock to be identified as Author of this work has been asserted by him in accordance with the Copyright, Designs and Patents Act 1988.

A CIP catalogue record for this book is available from the British Library.

All rights reserved. No part of this book may be reproduced or transmitted in any form or by any means, electronic or mechanical including photocopying, recording or by any information storage and retrieval system, without permission from the Publisher in writing.

Typeset in Palatino by SJmagic DESIGN SERVICES, India.
Printed and bound in India by Replika Press Pvt. Ltd.

Pen & Sword Books Ltd incorporates the Imprints of Pen & Sword Books Archaeology, Atlas, Aviation, Battleground, Discovery, Family History, History, Maritime, Military, Naval, Politics, Railways, Select, Transport, True Crime, Fiction, Frontline Books, Leo Cooper, Praetorian Press, Seaforth Publishing, Wharncliffe and White Owl.

For a complete list of Pen & Sword titles please contact

PEN & SWORD BOOKS LIMITED
47 Church Street, Barnsley, South Yorkshire, S70 2AS, England
E-mail: enquiries@pen-and-sword.co.uk
Website: www.pen-and-sword.co.uk

or

PEN AND SWORD BOOKS
1950 Lawrence Rd, Havertown, PA 19083, USA
E-mail: Uspen-and-sword@casematepublishers.com
Website: www.penandswordbooks.com

Cover photos:

Front cover:
Demonstrating its 'mixed traffic' potential, 'West Country' 4-6-2 34007 *Wadebridge* brings a sixty-wagon freight from Southampton Docks to London through Eastleigh in 1956.

Back cover top left:
War-time 'Austerity' Class Q1 0-6-0 33010 stands outside the shed at Hither Green on 16 August 1959, soon after overhaul at Eastleigh.

Back cover top right:
In May 1958, Bulleid's turf-burning 0-6-6-0 No CC 1 stands outside Inchicore works in Dublin ready for an inspection by the UK's Institution of Locomotive Engineers.

Back cover lower:
Still very new, 'West Country' 4-6-2 21C 102 *Salisbury* shows off its Southern Railway malachite green livery with three yellow stripes. *W.H.C. Kelland*

CONTENTS

The Author 7
Acknowledgements 8
Preface 11
Introduction 13

Chapter 1	The Key Characters 16
Chapter 2	The Southern Railway Inheritance 23
Chapter 3	The Southern Railway's First Diesel Shunters 32
Chapter 4	The Q Class 0-6-0s 35
Chapter 5	The 'Merchant Navy' Class 4-6-2s 41
Chapter 6	The Bulleid-Raworth Co-Co Electric Locomotives 66
Chapter 7	The Q1 Class 0-6-0s 73
Chapter 8	The 'West Country' and 'Battle of Britain' 4-6-2s 79
Chapter 9	The USA Class 0-6-0Ts 99
Chapter 10	The Bulleid/English Electric Diesel Shunters 107
Chapter 11	The Paxman 0-6-0 diesel shunter 110
Chapter 12	The 'Leader' Class 0-6-6-0Ts 113
Chapter 13	The 1Co-Co1 Diesel Electrics 124
Chapter 14	The Irish Inheritance 130
Chapter 15	The Prototype Bo-Bo Diesel Electrics 138

Chapter 16	The F Class B-B Diesel Mechanicals	142
Chapter 17	The A Class Co-Co Diesel Electrics	145
Chapter 18	The B Class A1A-A1A Diesel Electrics	153
Chapter 19	The C Class Bo-Bo Diesel Electrics	157
Chapter 20	The G Class 0-4-0 Diesel Hydraulics	162
Chapter 21	The E Class 0-6-0 Diesel Hydraulics	166
Chapter 22	The Turf-Burning Locomotives	169
Chapter 23	The Rebuilt Bulleid Pacifics	181
Chapter 24	Re-engining the A and C Class Diesel Electrics	203
Chapter 25	Mr Bulleid's Legacies	209

Appendix 1: CIÉ invitations to tender for diesel locomotives, 1952 ... 217
Appendix 2: Availability and reliability of CIÉ diesel traction ... 219
Bibliography ... 220
Index ... 222

THE AUTHOR

Colin Boocock is a life-long railway enthusiast and an experienced railway engineer. He remembers his first sight of a Bulleid 'Merchant Navy' pacific, around 1942 when he was four years old, when the rather dirty No 21C 2 came steaming into Platform 1 at Woking; Colin recalls announcing to his mother, 'It's the "Merchant Navy"!' to which his mother wisely responded, 'It's a "Merchant Navy".'

In some ways, the sight of this impressive machine was an influence in his future. Colin Boocock has remained impressed by Mr Bulleid's Pacifics and much else of his work, so much so indeed that in 1954 he eschewed the idea of going on to sixth form and then to university. Instead he opted to take up an engineering apprenticeship at Eastleigh Locomotive Works and at the age of sixteen he began what evolved as a career of forty-one years in full time work on the railways of Britain. He didn't let go completely even then. For another fourteen years, he did part-time work for a couple of consultancies, finally finishing paid work in 2009 at the age of seventy-one. That did not equal Oliver Bulleid's record however, because OVB, as he was often known, didn't retire from full time work until he was seventy-five!

The author was working at Eastleigh when the Bulleid Pacifics were being rebuilt. In addition to observing at first hand the significant changes being made to them, he was also keen to watch them in service and observe how their characteristics had changed following rebuilding. A period of three years at Brighton as John Click's technical assistant brought Colin into direct contact with people who had known Oliver Bulleid closely as Chief Mechanical Engineer, not only on the Southern Railway but also in Ireland.

Colin is therefore well placed to bring together in this book the history of OVB's original inputs to locomotive engineering during the two long periods when he was CME, from 1937 to 1949 on the SR, and from 1949 to 1958 in Ireland.

ACKNOWLEDGEMENTS

A lot of the information in this book comes from previously-published material either in well-respected earlier books or from responsible web sites. That is inevitable when dealing with a character who was born in 1882 and who died in 1970, and whose professional work was completed by 1958. My research took me to the publications listed in the Bibliography at the back of this book. All are recommended for further reading.

I must immediately acknowledge the inspiration that came from my having worked for John Click at Brighton for about three years either as his Technical Assistant or deputising for him when he was seconded to Eastleigh Locomotive Works as Assistant Works Manager. John knew OVB personally, admired him deeply, and told me a lot that helped me form the image I have of Bulleid as an enigmatic person with several sides to his quite complex character.

I am extremely grateful to Gerald Beesley for his help in ferreting out information in Ireland to add substance to the

Rebuilt 'Battle of Britain' 4-6-2 34077 *603 Squadron* pulls away from Pokesdown, a suburban station near Bournemouth, with a semi-fast from Bournemouth West to London Waterloo on 17 February 1962.

story of Oliver Bulleid's time as CME of CIÉ. Gerry not only shared items from his collection, but also spent some time with Mary and me in Dublin at the headquarters of the Irish Railway Record Society as we sought out drawings, diagrams, photographs and information for this book. I acknowledge the help from the IRRS's photographic archivist, Ciarán Cooney, for seeking out photographs to help complete the illustrations.

All photographs and diagrams used in this book are credited to the copyright owner if known. If there is no credit shown against a caption, the copyright holder is me. In one or two cases, particularly with old material, it is unclear who the original copyright holder is or was. In these cases, I plead tolerance and ask that he or she contacts the publisher. (If you sit in the waiting room at Dublin Connolly station and look at the historical information displayed in a frame on the wall, among the images is a picture of a J15 0-6-0 crossing the Liffey bridge with a suburban train taken in 1957. How Iarnród Éireann got hold of that picture I have no idea. IÉ probably doesn't know it's mine! Maybe I should make a fuss, but – hey – life's too short. I hope others may be so tolerant if I have unwittingly and similarly transgressed with their pictures.)

CPB

During diversions off the main line on 3 April 1960 due to engineering work at New Milton, 34009 *Lyme Regis* takes the Down Bournemouth Belle on a roundabout tour that includes approaching Bournemouth from the west! The light Pacific is crossing the former causeway at Poole Park and is banked by a BR class 4 2-6-0 for the climb at 1 in 60/50 towards Parkstone and Branksome.

Light Pacific 34041 *Wilton* approaches Broadstone, near Wimborne, about to leave the Somerset & Dorset route, with the southbound Pines Express from Manchester London Road to Bournemouth on 10 September 1960. This engine was one of a small number of Pacifics allocated to Bath Green Park depot at the time to handle some of the heavier trains on the S&D line that crossed the Mendip Hills and reached a height above sea level of 811 feet.

PREFACE

There are many books about Oliver Bulleid and his locomotives, but none, as far as I can see, that bring the whole railway story together, though one did come close. Also, I believe that no book describes adequately in one volume every locomotive class that was introduced within the field of Mr Bulleid's engineering and management responsibility during his unusually long career. I have enjoyed reading and re-reading a great deal recently of the published information about Oliver Vaughan Snell Bulleid and his products. These books are listed in the Bibliography. Naturally I have drawn much useful information from these books, as well as from my own experiences as a railway engineering apprentice and then a chartered mechanical engineer and from the contacts I have made over the past seven decades.

For many years, as a way of gathering funds for the wonderful charity Railway Children, I have been giving pictorial shows to societies and clubs. Two of the most popular of these are 'Bulleid's Pacifics', and 'Bulleid's Other Locomotives'. The idea for this book comes directly out of the positive response I have

On his arrival to take up his post in Ireland in 1949, Oliver Bulleid was faced with a national railway system that had only three large locomotives among a huge variety of different steam classes. The three big engines were the B1a class 4-6-0s introduced in 1939 by E.C. Bredin for the Dublin - Cork expresses, exemplified by this picture of 801 *Macha* heading towards Dublin at Clondalkin during the early 1950s. If only the rest of the CIÉ railway system had been up to this standard – but it wasn't! *Denis Morris/Irish Railway Record Society*

had to these talks. In particular, the audiences are always brimming with comments and questions about Mr Bulleid himself and about the more adventurous of his engineering designs.

This interest is hardly surprising. Oliver Bulleid was in many ways an enigma. Some people who knew him found him aloof; others admired him deeply; yet others did everything they could do to discredit his work. For years he appeared content not to strive to advance his own career, and yet was respected enough to be urged to take on the role of Chief Mechanical Engineer of the Southern Railway in 1937. To some people, his locomotives could not be beaten; to others they were extravagant, or unnecessarily complex. What is clear is that Mr Bulleid cannot be passed off as just another chief mechanical engineer. He was undoubtedly an interesting, unusual and in many ways outstanding engineer. The first chapter of this book attempts to highlight the many aspects of his character, and to relate them to his work. It also outlines two of the more significant engineers who had an effect on his locomotives, either in support of his work or in attempting to overcome his less successful innovations.

The rest of the book details all the different types of locomotive that were delivered to the railways over the period when he was a chief mechanical engineer, namely on the Southern Railway from 1937 and with Córas Iompair Éireann from 1949 to his retirement in 1958. One or two of these classes were 'in the pipeline' at the time he took office, and therefore are not technically his, but they are included for completeness. Others are locomotives designed by outside industry in the procurement of which OVB would have played a key role. The most interesting locomotives show how readily he designed them to meet specific needs, and yet how driven he could be to pursue a fundamental idea when he wanted to.

If this book can illustrate Oliver Bulleid's prowess and products in an honest and unbiased way, it will have succeeded.

INTRODUCTION

In the twenty-one years of his career in the posts of Chief Mechanical Engineer (CME) on the Southern Railway in England and on Córas Iompair Éireann in Ireland, Oliver Bulleid could lay some claim to have been responsible for the introduction of nineteen distinct locomotive classes. Not far from one new class of locomotive each year, this rate of design production is high, bearing in mind the vastly different designs involved, the absolute newness of many of them and the relatively small design teams at his disposal. Of these locomotive classes, seven were steam locomotives, eleven were diesels and one was electric. In addition to all this work, he also led the introduction of new designs of coaching stock, multiple units and wagons. He even made time to pioneer an innovative double-deck electric multiple unit design that ran for two decades on the Southern. This book, however, concentrates on his locomotive classes.

The name of Oliver Bulleid is synonymous in many people's

The name of Oliver Bulleid is synonymous with his 'Merchant Navy' class Pacifics. Looking smart in Bulleid's chosen malachite green with 'sunshine' numbers and lettering, 21C 20 *Bibby Line* stands at Nine Elms depot in 1947 when it was just two years old. The running number on the cabside is spaced correctly with the gap after 21C, but the number on the locomotive front has the space between the 21 and the C! *C.C.B. Herbert/Colour-Rail SR86*

minds with his 4-6-2 locomotives, especially the 'Merchant Navy' class. While not the most innovative of his designs, the 'Merchant Navy' class embodied some excellent engineering solutions to the problem of reducing the potential weight of a large locomotive to satisfy the wishes of a particularly cautious chief civil engineer. The result was a free-running locomotive at least as powerful as an LMS 'Duchess' but weighing ten tons less. His Pacifics did what was expected of them. What they cost was a different matter. We discuss their costs with the benefit of hindsight and some relevant facts in the chapter that considers their subsequent rebuilding in the late 1950s and early 1960s.

It is worth recording that the so-called 'light Pacifics' were each about eight tons lighter even than a 'Merchant Navy', an engineering feat that would have defeated many a competent professional. And yet it was Mr Bulleid who asked why the Southern Railway wanted to build 'such an unimaginative design' when confronted with plans for the Q class 0-6-0, and then went on to enlarge that self-same design to produce the successful war-time austerity Class Q1, also an 0-6-0.

Notwithstanding the railway's commitment to the war effort, which was intense under Bulleid's management, the SR succeeded in designing and building three innovative Co-Co electric locomotives to enable the railway's Central Section to move heavier freight trains, with an eye also on the post-war boat train traffic to and from Newhaven.

By the end of the Second World War, the SR was ready with the design for the 'West Country' class light Pacifics, production of which, mainly at Brighton Works, reached a total of 110 locomotives. Two diesel classes emerged just after British Railways had been formed. One was a simple update of the standard English Electric 350bhp shunter. The other included the interesting 1Co-Co1 layout for the SR's first main line diesel locomotives, a design format that was later copied by English Electric and by BR for nearly 400 new diesel main line locomotives.

Also finding time for some experimental work, the well-documented 'Leader' class double-bogie locomotive was paralleled by a relatively unsuccessful 500bhp diesel mechanical freight shunting and transfer locomotive. Differing views over the 'Leader' and other events encouraged Oliver Bulleid and the newly-formed British Railways to part company. Happily, by then he had become well-regarded in Ireland following his help given there as part of the Milne Commission's project to advise on the future for CIÉ's railways. He was offered the post of Consultant Mechanical Engineer there, which he took up in 1949; this was a natural lead-in to his becoming CME by 1951.

In Ireland, at the beginning of the 1950s, the transport operator CIÉ issued a policy document outlining its strategy for future rolling stock acquisition. Well ahead of BR, CIÉ began a comprehensive dieselisation programme based on buying diesel railcars for most passenger services and diesel locomotives for the rest of the traffic. Some steam traction was suggested for future emergency cover in case of oil shortages, and for seasonal traffic such as sugar beet. OVB seized on this latter idea to develop steam locomotives that could burn peat (the Irish call it 'turf'). He also used this opportunity to pursue his passion for full-adhesion double-bogie locomotives. This time the prototype worked, but when it did, the CIÉ Board had already decided to rely entirely on diesels.

The diesels that brought modernisation to Ireland also brought problems, at least in a couple of key cases. While the railcars that came in 1952 from ACV with AEC underframes and equipment and bodies by Park Royal were from an already proven pedigree, the A and C class locomotives that were built by Metropolitan-Vickers were disappointing because their Crossley engines proved to be unreliable. The B class locomotives built by BRC&W with Sulzer engines were successful. Mr Bulleid retired while CIÉ was still struggling to maintain adequate diesel locomotive availability for traffic. It was left to his successor, Dan Herlihy, to cope including having to absorb into the company in late 1958 the Éireann section of the partly steam operated Great Northern Railway, forcing CIÉ to acquire more new diesels urgently.

CIÉ's response to this locomotive crisis was initially to order a small batch of Bo-Bo diesel electrics from General Motors of the USA. Their success in traffic settled the future policy of CIÉ, which homed in on General Motors for all later locomotive orders. The policy led to the wholesale re-engining of the Metro-Vick/Crossley locomotives

Bulleid's turf-burner prototype 0-6-6-0T locomotive in Ireland was first given light trips and then loaded runs within Inchicore Works yard. CC 1 was to a large extent a balanced design, each half being an identical reverse of the other, with the boiler placed centrally and the driving positions in cabs just beyond either end of the boiler. This view in October 1957 shows it on load trials before smoke deflectors and numerals were added; smoke deflectors were soon found to be necessary during test running on the main line at speed. *CIÉ*

with General Motors engines, a fascinating story that we take up in a later chapter.

Rebuilding the Irish diesels was not, of course, the only expensive rebuilding given to Bulleid locomotives. Ninety of his 140 Pacific locomotives were rebuilt at Eastleigh locomotive works between 1956 and 1962 in a programme intended by BR to reduce operating and maintenance costs. OVB stated openly that the rebuilding was not necessary.

He had designed the locomotives for performance, something for which they were renowned. To Bulleid, fuel economy was a secondary consideration. That the rebuilding actually gave BR *both* performance *and* economy was a credit to the Brighton-based team, led by Ron Jarvis, which did the redesign work. The pay-back time was subsequently calculated to have been six-and-a-half years, meaning that BR had got its money back, just.

Oliver Bulleid finally retired at the age of seventy-five. He had clearly enjoyed his work, particularly the solving of complex engineering problems. Indeed, locomotive engineering had been his adult life's interest and passion. The idea of retirement seemingly was alien to him, judging from his reportedly restless moving from one home to another during the twelve years that followed, in search of …. what?

Chapter 1
THE KEY CHARACTERS

Oliver Vaughan Snell Bulleid
'Consistency is the hobgoblin of little minds!'

This is probably the most difficult chapter to write. I was at school when OVB was active on the Southern Railway and Region, and then I became a very junior engineering apprentice in England when he was in charge at Inchicore in Dublin. Thus, though I was sometimes not far geographically from him, I never met the famous man himself. All I write therefore comes from what I have learned from older people who did know him, or from the two definitive published biographies, the one by Sean Day-Lewis and the other by his son, H.A.V. Bulleid, both of which are recommended reading.

Oliver Vaughan Snell Bulleid was born in 1882 at Invercargill in New Zealand. Early in his life, his family moved back to the United Kingdom. Interested in almost everything scientific from an early age, OVB's further education was as a premium apprentice at the Great Northern Railway works at Doncaster. This was a scheme where the young person's family paid the railway for the privilege of receiving a practical and theoretical education in mechanical engineering. British Railways phased this system out in the early 1950s in favour of the engineering apprenticeship in which the railways paid the young person for the work he or she did while undergoing the same or similar training and education, a scheme in which I took part. Bulleid followed this with a number of practical 'hands-on' appointments in the works and depots. By 1912, he had gained the trust of the Chief Mechanical Engineer H.A. Ivatt who appointed him as an assistant in his office, a position in which he clearly excelled. When H.N. Gresley succeeded Ivatt as CME of the LNER, Oliver Bulleid served as his personal assistant.

The between-wars period is a phase in Bulleid's life about which history appears to know little. Gresley was a powerful character, and clearly took credit for all the positive outputs from his team, as is usually the case with a prominent head person in any organisation. The developments that took place under Gresley, however, such as the changes that turned the mediocre performance of the original A1 4-6-2s into the highly successful A3 locomotives, have the ring of more than one brilliant brain supporting his own. One can only conjecture at this distance in time how much influence the relatively young Bulleid had with his esteemed chief. There is evidence that OVB was fruitful in developing contacts with outstanding engineers such as André Chapelon, Bugatti and Ricardo, and this enabled the success for example of the A4 class locomotives that embodied ideas learned from two of these contacts. Indeed, OVB is credited with the design of the aerofoil curves employed in the streamlining of the A4s. The use of internal streamlining of steam pipe runs, and the subsequent fitment of Kylchap exhaust systems, illustrates experience learned from Chapelon's work in France.

When the London & North Eastern Railway sent the

Oliver Vaughan Snell Bulleid, not long before his retirement. *John Click*

The Key Characters • 17

OVB's career on the GNR and LNER convinced him of the benefits of Gresley's 'big engine policy'. This was epitomised by the high speed successes of the A4 class Pacifics. Bulleid has been credited with the inspiration for the design of the aerofoil-shaped curves on these streamlined locomotives.

Sir Nigel Gresley's traction policy reached its zenith with the P2 class 2-8-2s, the first of these being the famous 2001 *Cock o' the North*. OVB was the engineer who led the team that took 2001 across to France for road testing and trials on the Vitry static test plant. *Internet*

Class P2 2-8-2 2001 to the Vitry test plant in France, Oliver Bulleid accompanied the locomotive. There is no doubt that this locomotive's power and performance was a significant influence on his thinking when not long afterwards he gained responsibility as the SR's new CME for taking forward the Southern Railway Board's aspirations for future new, more powerful locomotives.

While on the Southern, OVB gained a reputation for 'not suffering fools gladly'. People who could not keep up with him mentally, and there would have been many, could not connect with his fertile sifting of ideas, his sometimes seemingly dictatorial approach, and his ability to give one instruction early in the day only to change it completely a few hours later. John Click, who had for a while been Bulleid's assistant in Ireland during the development of the turf-burning locomotive, told me more than once of an incident with OVB. In response to a quick change to an instruction that he had given earlier in the day, someone made the mistake of saying, 'Mr Bulleid, you are not consistent!', to which OVB responded with the eminent put-down: 'Consistency is the hobgoblin of little minds!'[1]

OVB was by and large a good engineer with flashes of brilliance. He was practical in that he would incorporate in his designs existing practice where that was good; he was able to improve on what was mediocre, and if there was a need to develop something original he liked to go back to basic engineering principles. He learned from practices in France and in the USA, visiting those places to make direct contact with the engineers responsible. Hence it was not surprising that his 'Merchant Navy' class design included much that was identifiably French practice, and other features that came directly from American experience. We discuss this engineering background more in the forthcoming and quite long chapter on the 'Merchant Navy' class.

As a reportedly somewhat autocratic engineer, OVB nonetheless could be down-to-earth when necessary. He was adamant that his engines needed to be acceptable to drivers and firemen, and he made efforts to discuss with them personally many of his ideas, and indeed to extract ideas from his talks with them. Thus his Pacifics were seen to be in advance of other railways' locomotives with regard to the layout of controls in the cab, not just for the driver who could reach all he needed from his seat. He also made life easier for the fireman who was treated with a power-operated fire-door and two straightforwardly reliable live-steam injectors grouped together on the fireman's side of the cab, as well as electric illumination of important components.

OVB was present on many of the early test runs of his new creations, to learn from the experiences and also to advise on the locomotives' handling. In some ways, like many adventurous engineers, he needed to be thick-skinned. No-one ever made advances in engineering design without being challenged by performance issues, and OVB's designs were no exception. For example, he had been supporting the idea that a 'Merchant Navy' could pull a twenty-coach train from London Waterloo to Exeter, so one was laid on; this was attended by many of 'the great and the good' among senior management. While the early part of the run went as planned, the locomotive then proceeded to embarrass everyone aboard by breaking a rocker shaft, rendering the valve events such that the trial could not continue. In another chapter we discuss this issue in engineering terms.

One issue that bugged the Bulleid Pacifics, particularly before they were rebuilt, was their propensity to slipping when starting a heavy train, a feature they shared with some of the Thompson Pacifics at least. Around 1961, the small record company Transacord published an 'extended play' 45rpm record of the sounds of Bulleid Pacifics. John Click told me that he played this record to OVB one day in his office. After hearing the sounds of three departures by 'Merchant Navy' class locomotives on expresses from the Up main platform at Salisbury, each of which slipped its coupled wheels characteristically, he declared emphatically, 'Those are not my engines!'

He was equally dismissive of British Railways' project to rebuild the Pacifics on more conventional lines. One author tells that OVB suggested it would be better for the engines to be scrapped than rebuilt, though one suspects that this might have been said tongue in cheek.

---

1. This was a common misquotation of Ralph Waldo Emerson's assertion in a paper he wrote on the subject of self-reliance. It is accessible on the internet if you want to know more.

His move to Ireland surprised several people. Historically, the moves of Irish locomotive superintendents to English railways had been more usual, *viz.* J.A.F. Aspinall, H.A. Ivatt, J.G. Robinson and R.E.L. Maunsell, all of whom served in Ireland before moving to Britain as CMEs there. His appointment in Ireland was, however, unsurprising, following his earlier input to the Milne Commission's work, and Ireland did need some new thinking following so many years of partial stagnation in investment, bearing in mind how much change they knew the railways there were soon going to have to face. His arrival in Ireland shows another aspect of his character. It is written that, soon after he had arrived at Inchicore in Dublin, he had a crucifix placed prominently in his office. Oliver Bulleid had, as a young man in the First World War in Belgium, consciously moved across from the Anglican faith of his forebears to join the Roman Catholic church; in Dublin this allegiance would have been a help in breaking the ice that might otherwise surround an odd Englishman turning up in Ireland. Others have recorded that at Inchicore, his office fire was always ablaze with the temperature as high as 80 degrees Fahrenheit, such did the ageing OVB feel the cold.

Later chapters in this book cover the diverse fleets of locomotives that CIÉ introduced during his time there as CME. That his fertile brain was active right up to his retirement was evident, particularly in his singular attention to the prototype turf-burning 0-6-6-0T locomotive. Happily, in an appendix to another book, John Click has reported that the trials of this interesting machine showed that the turf burner achieved technically most of what it set out do. Like the 'Leader' before it, however, the locomotive was in the end too heavy for use across much of the railway system.

Retirement can be quite a shock for a person who has been so dedicated to his or her work as had OVB. He did not retire until he was seventy-five years old. To start a new life at an advanced age must have been difficult for him. Biographies show that in retirement he was somewhat restless as to where he wanted to set up home. He moved about, choosing houses in pleasant places in the south of the UK, and even spending time living in Malta where the climate might have suited him better.

But, for the purposes of this book's subject, Oliver Bulleid's locomotives, I believe we should remember OVB as the adventurous and dedicated mechanical engineer that he was. We can thank him that he gave the Southern Railway and Region the locomotives that they needed (with perhaps two exceptions), and if the Crossley two-stroke diesel engine type had lived up to what the manufacturers had promised, that accolade would have applied fully to Ireland, too.

Ronald Guy Jarvis

Ron Jarvis, as he was always known, had his early career on the London Midland & Scottish Railway and the LM Region of BR. Born in 1911 amid a family living in Harpenden, his engineering career began in 1928 as a privileged apprentice (similar to the premium apprenticeship enjoyed by Bulleid earlier on the GNR) at Derby locomotive works. As an LMS man through and through, it must have been with some curiosity that he moved to the Southern in 1950 as Chief Technical Assistant in the Chief Mechanical & Electrical Engineer's (M&EE) department at Brighton. At this time, Robert Riddles was BR's Member of the Executive for M&EE. His strategy to move forward on standardisation was to spread his ideas quickly around the design offices of the former 'Big Four' railways by ensuring that key people who supported his ideas were in place in all the M&EE design offices.

Ron Jarvis was put in charge of all M&EE design offices on the Southern Region. This placed him in pole position to recommend how or whether Bulleid's 'Leader' class project should further progress, and again he was the right man in the right place when BR decided to let the Southern proceed with its proposal to rebuild the Bulleid Pacifics.

Ron Jarvis was a very different man from Bulleid, having been brought up within the Midland Railway and the LMS, and it was thus not surprising that he more readily adapted to the requirements of Robert Riddles when leading the design of BR standard locomotives at Brighton. It was natural that Jarvis would be chosen to lead the Bulleid Pacific rebuilding project.
J.M. Jarvis collection

During my own time at Brighton, from 1960 to 1963, I was technical assistant to John Click, and got to know him and also Ron Jarvis sufficiently well. I could see that Jarvis was a very competent engineer, steeped in the practices of the former LMS Railway (as were many of BR's senior M&EE engineers) but not hidebound by them. Under his guidance, the Brighton drawing office had produced three excellent designs of BR standard locomotives: the competent Class 4 4-6-0s, the very successful Class 4 2-6-4Ts, and the brilliant 9F 2-10-0s. How the Southern got away with curved sides to the cabs and tanks on the 2-6-4Ts, one can only conjecture!

But that quirk gave these engines the distinctive appearance that marked them out as a winning design. Curved sides of course were a Bulleid feature on his Pacifics, Q1s, and main line diesels, and the Brighton design office managed later on to add the same feature to the Bo-Bo electric locomotives for the Kent Coast electrification scheme as well. No-one else did this, so the BR 2-6-4Ts, uniquely among BR steam locomotives, carried this distinctive Bulleid feature.

As a former LMS man who knew the aims of Robert Riddles at BR HQ, it was not surprising that Ron Jarvis managed to design the rebuilt Bulleid Pacifics in such a way that they looked a bit like Britannias (from a distance), and still incorporated curves where they looked right. That the rebuilds were so successful is a credit to the Jarvis design philosophy, which we discuss further in Chapter 23.

Jarvis also managed the design processes that developed the innovative electro-diesel Bo-Bos that the Southern insisted in calling JAs and JBs, the E6000 series locomotives, some of which are still seeing active employment in the twenty-first century as Class 73/9s.

On his return to Derby, by which time traction and rolling stock design had been centralised in the Railway Technical Centre there,

The result of rebuilding the 'Merchant Navy' class was a group of more efficient locomotives that retained good performance and improved running costs as well as gaining significant good looks. 35018 *British India Line* was photographed at Southampton Central soon after re-entering service after rebuilding.

Ron Jarvis was, I have read, deeply involved in the design of the high speed diesel train (HST) power cars, again an innovative and iconic piece of kit that is still with us.

In retirement, Jarvis moved house to live within easy distance of Porthmadog in North Wales. I met him there on one occasion when the Institution of Mechanical Engineers Railway Division, Midlands Section, ran a trip from Derby to the Ffestiniog Railway. The by-then rather frail Jarvis joined the party for the run on the two-feet gauge railway from Blaenau Ffestiniog to Porthmadog and discussed among much else the interesting work he was doing in physically restoring old four-wheeled 'vintage' carriages for the FR. The development of the curves joining the timber-framed roof and ends was, he said, taxing even his engineering knowledge, as he worked on one carriage at a time in his back garden.

John G. Click

When I met John Click for the first time it was at an interview in 1960 at Brighton where he was considering whether I, among others, was a suitable candidate to be his technical assistant. He was then thirty-five years old and I was twenty-two. I was installed in the office next to his in the former London, Brighton & South Coast Railway's HQ offices just beyond the platform ends at Brighton station. I was at his beck-and-call whenever he pressed the buzzer button on his desk! John was at that time Technical Assistant to the M&EE (Workshops) A.E. Hoare. That section of the Southern Region M&EE department HQ was tasked with managing the maintenance and overhaul of the SR's steam locomotive fleet, including its inevitable run-down and eventual elimination. The team also managed the SR's plant and machinery department, and actively took part in the development or closure of main works until the BR Workshops Division was formed in 1962 and took them over.

In 1955, John Click had been an active engineer within the Rugby locomotive testing station. He had been prised out of there to assist Oliver Bulleid on loan to CIÉ in Ireland when OVB had found a lack of the particular technical expertise and management energy he needed to make progress with the turf-burner project. We are indebted to John's reports and photographs as they form a useful background to that project.

During my stay at Brighton, John showed clearly his admiration for OVB and it is through him that a number of Bulleid's statements have come into the public arena. John Click was indeed a forceful character, and at times had upset people he worked with, many of whom could not cope with his mood swings. As it happened, I had had some experience of meeting that challenge in my earlier life; I had learned that the 'down' periods would eventually pass by; one just had to live through them. There would soon then be 'up' periods in which John would be a joy to know, and in a very productive way.

When a situation demanded action, John would confront any resistance head-on. I recall a day in late 1960 when I visited Lancing carriage works where we had been trialling USA 0-6-0T 30073 as a possible means of replacing the ancient Stroudley A1 0-6-0T that shunted there. The works driver had failed the USA on the grounds that, because the engine was right hand drive, it meant that the driver had to face backwards when shunting carriages in and out of the different shops due to the left hand curve. He did say, with a degree of admiration that, 'This engine could pull a house!' I studied the valve gear and reversing gear and realised that the Meccano-like assembly could easily be reassembled from right to left hand drive with almost no engineering input. However, the Lancing Works Manager would have none of it; his driver had failed the engine on safety grounds and that was that. When John Click arrived back in the office I briefed

John Click was photographed wearing a boiler suit while taking part in running trials of the 'Leader' 36001.
John Click collection, courtesy National Railway Museum

him on this. John was on the phone immediately to the Works Manager and soon had a plan. About that time, he was being asked to move across to Eastleigh locomotive works as acting Assistant Works Manager there and, soon after he had moved to Eastleigh, a USA dock tank was converted there to left-hand-drive as I had suggested, and to my surprise it was painted in lined SR carriage stock green, an input straight from John Click's enthusiasm for railways. DS236 looked superb and was immediately accepted with open arms by all at Lancing!

John Click was also deeply involved when 34064 *Fighter Command* was fitted with a Giesl ejector exhaust system at Eastleigh. He liaised on site with Dr. Giesl-Gieslingen himself and made sure the inventor's experience was put to good use and that the device was fitted correctly.

In 1964, John had a subsequent career move to a senior production engineering position in the recently-formed headquarters of the British Railways Workshops Division at Derby, an organisation to which I had been promoted a year before. His reputation went before him. One day I was asked by my boss, Jack Jones, if I would be able to work with John again as they were thinking of taking him on as a production engineer, and I said I would. On occasions while on the Southern Region, when facing senior management's resistance to some of his ideas, John had proffered his resignation at moments of high emotion. This was always declined, as his volatility was tolerated there. He resigned again during a contretemps at Derby, but senior management there was much less forgiving than on the Southern and John suddenly found himself out of a job.

John Click's next career move was into teaching, something he enjoyed as he had an affinity with bright children and coped with them better than he did with many adults. I realise in retrospect that his invitation to me some time in the 1970s to visit him in his modest flat in south London was actually a privilege, for me that is. In this role, as host, he was essentially a private man, and to be welcomed by him as a friend was something I shall continue to cherish.

In preparing for this book, I have been able to look through John's negatives that are held for posterity in the National Railway Museum. I already knew that he was an accomplished railway photographer. I did not know until seeing this collection that his interest had spread to the narrow gauge railways of North Wales, particularly the Talyllyn and the Festiniog (as it was spelled then) which he had photographed quite comprehensively.

Around 1987, I learned sadly that John had collapsed at a bus stop while going to work and had died aged just 62.

John Click liked nothing better than to support the sometimes imaginative engineering proposed by Mr Bulleid. He was called to Ireland to help OVB with the turf-burner project. The two engineers are seen in deep discussion at Inchicore Works in Dublin.

Chapter 2

THE SOUTHERN RAILWAY INHERITANCE

For someone who had spent a couple of decades working on a 'big engine' railway, to be suddenly taking over the mechanical engineering function on the Southern Railway in 1937 could have been quite a shock. That railway was intensely engaged in electrifying many of its suburban and shorter main line routes, entirely operated by electric multiple units. Steam locomotive building was at an unusually low ebb. The only large locomotives on the SR were the sixteen 'Lord Nelson' class 4-6-0s.

Recent history was also to affect O.V.S. Bulleid's work significantly. In 1927, there had been an accident at Sevenoaks, with significant loss of lives, in which a K class 2-6-4T hauling an express train at around 60mph had yawed or rolled at such magnitude that the track had given way under it. The SR Board wisely decided to split the responsibility for the crash equally between Richard Maunsell, the CME, and George Ellson, the Chief Civil Engineer (CCE). Each had to take specific action to ensure such a disaster could not happen again. Maunsell was tasked with altering the locomotives to remove the yaw characteristic for good, and Ellson had to upgrade the track on all the SR's main lines.

With electrification forging ahead, the need to rebuild the 2-6-4Ts into 2-6-0 tender engines and the cost of upgrading so many miles of track, no wonder the SR had not afforded to build many new locomotives in the 1930s. In that decade, it built only 74 steam locomotives and most of those were in the first few years.

R.E.L. Maunsell retired due to ill health, which is how the CME post became available to Mr Bulleid. George Ellson, however, was still in place as CCE when Bulleid arrived; George was to be doubly cautious when confronted with potential new designs for large locomotives that might cause damage to his track.

OVB was able quickly to assess what the SR Board and its Traffic Department wanted for future locomotive building. The key need was indeed some 'big engines' that could lead the way in improving journey times and timekeeping on the main lines to Dover and the south-west, lines that were not likely to be electrified in the foreseeable future. Later chapters in this book take this story to its fulfilment.

Most new CMEs also look to see what improvements they can quickly make to their inherited locomotive stock, and OVB was no exception. He saw potential for a cheap modification to the existing SR front-line fleet that would improve the steaming of those locomotives that needed improvement. The 'Lord Nelsons' were judged not to be achieving their potential, and some of the Urie 4-6-0s, then at half-life but still working important services, would benefit from better steam events and lower exhaust pressure. The new CME took a ride from London Victoria on a 'Lord Nelson' hauling a heavy Dover express. He expressed the view that it was basically a good engine but needed 'freeing up' at the front end.

The LNs received new cylinders with longer travel piston valves of larger diameter together with Lemaître five-jet blastpipes exhausting into much wider chimneys. The Lemaître system, developed in Belgium by Maurice Lemaître, was simple to apply. The single blast pipe casting was replaced by a new

The Southern Railway had put most capital funds into electrification during the 1920s and 1930s, and had done little in the later pre-war years to update its steam locomotive fleet. The biggest engines were the sixteen 'Lord Nelson' 4-6-0s. No 858 *Lord Duncan* heads the Golden Arrow boat train in pre-war years. *Internet*

casting with five smaller exhaust outlets arranged in a circle. The five exhaust streams shooting up through the smokebox had the effect of supporting each other as they entered the unusually wide diameter chimney, providing less resistance which reduced exhaust back pressure. The outside area of the five exhaust cones when compared with that from a single blastpipe presented a much greater area of suction in the smokebox, and so created a higher smokebox vacuum to draw the fire gases through the boiler tubes and flues. It worked on the 'Nelsons', which had long fire grates that some firemen struggled to cover evenly with coal.[2]

The first twenty 'King Arthur' locomotives had been built from 1918 as Class N15 for the London & South Western Railway under CME Robert Urie. While, in their day, these solidly-built two-cylinder 4-6-0s had been a great improvement on the Drummond 4-6-0s of previous decades, by the late 1930s they were regarded as

---

2. The blast pipe patented by Lemaître also had a central nozzle which was designed to be variable. OVB had clearly decided to dispense with that, probably in pursuit of the simplicity of a casting with a ring of five nozzles.

The Southern Railway Inheritance • 25

Under Bulleid's improvement programme, all 'Lord Nelsons' received Lemaître exhausts with the characteristically wide chimney. This is 30855 *Robert Blake* at Eastleigh in BR days; 30855 was one of fourteen that also were given new cylinders with better steam passages and corresponding extended smokeboxes.

Two 'Lord Nelsons' missed out on the new cylinders but at least had the new exhaust system. These were 30851 *Sir Francis Drake* and 30863 *Lord Rodney*, the latter seen at Eastleigh in 1959.

somewhat sluggish, heavy sloggers; they did not run with the panache of the later Maunsell N15s. OVB tried several solutions with these, including lining up the cylinder bores, different arrangements of piston valves, changes in steam and exhaust passages, and Lemaître blastpipes and chimneys. Different engines received different versions and mixtures of these modifications, some not being modified at all, so one assumes that the results were inconclusive. One Maunsell 'Arthur', No 792 *Sir Hervis de Revel*, received a Lemaître exhaust around 1946; this was removed in 1952, the engine being returned to standard.

The 'Schools' class (V) 4-4-0s, Maunsell's star design by all accounts, were excellent machines that British Railways classified 5P when calculating their place in the hierarchy of express passenger locomotives. They had been designed under Maunsell's guidance to work up to ten-coach express trains over the hilly routes from London to Hastings, Dover and Ramsgate, and were specifically short in length to fit on 50ft turntables. Nonetheless, the 'Schools' class were regarded as being as powerful as a 'King Arthur', their only drawback being their meagre 42 tons

The next biggest SR express engines were the N15 class, named as the 'King Arthurs'. There were three batches of these. OVB believed the earliest, the Urie machines from the London & South Western Railway, needed improvement. This is a pre-war view of 739 *King Leodegrance* at Winchester on a Down Bournemouth train. *Colour-Rail SR6*

The Southern Railway Inheritance • 27

30737 *King Uther* at Bournemouth Central displays the Lemaître chimney which a few Urie N15s received. On others were tried different cylinders with better steam passages, and a couple of the wide chimney ones had smoke deflectors angled outwards. 30755 had larger-diameter cylinders. Apart from 30755 which was thereafter known as a strong engine, the modifications were less than conclusive in terms of performance improvement.

None of Maunsell's first batch of N15s was modified by Bulleid, and only one of the later 'Scotch Arthurs' received a wide chimney. No 457 *Sir Bedivere* of the first batch remained basically in its original form throughout its life.

28 • OLIVER BULLEID'S LOCOMOTIVES

The most efficient express engines on the SR were undoubtedly the forty 'Schools' class 4-4-0s such as 30905 *Tonbridge* seen here at Bournemouth Central in 1957.

OVB had half the 'Schools' class fitted with Lemaître exhausts before it was declared unnecessary on such a good locomotive design. 30901 *Westminster* shows off its wide chimney at Eastleigh in 1955.

adhesion weight. OVB nonetheless began a programme of fitting Lemaître exhausts to the 'Schools' class. Experience soon showed that the effect was to enable the locomotives to run a bit harder, but at the cost of burning more coal and throwing cinders up through the wide chimney. As with the Maunsell 'Arthur', it proved difficult to improve on an already excellent locomotive design. In the end only half the forty 'Schools' class locomotives were so modified, there being no financial benefit from continuing.

In the 1930s, the Southern Railway was getting a bad press due to season ticket holders[3] complaining about frequent delays to their journeys (it was ever thus!). The General Manager sought to brighten up the railway's public image. Up to that time, the express locomotives were painted a drab shade of olive green, decorated with black-and-cream lining, and with somewhat classical if old-fashioned lettering. Carriages were in the same colour. Other engines were just plain black.

Oliver Bulleid is credited with finding a green colour that was bright enough almost to shock, yet was sufficiently durable to shine through layers of dirt reasonably well. Thus was born the shade of green we all know as 'malachite'. Bulleid is also credited with introducing the 'sunshine' lettering style of sans-serif, shaded bold letters and numbers that spoke of a 'modern' railway. Wartime intervened before all the SR's front line passenger locomotives and carriages had been so repainted, and indeed the war conditions decreed a general livery of plain black locomotives for the duration. But from 1946, malachite green engines quickly became the norm, including even medium-sized locomotives such as the Brighton Atlantics and the L1 4-4-0s which looked very fetching in their new, bright colours. A range of new carriages also appeared with their designer's characteristic curved profile.

A practical action that OVB introduced was the removal of snifting valves from the superheater headers of Maunsell and earlier engines. These were visible on the outside of the smokebox top, and would 'snift' whenever the regulator was opened or closed. Their purpose was to avoid a vacuum arising in the steam passages during coasting (i.e. running without power applied) with the accompanying risk of cinders and soot being drawn into the cylinders and causing scoring of the polished working surfaces. Their removal was to simplify maintenance, and was accompanied by an instruction to enginemen that they must coast with the regulator very slightly open.

---

3. 'Season ticket holders': We now use the term 'commuters', but in the 1950s this word was not in common use in the UK. A letter in the Daily Telegraph in the early 1960s offered a definition of the word 'commuter' as: "A regular daily passenger of long standing."

Otherwise, the Southern was largely populated by old, medium or small sized steam locomotives of a wide variety of types. This T9 4-4-0 leaving St Denys in 1956 with a stopping train to Portsmouth dated from 1900, for example.

Branch lines in the south-west and on the Isle of Wight were still served by Adams Class O2 0-4-4Ts, originally designed in the 1880s for Waterloo suburban services. This one had just received a full general overhaul at Eastleigh in 1959.

Goods engines were largely old 0-6-0s from the pre-grouping railways, though there were also the twenty Q class that the Southern had designed and planned to build at the time OVB arrived on the SR in 1937. One of these latter engines, after being fitted with the Lemaître exhaust to improve its free running, was engaged on boat train duty at Lymington Pier in summer 1958.

The Southern Railway Inheritance • 31

Among the most numerous SR steam locomotives, and also among the more modern in concept, were the Maunsell 2-6-0s. This is three-cylinder U1 No 31903 leaving Bournemouth Central with the daily train to Brighton in 1954.

'Lord Nelson' with Lemaître exhaust diagram

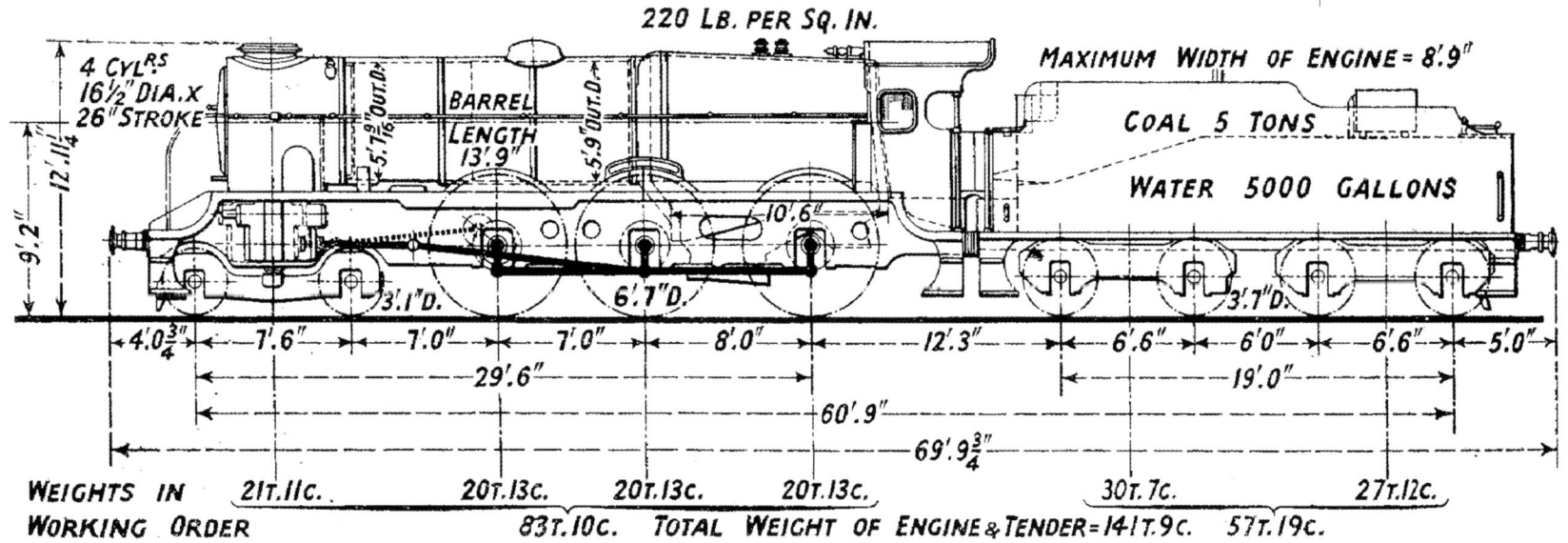

Chapter 3
THE SR'S FIRST DIESEL SHUNTERS

Introduced in 1937, it is certain that the Southern Railway's first three diesel electric shunting locomotives had been ordered before Oliver Bulleid arrived to take up his post of CME. They were built at Ashford works to a design not dissimilar to another small batch of locomotives introduced at that time on the Great Western Railway. The design clearly emanated from the firm of English Electric. It was an early example of 350bhp diesel electric locomotive that used two traction motors that rested on the outer axles and drove them through gearing. The locomotive design used outside frames (in the fashion of many nineteenth century steam locomotives) in order to provide enough room between the frames for the width of the traction motors and their drives. The wheels were coupled by means of coupling rods on fly cranks pressed and keyed on the outer ends of the axles. The traction motor-to-axle gear drive used single reduction gears which, according to Southern sources, had been intended to enable the locomotives' use on short-distance freight transfers between nearby yards. The gear ratio limited the starting tractive effort to 30,000lbf.

The diesel engine was the well-known naturally-aspirated four-stroke six-cylinders in-line English Electric 6KT model with 350 brake horse power output. It was coupled to a direct-current generator which fed current to the traction motors. Compared with more modern locomotives, the control system was simple. The driver's power handle, when moved forward one notch, linked the motors electrically to the generator, producing enough volts to begin movement. Further notching raised the engine speed progressively via its governor and thus increased the voltage and power available to the motors.

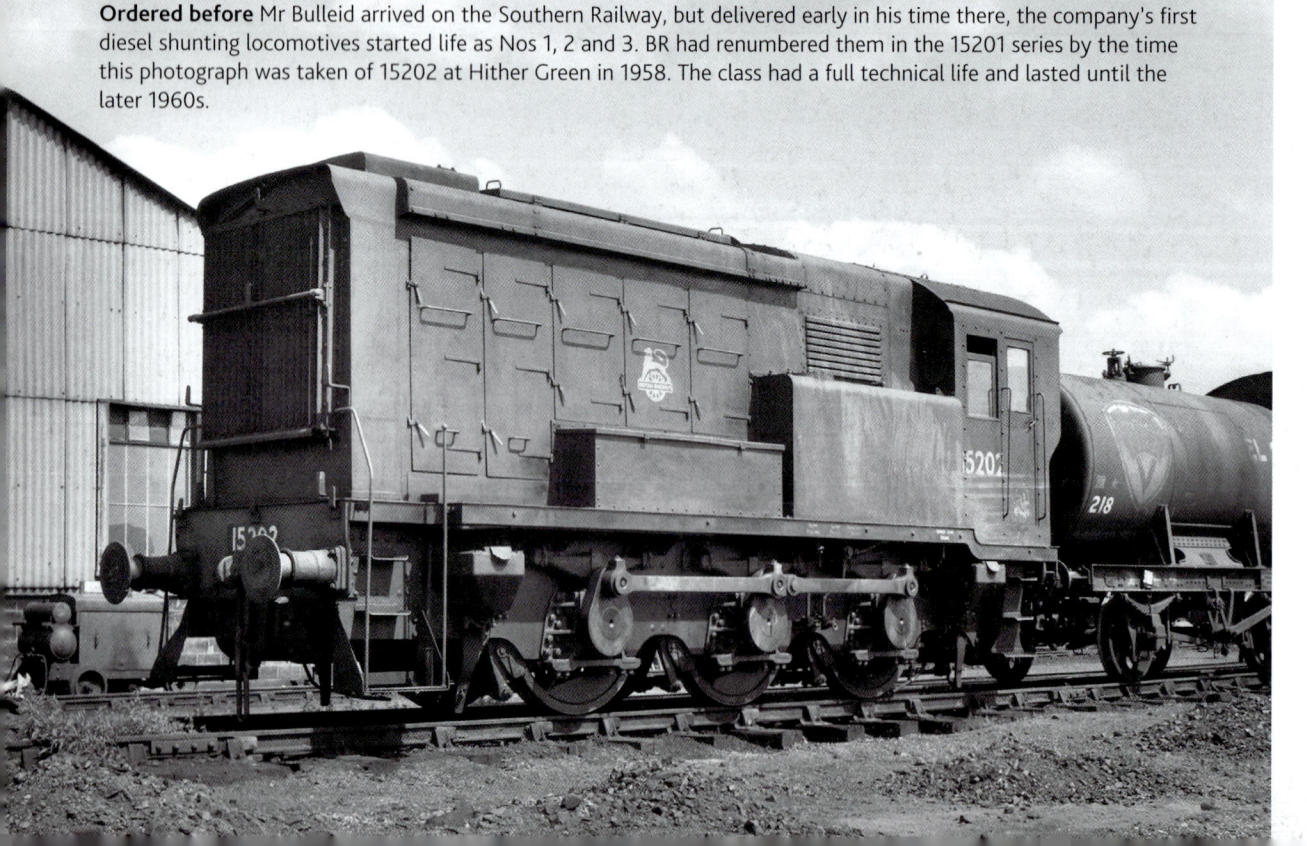

Ordered before Mr Bulleid arrived on the Southern Railway, but delivered early in his time there, the company's first diesel shunting locomotives started life as Nos 1, 2 and 3. BR had renumbered them in the 15201 series by the time this photograph was taken of 15202 at Hither Green in 1958. The class had a full technical life and lasted until the later 1960s.

The cab at one end of the frame was roomy and offered reasonable lookout for shunting and buffering up. At the front of the frame were wide steps on which a shunter could ride and be ready for coupling and uncoupling. There were sandboxes feeding the outer wheels, one each side for forward movement and one each side for backward.

In the front of the cab was an equipment compartment that contained the electrical control system and compressor for the locomotive air brakes. Beyond that, within the tall engine compartment, was the engine and generator, and forward of that was the cooling system with the radiator placed vertically at the front of the body. The body sides were mainly removable or hinged panels that enabled staff to gain access for servicing and maintenance. Outside on either side, immediately in front of the cab, were two fuel tanks, and forward of these the battery boxes.

Looking at the design of these locomotives with the benefit of hindsight, I have to admit the whole locomotive was a well-thought-through concept.

15203 of the same class was tried at Lancing Carriage Works in 1960 to assess its suitability for shunting the east yard there so as to replace the ageing A1X class 0-6-0Ts. The trial was successful, but the SR operators then declared that the diesel could not be spared for this duty. A BR Drewry 0-6-0 diesel mechanical was then tried, but proved to be unsatisfactory due to jerks from the gear changing process. In the end the works had to accept a steam shunter in the form of a modified USA 0-6-0T.

Knowing that it is rare for prototypes to last nearly thirty years in regular traffic, as these three machines did, they can be regarded as worthy precursors to the many similar such locomotives that flooded our railways in the post-war years.

The Southern Railway numbered these locomotives 1, 2 and 3, triplicating numbers carried by three Class T1 0-4-4Ts and also three of the four Class E1 0-6-0Ts on the Isle of Wight (though the latter numbers officially had a 'W' prefix that was not included on the painted numbers). BR renumbered the diesels 15201 to 15203. I am uncertain whether the three diesel shunters were painted black or olive green in Southern Railway days, but they were certainly always black in BR days. The three locomotives were based for most of their lives one each at Norwood Junction, Hither Green and Ashford for working in the large freight yards at those important locations. In 1963, one was sent for trial at Lancing carriage works when the Region wanted to replace the seriously ageing Stroudley 'Terrier' 0-6-0Ts that shunted the yard there. The trial of 15203 was successful, but then the operating department thought better of it and decided that the diesel could not be spared.

Class	0-6-0 diesel electric
Designed by	English Electric Co.
Builder	SR Ashford
Number in class	3
Introduced	1937
Diesel engine	English Electric 6-cylinder 6KT
Diesel engine rating	350bhp
Traction generator (dc)	EE 801/7D
Traction motors (dc)	DK129-2D (2) with single-reduction gears
Driving wheels diameter	4ft 6in spoked
Tractive effort	30,000lbf
Maximum speed	30mph
Train heat	None
Weight in w.o.	55tons 5cwt
SR number series	1-3
BR number series	15201-15203

Chapter 4
THE Q CLASS 0-6-0s

By 1937, the Southern Railway's Traffic Department was lumbered with large numbers of very old steam locomotives on its secondary routes, many dating back to the nineteenth century. This was a direct result of the SR channelling much of its recent capital investment into electrification schemes. A need to begin to build replacements for these old classes had prompted the production of drawings for a more modern freight locomotive that was large enough to be useful, yet light enough to traverse nearly all the company's railway lines. The Q class was to meet this requirement.

It was a neat locomotive with a big enough boiler pressed at 200lbf/sq in and fitted with a Belpaire firebox with a grate area just short of 22sq ft, giving it more power than other 0-6-0s on the SR. Weighing 49 tons 10cwt, the Q class was universally able to travel far and wide on the SR. It incorporated a design of inside cylinders that had developed during the period when Maunsell was rebuilding the mediocre Classes D and E 4-4-0s of the South Eastern & Chatham Railway into the high-performing D1 and E1 locomotives. The cylinders in these rebuilds used outside steam admission and inside exhaust emission, giving an almost straight, clear path for exhaust steam to escape from between the piston valves straight up the blastpipe. The performances put up by these modestly-dimensioned 4-4-0s were outstanding. This feature particularly was to give the Q class a free-running characteristic that belied the power classification that BR bestowed upon it, namely 4F. The 0-6-0s may have looked rather like an LMS 4F, but there the similarity ended.

There is indeed no doubt that the outline of a Southern Q bears resemblance to an LMS product.

In pre-war Southern Railway days, nearly-new Q 0-6-0 540 eases off depot, probably at Norwood Junction. The engine sports a standard Maunsell-style single chimney with capuchon. *John Neve/David Heys collection*

This resulted from the move in the early twentieth century from Derby to the Ashford drawing office of one James Clayton who brought with him some of the styling that the LMS was applying to updates of former Midland Railway designs. Of note were the shape of the cab sides and roofs and the flat tender sides with scalloped ends; Ashford applied some of these features to the D1 and E1 4-4-0s and to the new L1 class, as well as the Maunsell 2-6-0s. The visual similarity of the Q drawings to the LMS 4F was very likely what prompted Bulleid's comment about the Q as being an 'unimaginative design' when he first saw it on the drawing board. This would have been before he realised the significance of the cylinder and exhaust arrangement with outside admission, a feature he later incorporated in all his Pacifics.

The Southern Railway under Maunsell had fitted most of its new designs of locomotives with valve gear of the Walschaerts type that had proved over many decades to suit the fast running of passenger locomotives. For the Q class however the designers chose Stephenson's valve gear, a choice related to the engines' intended duties, namely slogging away on heavy freights for which

Mr Bulleid was keen to upgrade the Qs with Lemaître exhausts and wide chimneys. The chimney was fabricated in his relatively simplistic way rather than using a heavy iron casting as was traditional. In the later 1950s, 30531 stands at Eastleigh shed after overhaul in the nearby works. This picture illustrates the slight taper of the boiler barrel, as well as the typically LMS-style cab and tender shapes that sprung directly from the influence of one Clayton whom Maunsell had poached from Derby to Ashford drawing office in the early twentieth century.

As well as being useful general goods engines, the Q class were free-running enough to manage quite heavy special or seasonal passenger trains. This is 30530 arriving at Brockenhurst with a ten-coach boat train from Lymington Pier to London Waterloo on 25 June 1955. At this station the Q would give way to a main line locomotive for the trunk run to the capital.

the characteristics of Stephenson's gear were generally adequate. Walchaerts gear has fixed lap and lead, whereas Stephenson's gear gives a shorter lead at short cut-offs, not an ideal characteristic for running fast passenger trains where a longer lead at speed is beneficial. The use of Stephenson's valve gear did not, however, prevent the Qs putting up some splendid performances on occasions when hauling passenger trains, so versatile did these engines prove to be. The engines had steam reversers of the successful type inherited from the SE&CR.

The Q class locomotives were built at Eastleigh locomotive works and the first was delivered in 1938, a year after OVB had arrived on the Southern. It was probably the approach of war, as well as Bulleid's urgent work on designing the Pacifics and electric locomotives, that capped the production of the Q class to just twenty examples. After the war, they were generally allocated to the Western and Central Sections of the SR, mostly at Eastleigh and Norwood Junction sheds, though a few were scattered elsewhere within the two Sections. Their omission from the Eastern Section can be explained by the fact that that area was already well served by the competent Wainwright C class 0-6-0s; the Qs would displace some of the ancient LSWR Class 0395 0-6-0s and the former LB&SCR C2 class.

30549 was experimentally fitted with a BR standard Class 4 blastpipe which exhausted up a stovepipe chimney to check that steaming would still be sufficient. The locomotive was photographed shunting at Bournemouth depot on 25 August 1955; it kept this chimney until withdrawn from service.

British Railways then fitted most of the Q class engines with BR standard Class 4 type single blastpipes and cast chimneys, which improved their appearance as well as enabling them to continue with their normal work.

Early on in their lives, OVB stamped his mark on the Q class by having them all fitted with Lemaître blastpipes and wide chimneys. This might have made them a little freer running in view of the lower back pressure, but at the price of more sparks from the chimney. In the mid- to late-1950s, Eastleigh drawing office schemed an idea to fit the class with BR standard Class 4 single blastpipes and chimneys. At first an experimental single blastpipe and a particularly ugly stovepipe chimney were fitted to 30549; this modification was successful enough for the class to be altered this way, but with proper BR cast iron chimneys and petticoats.

Some of the Qs came to be scrapped before being modified. The last Q class locomotive to work for British Railways was withdrawn in 1965, just two years before steam finished entirely on the Southern Region.

The Qs were generally used as goods engines, but summer weekends in particular found them drafted to holiday specials. One duty they performed regularly was to work boat trains along the Lymington branch on summer Saturdays. These were ten-coach trains from London Waterloo carrying holidaymakers bound for the western end of the Isle of Wight. On arrival at Brockenhurst, the main line express engine would detach and usually it was a Q class 0-6-0 that coupled on to take the quite heavy train on to Lymington Pier where the passengers could transfer quickly to the waiting ferry for Yarmouth. Some runs on this branch line showed the Qs to have a good turn of speed.

On one occasion in 1953, I wanted particularly to photograph the Bournemouth Belle Pullman car train between Bournemouth Central and West stations. This was at the time that V2 class 2-6-2s and others were temporarily allocated to Nine Elms depot to replace 'Merchant Navy' Pacifics withdrawn for axle examinations (see Chapter 5). On this day the V2 had failed;

Quite exceptionally, a Q 0-6-0 did replace a bigger locomotive when a former LNER V2 2-6-2 failed on the Bournemouth Belle Pullman train in early summer 1953. 30542 was manfully spiriting the 500-tons train between Bournemouth Central and Bournemouth West. It is seen at the approach to Gas Works Junction. (Chapter 5 explains the reason why V2s and other exotic types were running on the Southern Region at that time.)

it was taken off the heavy train at Bournemouth Central. My photograph shows this heavy prestige train trundling along towards Gas Works Junction about twenty minutes late behind nothing bigger than a Q class 0-6-0!

Many nice things have been written about the preserved Q 0-6-0 that is normally to be found on the Bluebell Railway in Sussex. No 30541 with its BR 4 chimney is an ideal engine for running trains on a preserved railway that demands heavy pulling up hills with speed limited to 25mph by the light railway regulations. For some of its preserved life, the engine was running as Southern Railway 541 in pre-war Maunsell livery style. It looked nice, but the purist will always comment that the BR chimney which it carries does not look the same as its original Maunsell chimney. At the time of writing, the locomotive is in BR livery as 30541 and has gained accolades when visiting other heritage railways around the country.

Class	Q 0-6-0
Engineer	R.E.L. Maunsell
Built by	SR Eastleigh
BR power class	4F
Number in class	20
Introduced	1938
Cylinders (2 inside)	19in x 26in
Coupled wheels	5ft 1in
Boiler pressure	200lbf/sq in
Grate area	21.9sq ft
Tractive effort	26,160lbf
Weight in w.o.	49tons 10cwt
SR number series	530-549
BR number series	30530-30549

Weight diagram for Q1 0-6-0

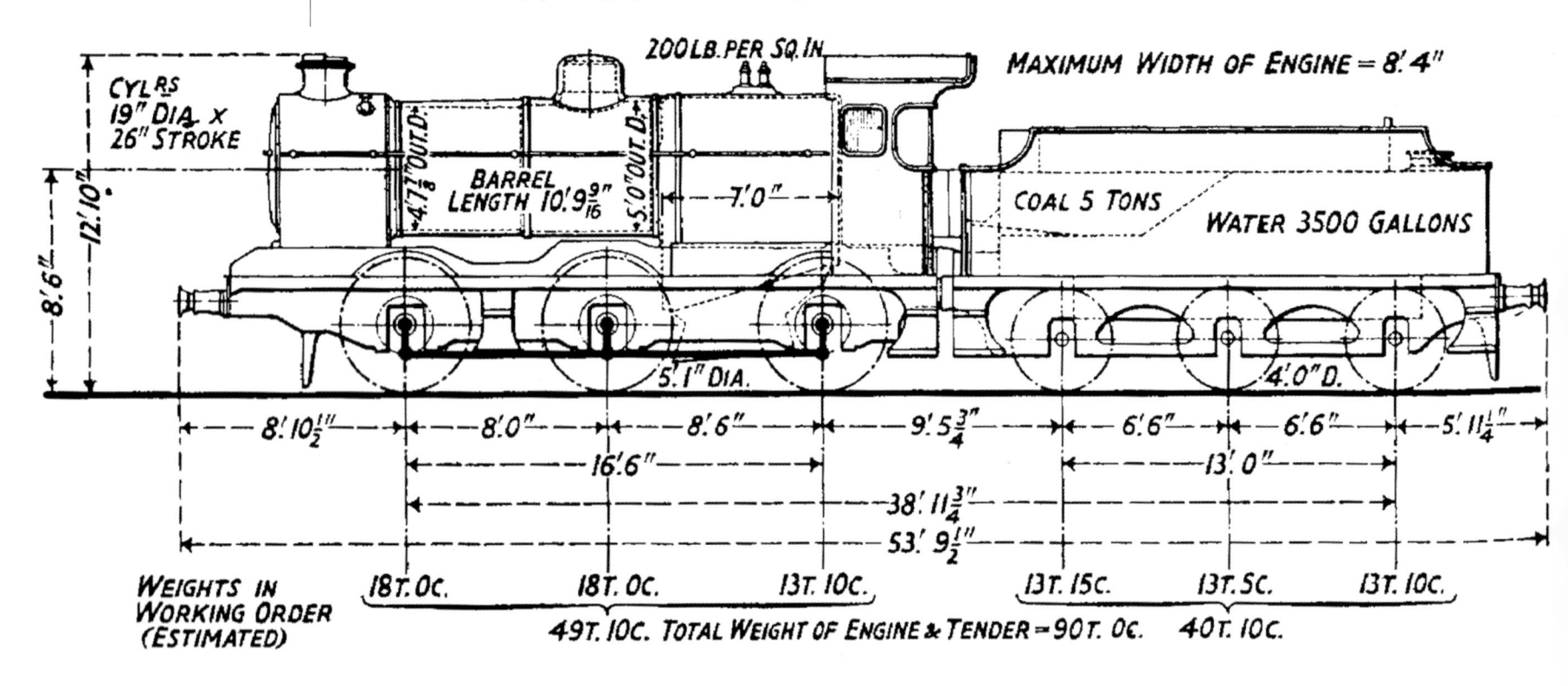

Chapter 5
THE 'MERCHANT NAVY' CLASS 4-6-2s

One of the interesting aspects of Bulleid's time on the Southern Railway is the close relationships and excellent accord that he was able to build up with SR Board members. He quickly realised after his appointment as CME of the SR that he and they had the same long-term view, namely that the Southern Railway should develop plans for motive power that could raise the speeds and loads of express passenger trains across the railway. The urgent need was to eliminate expensive double-heading of the London Victoria to Dover boat trains, but of almost equal importance would be speeding up the fast trains on the lines from Waterloo to the West Country and to Bournemouth.

The Southern's heavy load pullers were the sixteen 'Lord Nelson' 4-6-0s, but the need was for a locomotive type that could exceed the 'Nelsons'' performances by a significant margin. Something was needed that could pull at least 550 tons up to an average speed of 60mph. Richard Maunsell had indeed

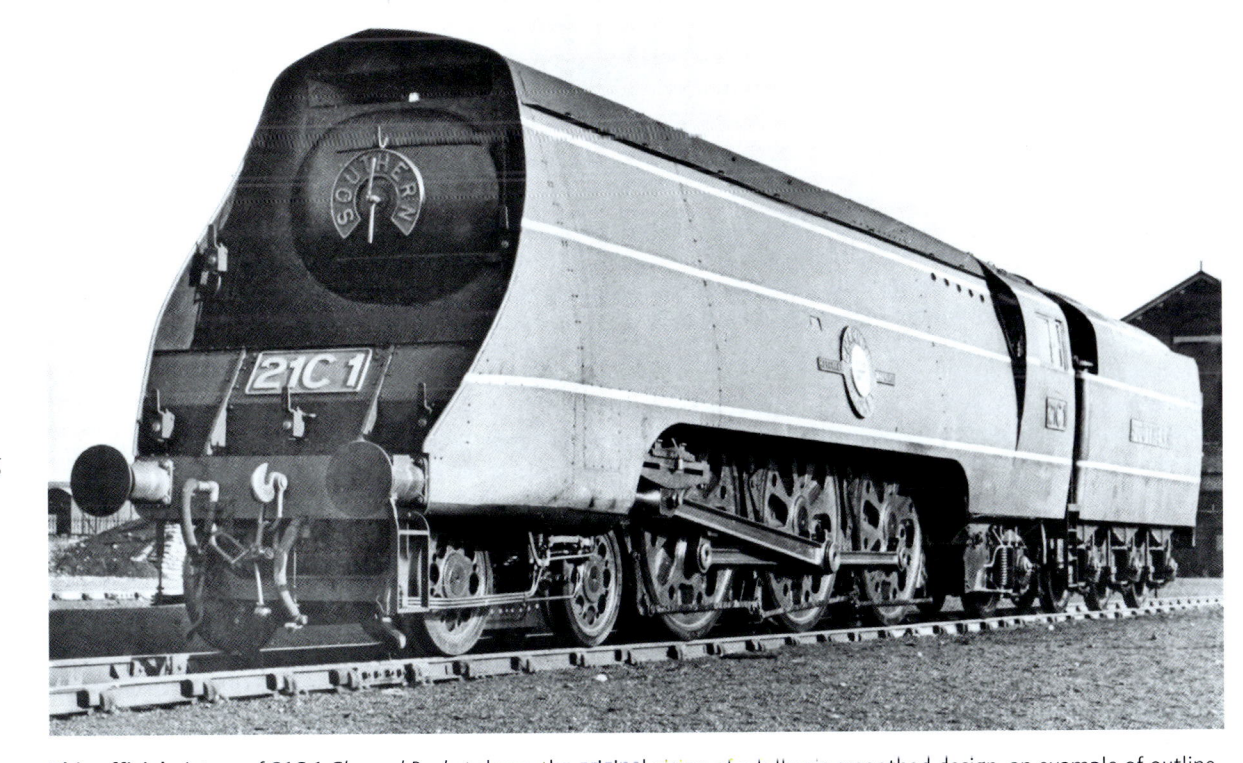

This official picture of 21C 1 *Channel Packet* shows the original vision of a fully air-smoothed design, an example of outline simplicity without the constructional complication of full streamlining. The slot near the top of the smokebox front sheet was to allow air to flow upwards past the chimney in an attempt to reduce drifting of steam into the driver's view. Only 21C 1 and 21C 2 had the numbers on brass plates on the front and cabsides, and 'Southern' plates on the tender sides. These were sacrificed to aid the reduction of locomotive weight to the design value, and were replaced by transferred numbers and decals. The name commemorates the Southern Railway's own cross-Channel shipping services. The locomotive is standing outside Eastleigh Locomotive Works and appears to be painted in photographic grey rather than the malachite green of the first few MNs before war-time black took over. *SR*

sketched out a proposal for a 4-6-2 based on an extended 'Lord Nelson' with wide firebox. There was also a diagram of a 2-6-2 three cylinder mixed traffic engine, like an enlarged U1 with wide firebox, that might have had useful potential west of Exeter. Neither type, however, was approved and Maunsell's ill health almost certainly had got in the way of his continued involvement in locomotive development.

Building on his experiences as Gresley's assistant, OVB's early inclination was that, for the SR's heaviest passenger services, there should be a large 2-8-2 tender locomotive in order to incorporate enough adhesion weight on the coupled wheels. Among other ideas being discussed, a diagram was drawn up that harked back to the Gresley P2 2-8-2 in several features. This proposal had eight coupled wheels of which the leading pair were part of a Helmholz truck in concert with the front pony truck, a system which was established in continental Europe as a way to combine the flexibility of a leading bogie with additional adhesion from an extra pair of coupled wheels. The coupled wheels were to be 6ft 2in diameter and they would be driven by three cylinders. The locomotive would weigh a little over 100 tons in working order. (Gresley had apparently denied Bulleid the satisfaction of using a Helmholz truck in the P2, probably to the chief's lasting chagrin in view of later, possibly unsubstantiated, rumours of spread track north of Edinburgh.) Apart from the Helmholz truck and a crude attempt at an air-smoothed casing, the locomotive OVB was promoting was very much a P2 variant.

The Chief Civil Engineer, George Ellson, was unconvinced about the better curving that a Helmholz truck would encourage. He was absolutely against any express locomotive that appeared to have anything like a single-axle pony truck at the front. The locomotive was in any case too heavy.

The development of Gresley's P2 2-8-2 would have been a strong influence on O.V. Bulleid in thinking through the introduction of a large locomotive design for the SR that would serve the war effort in moving freight as well as being good for a high speed future when the war was over. *W.H.C. Kelland collection courtesy Bournemouth Railway Club Trust*

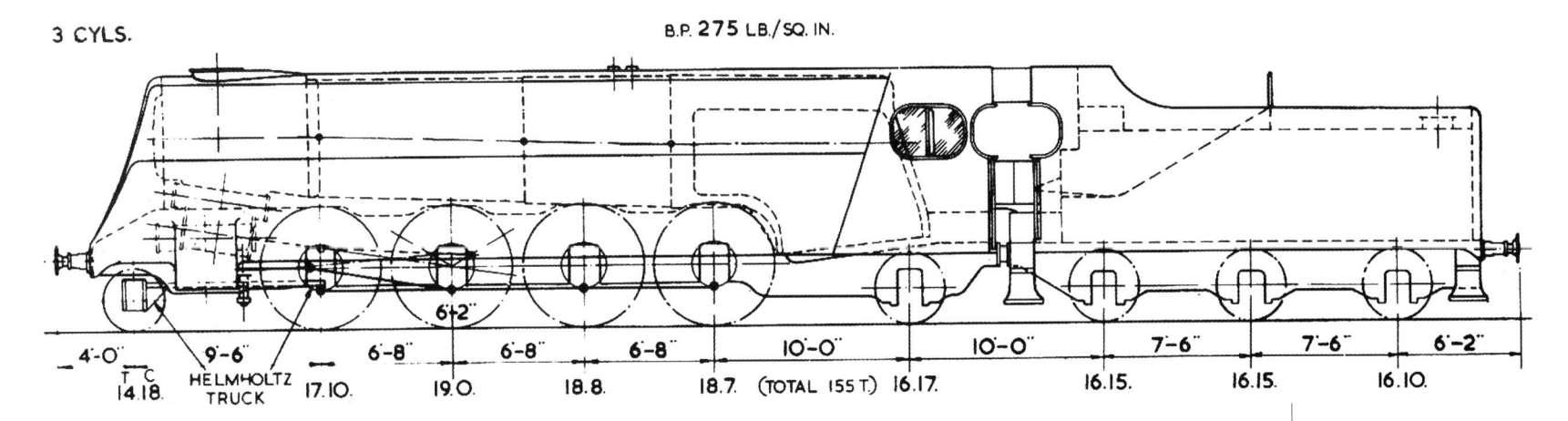

OVB had a quietly persuasive nature and managed to get the General Manager to relent slightly in that he was minded to allow up to three 2-8-2s to be built experimentally and be given a fair trial. Aware that this holding operation might result in untold delay in progressing a full fleet build, OVB decided, perhaps impetuously, that if they really wanted the requested batch of ten locomotives, then he would provide ten 4-6-2s. Thus the big, powerful 2-8-2 with high adhesion and the ability to run fast with loads of up to 550 tons was kicked into the lengthening list of 'locomotives that were never built'.

There were in fact several restraints on the designers who were by now concentrating on creating a powerful 4-6-2 for the SR. The SR's general loading gauge restricted locomotives in height to 13ft 1in and width to 9ft. The permitted height of the cab cornice above rail was 10ft 11in, and the maximum width over cylinders 8ft 10in. George Ellson was insisting on a maximum axleload of no more than 21tons, two tons less than other UK railways allowed.

He was also adamant that hammer blow, the vertical forces transmitted to the rails arising from unbalanced rotational forces within the locomotive, should be at a minimum. All the biggest express passenger locomotives on the other three principal railways, LMS, LNER and GWR, exceeded one or more of these limits. So the new SR locomotive would have to fit into a smaller space, be lighter on the track and yet produce the same level of power as a 'Duchess', A4 or 'King'. What a challenge!

While this challenge might have been daunting for some, it was just the sort that fired up OVB's inventiveness. He had clear views on what any locomotive design should embrace. Central to this was his insistence that the boiler's ability to produce enough steam was absolutely key. Whatever the rest of the locomotive could do, it was totally dependent on the boiler's performance. He had learned this from his time on the GNR and LNER. Gresley always provided enough boiler power to feed the cylinders on his engines whatever they were called upon to do. With OVB's contacts in France, he would also have learned André Chapelon's maxim that a locomotive had to be considered as a complete and integral system. So the way the steam was used was also important if the engine part of the locomotive was to perform as desired. Chapelon used streamlined, large diameter steam pipes and large steam chests to ensure that maximum steam pressure at the entry to the cylinders was as close as possible to the actual boiler pressure when the regulator was wide open. He also aimed to keep exhaust pressures low with an exhaust system that did not choke back the flow of used steam out of the engine. Creating enough smokebox vacuum to pull the fire gases through the boiler tubes and enough air through the grate was another part of the science of draughting steam locomotives. And dare I suggest that, while the science was becoming more widely understood in Bulleid's time, there was still room for the art of good engineering to play its part? Design is not all mathematics; there is still room for trial and error, even in something as apparently well understood as a steam locomotive.

Among many diagrams showing heavy express locomotives that Mr Bulleid was proposing for the Southern Railway was this large 2-8-2. It has a direct lineage from the LNER P2 design in the 6ft 2in diameter coupled wheels and three-cylinder layout. It incorporates a Helmholtz truck linking the front pony truck with the leading coupled wheelset to assist in entering curves, a feature that OVB had wanted to use on the P2 but which Gresley had disallowed. It was but a short step from this promising layout to the 'Merchant Navy' 4-6-2 design. *SR*

44 • Oliver Bulleid's Locomotives

The first ten 'Merchant Navy' locomotives were distinctive in several ways from the twenty locomotives that followed later. The curves over the wheel space, deeper side sheets on the cab and tender, and higher side sheets almost embracing the coal bunker marked them out, as did the narrower curve of the main casing towards the buffer beam. In this view of 35005 *Canadian Pacific* at Bournemouth Central in 1953, the forward sweep of the cab front has been changed to bring the outside of the windscreen within reach of the crew in the cab for cleaning, and the side plates shrouding the outside cylinders have been removed to ease access for maintenance. Not long after the war ended these locomotives had received the full-length smoke deflectors shown here.

The simplified diagram of a 'MN' boiler shows clearly the two main barrel rings and the large firebox with its thermic syphons linking the water spaces in front and above the inner firebox. The regulator in the dome sent the steam through to the superheater header in the smokebox and thence through the superheater flues before reaching the cylinders. Hence it was less than responsive when a driver was trying to control bouts of wheelslip.

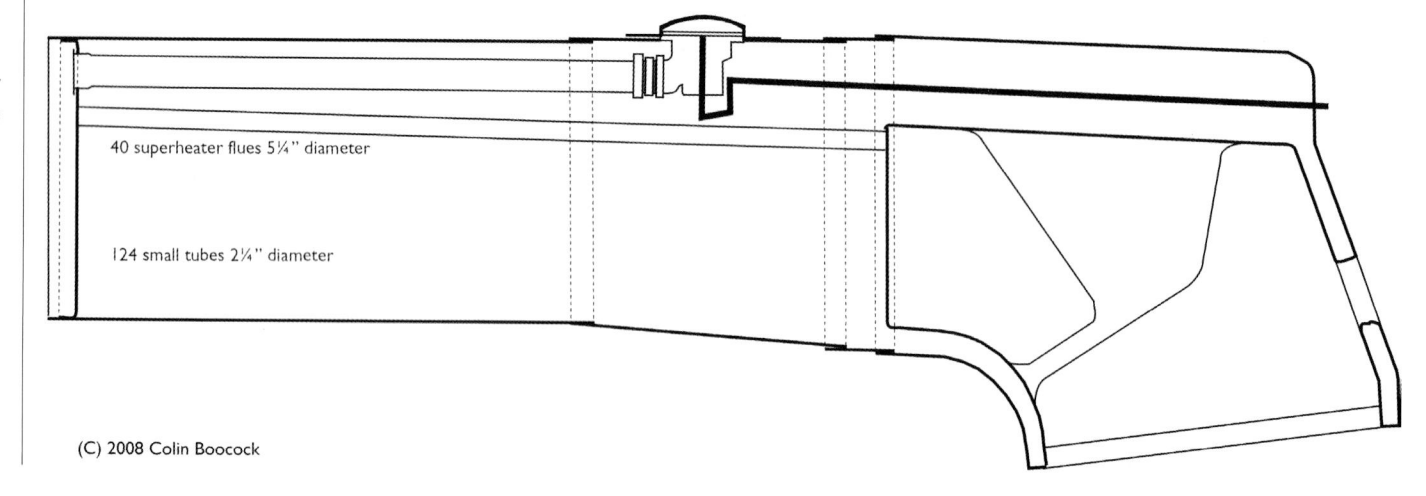

40 superheater flues 5¼" diameter

124 small tubes 2¼" diameter

(C) 2008 Colin Boocock

The boiler

The 'Merchant Navy' boiler was clearly not a copy of any previous boiler, though its size related well to the Gresley influence. Its heart was a wide grate with an area of 49.5sq ft, almost as big as an LMS Pacific. The firebox had a forward combustion chamber and the crown was of Belpaire shape. The barrel contained five rows of superheater flues, forty in number (like a 'Duchess'). The barrel was not overlength and the front ring of the barrel was tapered, unusually at the bottom so as to clear the height of the inside cylinder casting. Tapering the barrel helps to keep down the volume of colder water at the front. A relative innovation for the UK was the use of steel for the inner firebox plates. Steel fireboxes were the norm in the USA. Their weight was less than copper fireboxes, and steel facilitated the use of welded construction. By using welding, Bulleid was able easily to include in the firebox design a pair of large thermic syphons. These assisted the circulation of hot water from the lower front tubeplate and up over the firebox crown, and added to the total heating surface available to heat water and create steam.

A disadvantage of steel fireboxes is the risk of corrosion from the water. On the SR, Bulleid introduced the TIA type of water treatment that he had admired in France[4]. This was fitted to the locomotive tender and measured the water hardness which it countered by injecting the correct volume of softening chemical into the feed water. The Southern Railway and Region were small enough to enable management to manage the water treatment thoroughly; other regions with more widely dispersed depots might have struggled. Otherwise, steel's advantages include the ability to weld plates together during construction, and to repair them by welding in patches where necessary; the ability to weld boiler tubes to both tubeplates, and the use of ferrous or monel metal stays that avoid expansion differences, and thus keep stresses, and possible cracking, to a minimum. On the 'Merchant Navy' class, the firebox foundation ring was a conventional, rivetted solid ring. The boiler barrel was also conventionally of rivetted construction. (Beware of authors who unthinkingly write about all-welded boilers. Bulleid's Pacifics did not have these; only the fireboxes were welded.) The three safety valves were unusually situated towards the back of the front ring of the barrel. This was presumably to keep the valves away from the areas of greatest water turbulence such as over the firebox crown where the thermic syphons were active. An unfortunate consequence was that, when a train came to an unusually abrupt halt, say at a station on a fast main line, the water surging towards the

---

4. TIA = Traitment Intégral Armand, named after M Louis Armand, chief engineer of SNCF at Bulleid's time on the SR.

This 'Merchant Navy' boiler in the boiler shop at Eastleigh shows off its forty superheater flues and the heavily riveted construction of the boiler barrel, designed to withstand a working pressure of 280lb/sq in (later reduced to 250lb/sq in). The water space between the inner and outer fireboxes was held by monel metal stays. On the 'MN' boiler the firebox foundation ring was conventionally riveted.

front of the boiler lifted the safety valves and sprayed everything and everybody around with warm water! (This was corrected during rebuilding – see Chapter 23.)

Cylinders

If the heart of a locomotive is its boiler which produces the steam, the limbs are surely the cylinders that put it to use. On the 'Merchant Navy' class, OVB opted for a short piston stroke; this was 24 inches which compares with 26 and 28 inches on previous SR locomotives such as 4-6-0s, and 30 inches on many GWR engines. The cylinders were fed by large diameter piston valves with a reasonably long throw. Bulleid had learned about outside live steam admission, a feature of more recent and successful locomotive designs from Ashford, and he incorporated this in his Pacifics. Outside steam admission goes in tandem with inside exhaust emission. The steam exhausted from the cylinders has a direct path from the space between the piston valves to the base of the blastpipe, giving it a freedom from back-pressure that even well-designed inside admission cylinders provide less well. It is essential that a large locomotive exhausting in this way should have an equally free passage through the blastpipe and chimney, another source of increased back-pressure in many older locomotives. Mr Bulleid made sure the exhaust passages were large and obstruction-free. The Lemaître five-jet blastpipe was simple yet effective, and the wide petticoat and chimney offered little resistance to exhaust escape. Thus emerged one characteristic of Bulleid Pacifics – the sound of their exhaust when running was often surprisingly soft. When opened up, they emitted what the writer O.S. Nock once described as the sound of 'rhythmic sandpapering'. The soft exhaust had a major disadvantage in that it proved difficult to raise the exhaust steam and smoke sufficiently high above the cab for the crew to see forward, a problem on occasions when picking out signals. This is discussed later.

For the power needed from the new SR Pacifics, there was a choice between three and four cylinders. To have just two cylinders was not a sensible option if the engines were to meet the Civil Engineer's demands for low impact on the track, even though the German railways had already shown that two-cylinder Pacifics, if large enough, could produce 2,000-plus horse power. Three cylinders was the useful minimum for the power output needed in SR conditions. Three cylinders would bring useful side benefits in that the natural balance of a three-cylinder locomotive could enable a reduction in the weight of balance-correction measures, something we discuss later in the chapter. Four cylinders would be perhaps a complication too far; why pay for four of something when three will do? So Oliver Bulleid chose three cylinders of 18 inches diameter, all driving on the centre coupled axle. A shorter piston stroke enables a cylinder casting to be a few inches shorter than otherwise, just one of many actions that saved weight in this most interesting design.

The arrangement of cylinders was something that clearly came from OVB's experience with Gresley locomotives, where the three-cylinder types were arranged to drive the centre coupled axle. To achieve this, Gresley had raised the inside cylinder sufficiently and set it further back to enable the inside connecting rod to clear the leading coupled axle. The different angle of approach of the inside cylinder to the axle being driven when compared with that of the outside cylinders was seen as not sufficient to cause undue mismatched force couples. The clearance issues over the leading coupled axle encouraged the use of conjugated gear for the inside cylinder which drove the inside valves from the front; it would have been difficult, though not impossible, to fit in a normal inside Walschaerts gear with the leading coupled axle in the way. Thompson and Peppercorn did go on to achieve this after Gresley's departure.

Inside a smokebox is the Lemaître five-jet blast pipe exhausting up into the wide, fabricated chimney petticoat. SR

In the case of the Bulleid Pacifics, the inside cylinder was raised such that the piston rod drove the centre couple axle at an inclination of 1 in 7.75 from the horizontal. This compares with the drives for the two outside cylinders which were almost horizontal at 1 in 40. OVB chose not to use conjugated gear, however, but invented his own valve gear that eliminated completely the problems normally associated with outside steam admission (high pressure piston rod glands) and tight clearance over the leading coupled axle, and yet contained all the components of Walschaerts gear[5].

Bulleid valve gear

What OVB achieved was to miniaturise Walschaerts gear such that all three sets of valve gear would fit between the locomotive frames. The resultant short throw had to be enlarged to that required for long-travel piston valves, and this was done using a rocker shaft for each cylinder carrying levers set at a ratio of three to eight, that is three units of throw of the lever driven by the valve gear was enlarged to eight units throw for the link to the piston valves. Because the rocker shaft entered the cylinder valve chest in the exhaust cavity, there were no high pressure piston valve rod glands.

To keep the valve gear compact, the main valve gear drive shaft that contained the three eccentrics was driven by a chain from a lay shaft which in turn was driven by chain from a sprocket wheel shrunk on the crank axle. These were by no means small chains but were of industrial size and strength and were proven to be strong and reliable in service. The lay shaft was adjustable (with some physical contortion by a fitter) so that any chain slack could be minimised periodically.

The drive shaft drove the valve gear components as shown in the diagram, the final movement being via long push rods to the lower pins in the rocker arms. Unusually for railway practice, the valve gear joint pins were shorter than usual and were held in by circlips which expanded into grooves cut in the inside of the valve gear components. This system did away with the conventional method of securing pins by means of cotter pins and/or split pins which can sometimes work loose. The circlip method worked well in practice. It was yet another of OVB's ideas that saved just a little bit more weight. Reversing was by means of a conventional steam reverser.

Lubrication of the valve gear and all key inside moving parts was by oil pumped mechanically from the oil in the part-filled oil bath. In fact it was more of an oil sump. The valve gear, inside connecting rod and big end did not slosh about in oil in the oil bath as some commentators believe. The oil was piped to the right places and sprayed where it was needed. The sump was made up of thin steel plates at the ends and bottom, and it used the frames themselves for its sides. Flexing of the frames was to prove to be a source of weld cracking and oil leakage, as well as the cut-out at the front that enabled the inside connecting rod to clear.

The lightweight valve gear had advantages and disadvantages. In its favour was its compactness and therefore its much lighter weight than a conventional arrangement of Walschaerts gear. This lighter weight also meant that any imbalance of forces within the valve gear would have less effect on the forces felt within the locomotive as a whole, enabling any applied balancing to be reduced. When newly overhauled, a 'Merchant Navy' locomotive performed effectively and with reasonable efficiency. As the valve gear components wore, clearances within joints naturally increased. The three-to-eight multiplication of throw also multiplied the effect of these looser clearances. Opinions differ as to whether slacker chains would give rise to misplaced valve events, though I am certain that they could do just that. The upshot was a clear deterioration in the valve events, which were not spectacularly accurate anyway. The later British Railways test reports published indicator diagrams showing the pressure variations inside the cylinders on a test roller bed and when working controlled road test trains. These illustrated how poor steam distribution actually was when compared with locomotive classes with conventional valve gear.

Poor steam distribution, exacerbated by overrunning of piston valves at higher speeds (sensed by drivers as 'free running'), appeared to me and some other engineers as the root

---

5. When giving my slide show on Bulleid's Pacifics, at this point I usually misquote the comedian Eric Morecambe by saying, 'Bulleid valve gear has all the right components of Walschaerts gear, but not necessarily in the right order.' Strictly true or not, it drives home the point.

48 • Oliver Bulleid's Locomotives

The Bulleid valve gear layout was basically a miniaturised version of Walschaerts gear. Each set drove a rocker arm which in turn, via a shaft, drove the longer arm connected to the piston valve rod within the exhaust cavity above the cylinder. This applied a movement to the piston valve that was greater than the throw of the valve gear by a ratio of eight to three.

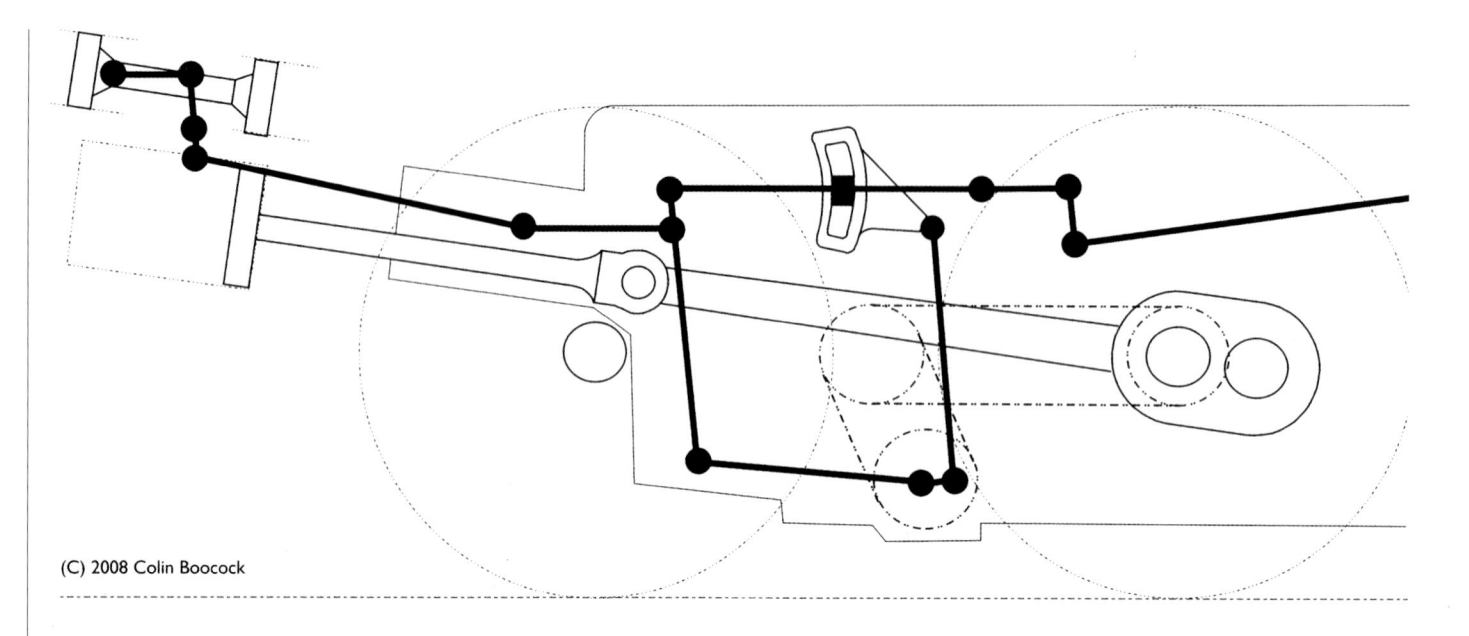

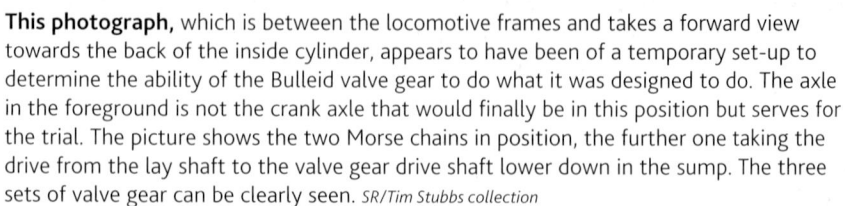

(C) 2008 Colin Boocock

This photograph, which is between the locomotive frames and takes a forward view towards the back of the inside cylinder, appears to have been of a temporary set-up to determine the ability of the Bulleid valve gear to do what it was designed to do. The axle in the foreground is not the crank axle that would finally be in this position but serves for the trial. The picture shows the two Morse chains in position, the further one taking the drive from the lay shaft to the valve gear drive shaft lower down in the sump. The three sets of valve gear can be clearly seen. *SR/Tim Stubbs collection*

Looking in the opposite direction, towards the rear, the chain drives are low in the photograph in the distance. The three vertical combination levers are prominent, as are three rods which they drive towards the rocker arms which are out of sight above the camera. The middle cylinder slide bar takes up the centre of the picture, but without the crosshead and piston rod in place. *SR/Tim Stubbs collection*

cause of the higher-than-normal coal and water consumption of the 'Merchant Navy' class locomotives in service.

Frames and wheels

The rest of the locomotive design was more conventional, though not without its originality. The main frames were spaced closer together than had been normal practice across UK railways. Normally, steam locomotive frames were spaced such that a narrow firebox between them could be of maximum width; the coupled wheels would have adequate clearance from the frames, but no more. With Bulleid's narrower frame spacing, the horn guides between which the coupled axleboxes slid up-and-down were thus held firmly on their vertical centreline and avoided the bending moments that 'conventional' locomotive horn guides had to endure. Another advantage of this arrangement on the MNs was that the frame stretchers would be that much shorter, and thus lighter. This closer frame spacing was later applied to the BR standard Pacifics and 2-10-0s.

The coupled wheel axleboxes were solid gunmetal (brass) castings with whitemetal inserts and whitemetalled guides. The whitemetalled areas were machined smooth. The axleboxes' vertical movement was controlled by leaf springs.

Many commentators have made much of the so-called 'Boxpok' wheel design. In fact, locomotive wheels without spokes have been relatively popular in some countries such as the USA, Russia and China. Spoked wheels have a disadvantage in that the wheel rim stresses are uneven. In a Boxpok-type design, the wheel centre can be designed with metal in the right places to even out wheel stresses. OVB was able to patent the design which he had developed in concert with the steelmakers Firth-Brown. The B-F-B (Bulleid-Firth-Brown) wheels were indeed steel castings (a fabricated set was welded up for comparison and installed on one locomotive, but that idea was not pursued any further). The full set of B-F-B wheels lowered the locomotive weight by around two tons, a significant contribution to the demand for a lighter-weight locomotive to suit the SR's CCE. The crank axle had no additional balance weights, not even on the crank webs. OVB was pursuing his conviction that these three-cylinder locomotives would be self-balancing.

A sensible change that was later copied for BR standard locomotive designs was the method for fixing steel tyres on the wheel centres. Conventionally, railways had used the process of heating up the tyres and then shrinking them onto the wheel centres, fitting a steel ring, known as a Gibson ring, onto the wheel centre and then rolling a lip at the back of the tyre over the ring to add security. Bulleid's idea was so simple in comparison. Each tyre bore was machined to have a small lip either side; the tyre was heated as before to expand it sufficiently to clear the inner lip; the tyre was then shrunk on to the wheel centre which gave it an interference fit, and the two lips acted to prevent any subsequent lateral shifting of the tyre in service.[6]

On the Bulleid Pacifics, the coupled wheelsets were spaced further apart than might be expected, but this was to enable another Bulleid feature to be accommodated. He wanted to minimise forces on the axleboxes, and a sensible way to do this was to fit clasp brakes on the coupled wheels. On 'conventional' locomotives in the UK, a single brake block was applied to each coupled wheel, leaving the axlebox and horn guides to take the reaction force each time the block was applied to the wheel. Bulleid's thinking was clearly to take the stress off the axleboxes by applying a balanced brake force on each coupled wheel. Smooth braking was an attribute of the Bulleid Pacifics.

Driving cab

In the relatively commodious cab, which was more enclosed than earlier SR design cabs, both crewmen had seats, even though the fireman might well not use his seat as much as the driver would use his. The driving controls were accessible and operable from the driver's sitting position. The regulator, which was located under the boiler dome, was worked by a pull-out lever pivoted at the top. Forward and reverse gear and notching-up were achieved by means of a steam-operated reverser. (This proved less

---

6. Three decades later when I was Rolling Stock Engineer on the Scottish Region, we were still experiencing the failure of tyres fitted with Gibson rings because designers at Derby and Swindon had continued to include them in the BR diesel mechanical multiple units even though OVB's simpler solution was available to them.

The 'Merchant Navy' cab layout had the driver's seat on the left; the fireman had a similar one on the right side, stowed upwards in this picture. Note the brake handle and ejector controls above the driver's position, almost getting in the way of a clear view forward. The steam reverser control lever is just in front of the driver's seat. The firehole doors are shown cocked open, their manual operating lever set in the horizontal position. Normal operation in service was via the foot pedal which is only just visible at floor level. The fireman has all the injector controls at his fingertips below his seat. The regulator handle is the large vertical lever above the left side oil box. Among the gauges is a steam chest pressure gauge to indicate to the driver how effective is the regulator opening he has set. (This cab has additional equipment set up for testing purposes.)
Tim Stubbs collection

reliable unless it was assiduously maintained – it would creep away from a setting, sometimes in a wrong direction, a source of many apocryphal tales!) There was a water gauge on each side of the firebox backplate, each gauge being electrically lit from behind. The manifold valve was located towards one side of the firebox front. Two displacement oil feeders were prominent either side of the firehole. There were also mechanical oil pumps on the locomotive front under the casing beneath the smokebox door.

The water injectors were both of the live steam type, simple and reasonably reliable. They were grouped vertically as a pair under the fireman's side of the cab with the controls easily accessible. The pipes from the injectors fed two clack valves on the right hand side of the boiler front ring. An original feature, not seen on other British locomotives in my experience, was the pedal-operated firehole door. This was an American idea imported by Bulleid and modified to use steam as its propellant (the US versions used air from the air brake systems). The idea was that a fireman would lift coal from the shovel-plate at the front of the tender, and as he swung round his right foot would press the pedal, the firedoors would open and his shovelful of coal would enter the firebox. Releasing his foot would allow the doors to close by gravity, thus avoiding the entry of more secondary air than might be wanted. Using steam instead of air proved a problem at times, as condensate would prevent the doors operating effectively. I have seen a competent fireman on a 'Merchant Navy' make good use of the power-operated doors, however, and it was a pleasure to watch.

Under the cab was fixed a Stones turbo-generator that used a steam turbine to drive a 24Volts dc generator. This supplied lighting to the cab, water gauges, injector overflow pipes, lubrication points and areas where crew needed to see in the dark to prepare, lubricate and dispose of their locomotive. Why the BR standard engines did not have electric lighting, I shall never know! The generator also supplied six electric marker lamps at each end of the locomotive and tender. These could be lit for night travel in place of oil lamps. (During the day the SR used prominent white discs to display headcodes on steam trains.)

Looking back from the cab, when running tender-first, there was a wind shield with windows in it which enabled a crew member to see past the narrowed coal bunker, there being a gap between each bunker side and the adjacent tender side rave. In service, this gap tended to fill up with stray coal pieces and fire irons, thereby restricted the view. Looking forward from the driver's perspective, the cab front windows were difficult to reach until they had been modified and moved back to a position closer to the driver and fireman and angled; the closer and angled glass gave a slightly wider view of the way ahead. The new position enabled the crew to lean forward out of the cab side window to clean the front surface of the windscreen. Even then, the wide shape of the locomotive casing and the downward drift of steam towards the cab could sometimes restrict the forward view from these engines.

The whistle was a single-note steam whistle with its tone pitched mid-way between a conventional high-pitched whistle and a hooter. This mellow tone was used only on Bulleid Pacifics and was not copied for any other SR or BR locomotive types.

Air-smoothing

The term 'air-smoothed' as applied to the Bulleid Pacifics can be construed as a mischievous way of convincing publicity people that a locomotive might be streamlined when in fact it is not! The flat front of a Bulleid Pacific is in no way an example of streamlining. What the all-over air-smoothed casing on a 'Merchant Navy' did do was to enable the designer to eliminate yet more metal structures such as

Starting trains in the Up direction was particularly difficult at both Salisbury and Bournemouth Central due to the trains being on a tight curve in each case. This is Salisbury on 27 April 1957 where 35006 *Peninsular & Oriental S.N. Co.* has its steam sanding working as it gets to grip with an Exeter to Waterloo express. 35006 demonstrates the modifications made to the plating in front of the cylinders and around the wheel space to improve access for maintenance. The aged T9 4-4-0 30702 sits in the bay platform with a train to Bournemouth via West Moors and Poole.

35009 *Shaw Savill* rolls into Bournemouth Central on 10 July 1955 with an express from London Waterloo. This view emphasizes the narrower, straighter curve of the side plates of the first ten locomotives when compared with the front view of locomotives from the second and third batches.

side footplates and valances and the brackets to hold them, boiler lagging plates, and decorative castings shrouding the dome and safety valves. The overall casing was shaped to fit the outline of the wide firebox, extended to near the front of the locomotive. The casing was made up of thin steel plates carried on a lightweight framework that was of limited structural significance. The cab sides were likewise made up of lightweight plating. The tender and cab sides were given a gentle curve to maximise their width within the loading gauge at the point where width was useful, a feature OVB was applying to passenger rolling stock to maximise their passenger-carrying capacity. So the locomotives matched the stock they were designed to haul.

The smokebox front was flat, but above the smokebox door there was a wide gap to let trapped air flow up to pass the chimney in the hope that it would deflect the downward drift of exhaust. To contain the air and channel it towards this gap, the space in front of the smokebox was given side plates that swept upwards from the front buffer beam and wrapped around the smokebox frontal area. A modification applied during the war due to its urgency was to fit separate smoke deflectors each side of the smokebox front, allowing additional air to flow

The 'Merchant Navy' Class 4-6-2s • 53

up the sides of the locomotive. The second and third batches of the class were built with separate smoke deflectors from new.

Access from the ground to the cab, to the locomotive front and to the tender top was by a set of steel steps welded out of steel tube with no backplates, again a lighter weight alternative to what had gone before; this feature was adapted for BR standard locomotives, too.

Construction

The first batch of ten locomotives was built at Eastleigh Locomotive Works from 1941 to 1942. 21C 1 *Channel Packet* was outshopped late in February 1941, its peculiar numbering being OVB's less logical slant on the French system that numbered all SNCF Pacifics with a 231 prefix. Fitted with 5,000 gallon three-axle tenders, the ten locomotives delighted their crews from early on in view of their free steaming and the ability to haul whatever loads they were given.

The second batch was authorised late in the war and constructed during 1945. Externally, they could be distinguished from the first ten by a number of changes to the air-smoothing. The side plates that swept up from the buffer beam started off with a smaller-radius curve to take up the full width lower down. The cab and tender side sheets were cut higher from rail level at the bottom edge. The space over the coupled wheels, which had curved ends on the first batch, was angular on the second. The backwards slant of the first batch cab front when viewed from the side was changed to be vertical on the second. And the tender side-rave tops, which almost reached the top of the bunker on a first batch tender, were rounded off and finished lower down.

The third batch of ten locomotives was ordered by the Southern Railway but emerged

The Royal Wessex was a thirteen-coach train of three parts: five coaches for Weymouth behind the train engine, then two for Swanage that would be dropped off at Wareham, followed by the six-car restaurant set for Bournemouth West that would be detached at Bournemouth Central. In 1957, 35010 *Blue Star* rattles past Eastleigh and the exit from the wartime Stoneham sidings with the Down train.

The second locomotive of the second batch, built in 1945, poses in photographic grey with white stripes. 21C 12 *United States Lines* illustrates the full length of the original cab before the front windscreens were moved back for crew convenience. It also has side plating in front of the outside cylinders that would later be removed to assist in servicing. The original short smoke deflectors are in place, and the picture also shows how the tender side raves do not envelop the sides of the coal bunkers like the first batch ones did. *SR*

from Eastleigh works in 1948 after British Railways was launched. This batch to all intents and purposes was to the same design as the second, with the key exception that the third batch tender rode on a longer frame to accommodate a 6,000gallon water tank.

All the class were ceremonially named, usually by senior representatives of the shipping lines after which they were named, with the SR gaining much publicity from this exercise.

Liveries

When new, the earliest first batch engines appeared in malachite green with three yellow stripes along each side and looked most impressive to lineside onlookers. Lettering was the SR's 'sunshine' sans-serif style. Wartime conditions forced repaints into plain black, a colour in which second batch engines were delivered.

The first locomotives were adorned with an almost circular brass plate with the word SOUTHERN on it wrapped round the smokebox door dart handles. This had a gap in the bottom that made it look like an inverted horseshoe. On the grounds that this appeared to be a bad-luck symbol to some enginemen, the gap was later filled in so that the plate was completely circular. The new section carried the locomotive's building date and works in small capitals (e.g. EASTLEIGH 1945). Nos 21C 1 and 21C 2 had their numbers

The 'Merchant Navy' Class 4-6-2s • 55

on brass plates on the cab sides and on the locomotive front above the buffer beam. There were also SOUTHERN plates on the tender sides. These number and railway name plates were omitted on later locomotives and replaced by transferred letters and numerals, allegedly to save a little more weight.

The locomotive nameplates were shaped with a central disc for the name, fixed between two straight pieces that carried the MERCHANT NAVY CLASS term, very like the outline of the Plimsoll mark on a ship. Inside the name was a vitreous enamel badge showing the flag(s) of the shipping line after which the locomotive was named. The flag(s) always flew towards the rear of the locomotive. The Southern Railway painted the nameplate backing red, but BR from 1949 adopted its standard black, a colour that Eastleigh works in the early 1960s quietly substituted with red again, probably under John Click's influence when he was acting Assistant Works Manager there.

The third batch of locomotives came along in malachite green but without designations on the tenders until some appeared with BRITISH RAILWAYS in the nationalised railways' Gill Sans style. The third batch, of course,

Most of the second batch emerged new from Eastleigh Works painted in wartime black with green shaded lettering in the 'sunshine' style. The relatively new 21C 17 *Belgian Marine* at Salisbury still had its short smoke deflectors and as yet carried no nameplates. *W.H.C. Kelland collection, courtesy Bournemouth Railway Club Trust*

arrived with their new BR numbers from 35021 to 35030 on the cab side and with BR smokebox door numberplates from the start, a condition quickly applied to the rest of the class in 1948. The new BR Prussian blue colour with just two side stripes in black edged in white began to appear on all the class in 1949, with the tenders adorned with the largest size lion-over-wheel BR emblem. I believe that this was the livery that suited the 'Merchant Navy' class engines best. From 1952, blue gave way to standard BR 'Brunswick' green with black-and-orange lining.

Once painted in the bright malachite green with yellow stripes and with red-background nameplates attached, the 'Merchant Navy' class locomotives looked striking. This is 21C 18 *British India Line* at Southampton Central with a Down express to Bournemouth and Weymouth. It still has the short smoke deflectors and full length cab side sheets. *W.H.C. Kelland collection, courtesy Bournemouth Railway Club Trust*

The 'Merchant Navy' Class 4-6-2s • 57

21C 13 *Blue Funnel Certum Pete Finem* approaches Basingstoke with the Down Devon Belle Pullman train in September 1947. It now has full length smoke deflectors, but other plate modifications are still to take place. *H.N. James/Colour-Rail SR4*

While working the Bournemouth Belle service there was little time at Bournemouth West for locomotive turning and servicing so, rather than run all the way back to Bournemouth depot, the 'Merchant Navy' off the Down 'Belle' used to visit Branksome, turn on the triangle there, and take water at the small sub-depot that was normally used only by locomotives off the Somerset & Dorset route. That is what 35015 *Rotterdam Lloyd* was doing in 1952. This locomotive demonstrates its cut-back cab windscreen. *Stephen Townroe/Colour-Rail BRS373*

Reliability

Apart from the early failures of rocker shafts, which were dealt with by strengthening the original design, maintenance at depots had to concentrate on keeping the valve gear chains sensibly tight, correcting oil leaks from the welds around the oil bath and ensuring the steam reverser and firehole door mechanisms were in good order. OVB's desire that maintenance costs would be kept low by using enclosed, miniaturised valve gear proved unrealistic in practice. The valve gear components showed signs of being stressed, and clearances became greater than desired, leading to erratic valve events and adding to the costs of running.

The crank axle of 35020 broke when it was passing through Crewkerne station at speed on a West of England express in spring 1953. Luckily, the engine stayed on the track, but management decided not to risk more such incidents until all the 'MN' crank axles had been inspected, and quickly withdrew all thirty locomotives from service. Other Region's locomotives were drafted in to help out during the few weeks of this potential disruption. WR 'Britannias', ER V2s, and LMR and BR Class 5s came to the Western Section, and some ER B1s worked for a while on Kent lines to enable 'West Country' class 4-6-2s to deputise for MNs elsewhere on the Region. Two other crank axles were found to need replacement and all the others were put under an on-going regime of ultrasonic testing, probably the first time this technique had been used on railway locomotives in this country. The testing system was thereafter standard across BR. The V2s settled in well at Nine Elms and were the last 'foreign' locomotives to be released back to their home areas once the 'Merchant Navy' class was fully back in service.

Looking up at the front of 35020 *Bibby Line* as it takes water at Salisbury while working the Down Atlantic Coast Express, the space above the smokebox front to channel air past the chimney is visible. This view also shows the wider side sheets that curve sharply to almost touch the ends of the buffer beam. Note the six electric marker lamps on the locomotive front that were repeated on the back of the tender for reverse running.

The 'Merchant Navy' Class 4-6-2s • 59

Standing at Bournemouth Central Up main platform on 1 September 1954 is 35020 *Bibby Line* showing off its long smoke deflectors and the 6,000 gallon tender it had acquired from a third batch locomotive. *Bibby Line* was the only 'Merchant Navy' to have extended smoke deflectors fitted at the time of the 1948 locomotive exchanges, though three 'West Country' class engines were also so adorned. This was the engine that broke its crank axle in spring 1953 while passing Crewkerne at speed, causing the summary temporary withdrawal of the whole class.

35020 was caught on camera on 30 August 1955 working a train of twenty parcels vans from Southampton Docks towards London passing the war-time sidings alongside Eastleigh Airport. The latter had just a grass landing strip in those early years. 35020's tender was by then running with cut-down side raves for a better rearwards view. The locomotive had had the side plates in front of the outside cylinders removed.

The breaking of a crank axle in 1953 prompted management to withdraw all thirty 'Merchant Navy' Pacifics almost precipitously. Replacement power from other Regions included half-a-dozen Gresley V2 2-6-2s, which settled down well on Nine Elms duties, including the Bournemouth Belle. On 3 June 1953, V2 No 60893 passes through Boscombe station with the Down Pullman train.

Modifications

I have already mentioned the modification to reposition the cab front windscreens for ease of cleaning and forward vision. To improve the view from within the cab to the rear for tender-first running, from early 1953 Bulleid Pacific tenders began to appear after overhauls with the side raves cut down to the level of the tank tops, but with covered channels alongside the bunkers in which to store fire irons. The tops of these channels were angled such that any loose coal that dropped over the top edges of the bunkers would be deflected and fall to the ground. These tenders, and the adjoining cab sides, were given the BR standard form of lining out as a panel with the orange lines spaced from the central black line; the black lines with orange edging remained in place on the air-smoothed sides of the locomotive.

For a time, 35005 *Canadian Pacific* was tested with a Berkeley screw coal feeder to the fire grate. This was not pursued, the understood reason being the need to use coal specially graded in small lumps. This additional activity in sorting small coals from larger lumps would be onerous to most depots and would add to running costs.

35019 *French Line CGT* ran a period between overhauls fitted with a single blastpipe and chimney, ostensibly to reduce spark-throwing. The single blastpipe was proved to restrain the locomotive's performance at higher outputs; the locomotive later reverted to the Lemâitre system.

From 1947, all the 'Merchant Navy' class locomotives had unobtrusive narrow bars fitted near the tops of the smoke deflectors; these were to support the side name-boards when hauling the Devon Belle Pullman train.

The TIA water treatment was replaced in the 1950s by a simpler system using chemical briquettes. Each tender was fitted with a perforated drum below the tender water filler, into which a depot would place the correct number of briquettes to ensure the softness of the water was maintained. The owning depot was responsible for measuring the softness of the water in the tank when the locomotive was on the depot, and for making sure enough briquettes were added. The system worked very well indeed. It prevented the build-up of lime scale in the boiler; the impurities instead sank to the bottom of the boiler barrel as a sludge. By blowing down the boiler periodically at depot (a valve under the barrel enabled this to be done) this sludge would be blown out of the boiler, enabling depot wash-out intervals to be extended.

The 'Merchant Navy' Class 4-6-2s • 61

Apart from having 6,000gallon tenders on slightly longer underframes, the third batch of 'Merchant Navy' locomotives were basically the same as the second batch, incorporating most of the modifications during their build. 35022 *Holland America Line* calls at Bournemouth Central on 10 March 1956 with the up 10.40 express to London Waterloo. Looking somewhat careworn externally, 35022 was an excellent performer and laid claim to an authenticated 104mph through Axminster.

35021 *New Zealand Line* with a cut-down tender is seen climbing Parkstone bank tender-first between Poole and Bournemouth with empty stock. One might be forgiven for asking why the driver still preferred to lean out of his cab side window to observe signals (and the occasional lineside photographer!) instead of looking through the rear view spectacle on the tender front!

Late in the life of the unrebuilt 'Merchant Navy' class, 35029 was surprise power for the Bournemouth Belle on 2 November 1957. The Down train is passing through Eastleigh station. 35029's black exhaust is evidence of the incomplete combustion of coal that these engines were accused of when being considered for rebuilding. The lack of a named train headboard on the smokebox door suggests that 35029 was a last-minute substitution at Nine Elms this day.

Only a few months before it entered Eastleigh Works for rebuilding, 35029 *Ellerman Lines* was still coupled to a tender that had not been modified with cut-down side raves. It calls at Eastleigh station with a Down semi-fast service to Bournemouth in summer 1957.

The 'Merchant Navy' Class 4-6-2s • 63

Performance

Engine crews welcomed the 'Merchant Navy' locomotives with open arms once the early reliability problems had been resolved. They now had locomotives that could haul all the trains on offer on the Southern and keep time with them. They liked the cab environment, and particularly the convenient grouping of controls and the electric lighting. The free steaming boilers and apparent 'free running' of these engines at speed soon became legendary.

In service, on the footplate a 'Merchant Navy' was as smooth riding as any steam locomotive I have experienced. The absence of detectable hammer-blow or in-built oscillation was distinctive. The 'mixed traffic' sized coupled wheels at 6ft 2in diameter proved to be no hindrance to fast running. On the long, well-aligned route between Basingstoke and Woking, a 'Merchant Navy' with twelve or thirteen coaches would usually bowl along at between 80mph and the line speed limit of 85mph. From an observer's viewpoint, the engines did not appear to be worked that hard, yet these speeds were indeed common. The presence of the 'Merchant Navy' class enabled BR to take ten minutes off the timings of the principal London Waterloo-Bournemouth Central expresses to achieve a regular journey time of two hours for this stretch of 108 miles, with one stop at Southampton Central. These were not lightweight trains, and included the luxury Pullman train, the Bournemouth Belle, which often loaded to over 500 tons.

The Southern Region possessed a self-weighing tender that was attached to any MN class locomotive when required. Otherwise it carried on in general service behind 35014 *Nederland Line*, and later 35024. This tender's coal bunker was carried on springs which allowed the bunker to rise gently as the coal was fired from it; a gauge on the tender front gave an approximate indication of the weight of coal in the bunker.

In the 1948 locomotive exchanges the 'Merchant Navy' class competed against such stalwarts as LMS 'Duchesses' and 'Royal Scots', LNER A4s and GWR 'Kings'. While other locomotive crews tended to drive for economy, the Southern engines were driven by their SR crews to keep time where possible, and inevitably suffered in the fuel economy comparisons with other classes. Even so, the 'Merchant Navy' average figure of 3.60lb of coal per drawbar horsepower hour was almost the same as the 'King' (3.59), and was better than that recorded with the WD 2-8-0 (3.77) and the WR 'Hall' (3.94). The 1948 trials had too many variables to produce truly definitive comparisons of locomotive efficiencies; tests on

'Merchant Navy' 4-6-2 35022 *Holland America Line* was tested on the static plant at Rugby and exhibited some poor indicator diagrams showing the steam distribution in the cylinders to be uneven. However, the highlight of the tests of this engine was the achieving of a higher boiler steam output than any other locomotive tested. *British Railways*

a roller test plant against a dynamometer, or with a controlled road test train, would have been more scientific. So, following these events, 35022 was tested on the rollers in Rugby testing station. With two firemen trying to feed the large fire grate, the highest potential output of the boiler was never reached. It had exceeded 42,000lbs of steam per hour when damage to coupling rods caused the test to be stopped. We can only speculate what the upper output limit of a 'MN' boiler might be! The indicator diagrams produced at these controlled tests for the Bulleid engine were frankly awful, indicating that the valves and valve gear were not properly distributing steam in an efficient manner.

There are recorded exploits by 'MNs' at higher speeds than the 85mph limit at that time on SR main lines, in particular an authenticated one accredited to 35022 *Holland America Line* in passing Axminster at 104mph. So why was there so much pressure in the 1950s that railway management should 'do something' about these locomotives' high fuel and water consumption and high maintenance costs? Chapter 23 explores this issue.

Class	MN 4-6-2
Engineer	O.V.S. Bulleid
Built by	SR and BR Eastleigh
BR power class	8P
Number in class	30
Introduced	1941
Cylinders (3)	18in x 24in
Coupled wheels	6ft 2in
Boiler pressure	280lbf/sq in*
Grate area	49.5sq ft
Tractive effort	37,500lbf
Weight in w.o.	94tons 15cwt
SR number series	21C 1-21C 20
BR number series	35001-35030

* Boiler pressure was reduced in the early 1950s to 250lbf/sq in, reducing tractive effort to 33,480lbf.

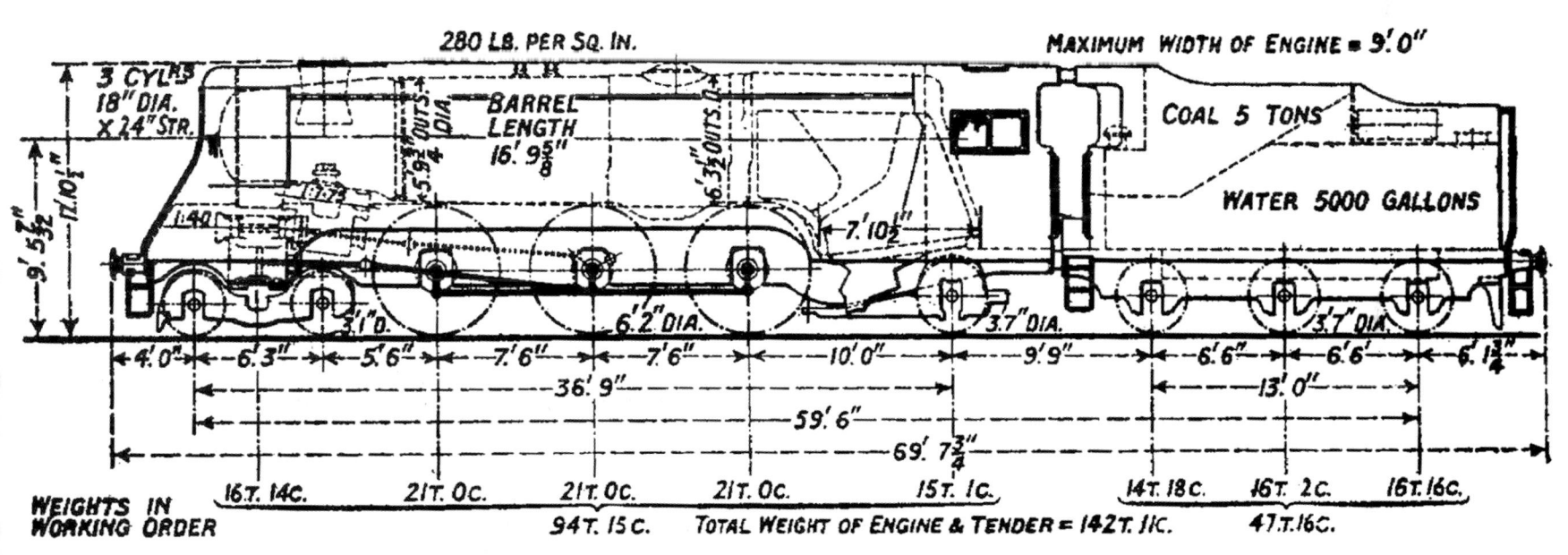

'Merchant Navy' class diagram for first batch. *SR*

Chapter 6
THE BULLEID-RAWORTH CO-CO ELECTRIC LOCOMOTIVES

Another completely new locomotive design emerged from Ashford Works in 1941, namely the Bulleid-Raworth Co-Co electric locomotive, the first two being numbered CC 1 and CC 2 in true Oliver Bulleid style following the continental system. Apart from its rather austere-looking body shape, this locomotive was innovative in its mechanical and electrical design. After some debate among general management, Oliver Bulleid assumed responsibility for the mechanical design of the locomotives. The Southern Railway's Electrical Engineer, Alfred Raworth, was responsible for the design and procurement of the electric traction equipment. The locomotives were intended for mixed traffic work; war-time freight was initially to

Bulleid/Raworth Co-Co electric locomotive No 20002 leans to the curve at Clapham Junction with a Newhaven boat train from London Victoria. This was British Railways' first national livery for non-steam main line locomotives, and was quite striking when kept clean. The carriage stock, a mixture of Bulleid and Maunsell types, is in carmine red-and-cream livery, the consist being eleven coaches plus a SR B van. *W.H.C. Kelland collection, courtesy Bournemouth Railway Club Trust*

The Bulleid-Raworth Co-Co Electric Locomotives • 67

be their main occupation but with an eye on future post-war work on heavy passenger services such as the London Victoria-Newhaven Harbour boat trains.

The two bogies dispensed with conventional bolsters, secondary springs and spring planks and instead relied for vertical ride solely on the primary leaf side springs with supplementary coil springing. The body was carried on side bearers, and the bogies relied on a centreless arrangement of sector plates and centring springs for lateral ride and curving. In service, this unorthodox arrangement proved to be successful. Each bogie rode on three wheelsets with 3ft 7in diameter wheels, each wheelset being driven by one 245hp traction motor supplied by English Electric. The locomotive bodies were mounted on heavy girder underframes.

The locomotives were designed to run on the SR's conductor rail network which was pressed at a nominal 660V dc. In some freight yards it was deemed unsafe to have conductor rails around the yard at ground level where shunters might come into contact with them in the course of their duties. Simple tramway-type overhead wires were erected over specific reception sidings and run-round loops, for which each locomotive was equipped with a central pantograph of the box type mounted in a recess centrally on the roof. Modern axle-hung traction motors that were suitable for this type of locomotive were already capable of absorbing higher voltages than 660, 1,500V dc being typical.

Another issue that stemmed directly from the SR's third rail system, was the need for a locomotive to continue moving whenever it came across a gap in the conductor rail. Gaps were necessary at points and crossings to allow train wheels to pass across the alignment that the third rail would otherwise occupy.

20002 stands at Eastleigh depot on 10 May 1959 after outshopping from Eastleigh Locomotive Works, the first electric locomotive to be overhauled there after the closure of Ashford Works. The livery is BR/SR coaching stock green with a red side band edged in white, a livery for SR electric locomotives also used on the Doncaster-built E5000 series locomotives. The centrally-located pantograph is just visible above the roof line.

Passing Lancing on 20 April 1960, Co-Co electric 20002 heads an Up freight. The headcode displayed by the white discs is for Brighton & Hove via the Preston Park spur, so the train is probably from the Portsmouth area and eventually bound for London's Norwood yard after remarshalling.

On typical electric multiple units, the collector shoes were far enough apart to bridge such gaps. Locomotives were too short to bridge the gaps with their collector shoes.

Raworth's team, together with English Electric, demonstrated inventiveness in meeting these two problems with one solution. No CC 1, and subsequent Southern straight electric locomotives, employed large motor-generator sets within the locomotive bodies, two such in the case of the Bulleid-Raworth Co-Cos. On each motor-generator set, the motor part received the full 660V dc current from the conductor rail. This motor was able to drive the generator at variable speeds so that the latter would output current at variable voltages suitable for starting and accelerating a train. By adjusting the field strengths on these machines, a driver, who had 26 notches on the traction controller, could adjust the output voltage to the traction motors from near zero to maximum.

Once again, there was innovation in this arrangement, because the output feed to the motors could be switched such that it was added to the 660V direct current from the third rail to feed up to 1,200V dc to the traction motors. Locomotives CC 1 and CC 2 were

The Bulleid-Raworth Co-Co Electric Locomotives • 69

New in 1948, 20003 was quickly repainted from SR green into BR's standard livery of black with stainless metal numerals and side stripes. This view is of it at Waterloo for an official inspection. The different cab front is evident. The locomotive was slightly heavier and more powerful than the first two of the type. All three worked on the Central Section of the Southern Region. *W.H.C. Kelland collection, courtesy Bournemouth Railway Club Trust*

rated at 1,470bhp continuous, with a maximum tractive effort of 40,000lbf. With an overall locomotive weight of almost 100 tons, these locomotives at that time had the highest haulage capacity of any locomotives on the Southern. While their horse power was lower than a Bulleid Pacific could produce, the electric locomotives' maximum speed of 75mph was readily attainable on the passenger loads offered to them. The two electric locomotives proved their worth with reliable operation and they competently handled the trains they were required to haul.

The other innovative feature of the motor-generator sets was the use of a heavy flywheel fitted on the same shaft and between the motor and the generator. This had the effect of enabling an admittedly-reducing voltage to continue to be fed to the traction motors when a locomotive was

The BR/SR green livery looked rather drab when applied to 20003, seen at Eastleigh Works after an overhaul in 1966. One of the Doncaster-built (1957) E5000 series locomotives is behind it.

temporarily moving across a gap in the conductor rail.[7]

A third locomotive of updated design was delivered from Brighton Works in 1948. No 20003 was too late to receive its Southern Railway number CC 3, and BR included it in its new scheme, the other two being renumbered 20001 and 20002.[8] 20003 was heavier and longer than the first two, and in appearance a little more stark with its straight-fronted cab. All three locomotives served competently on Central Section freight and passenger work. Whatever reason BR had to give these locomotives the power classification 7P 5F,

---

7. Most commentators have seized upon this feature as the reason for the use of motor-generator sets on these locomotives. I am convinced that the traction advantages, including buck-and-boost, were the main reasons for their employment, the flywheels being an important addition to an innovative approach.

8. British Railways actually had three locomotives that carried the number 20002, though not at the same time. BR inherited a Kirtley 2-4-0 tender engine from the LMS that carried the number 20002 until withdrawn in 1948; it never received its BR number. BR also numbered a Bo-Bo Type 1 diesel as 20 002; that was after the electric 20002 had been withdrawn. The aesthetic gap between the 20 and 002 on the diesel was no doubt eliminated on subsequent repaints.

The Bulleid-Raworth Co-Co Electric Locomotives • 71

the power and high tractive effort actually available would, in my opinion, justify this being revised to at least 7P 9F.

Their early livery was SR malachite green, initially with narrow lining and 'speed whiskers' (CC 1 and CC 2). From 1949, BR imposed its livery of black with a silver band along the bodysides that it had inherited from diesels 10000 and 10001. Later, from 1956, the Southern Region broke ranks and painted its electric locomotives SR carriage stock green (a slightly darker shade than malachite) with a red band along each side edged in white. Nos 20001 and 20002 received a few modifications during their lifetimes, including fitting BR-SR air horns and roller-blind route indictors on the cab fronts to replace the electric marker lamps originally fitted. Only No 20001 received BR rail blue livery, at the last major overhaul given to this type in 1966. After July 1967, when all steam working had ceased on internal SR services, 20001 was the SR's only smart-looking locomotive that could still deliver steam heat to a vacuum braked train, and so it enjoyed occasional use when the Royal Train visited south of the Thames. After that train had been modernised with air brakes and electric heating, 20001 was withdrawn in 1969 as the last of its class. None is preserved.

Class	Co-Co electric
Engineers	O.V.S. Bulleid and A. Raworth
Built by	SR and BR Ashford and Brighton*
Traction equipment	English Electric Co.
BR power class	7P 5F
Number in class	3
Introduced	1941, 1948*
Wheels diameter	3ft 7in
Electric supply	660Volts direct current
Current collection	Conductor rail/overhead wire
Control	Motor-generator sets and flywheels
Power output	1,470 brake horse power
Tractive effort	40,000lbf, 45,000lbf*
Maximum speed	75mph
Train heat	Electrically-heated steam boiler
Weight in w.o.	99tons 15cwt, 104tons 14cwt*
SR number series	CC 1, CC 2
BR number series	20001-20003

* Asterisked data refer to 20003.

Eastleigh Works had a rudimentary electric locomotive test facility at first, to check such things as traction motor rotation. This view of 20001 in 1966 shows it equipped with BR/SR roller-blind indicators on the cab fronts, and standard 'raspberry' air horns on the cab roofs. Accordingly, the clutter of headcode discs on the cab front has been removed. 20001 was the only Bulleid locomotive to be painted BR rail blue. As such, its duties included hauling the Royal Train until the latter was modernised with air brakes and electric heating.

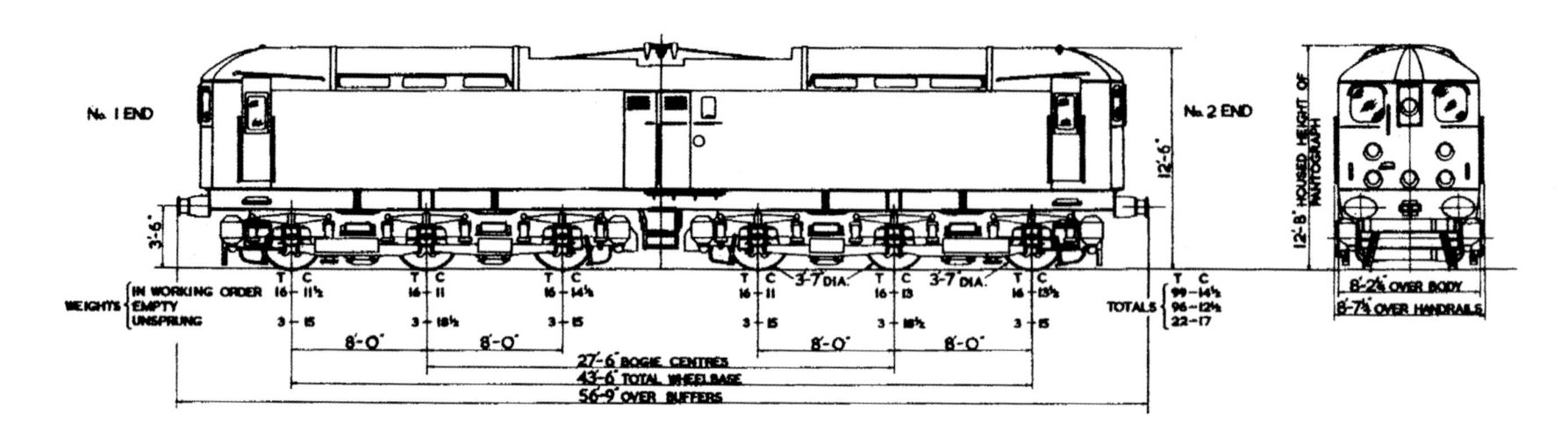

72 • OLIVER BULLEID'S LOCOMOTIVES

Co-Co electric locomotive CC 1 diagram
SR

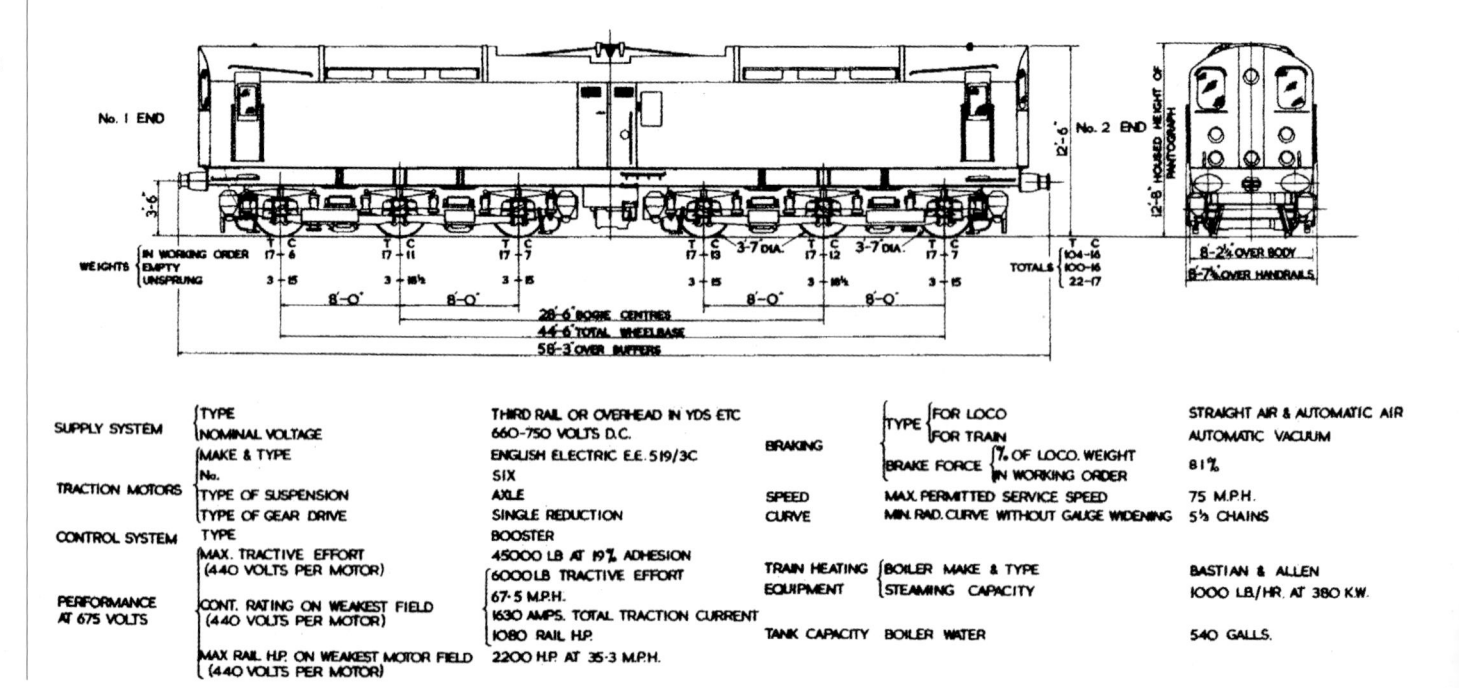

SUPPLY SYSTEM	TYPE	THIRD RAIL OR OVERHEAD IN YDS. ETC.	BRAKING	TYPE { FOR LOCO. / FOR TRAIN }	STRAIGHT AIR & AUTOMATIC AIR / AUTOMATIC VACUUM
	NOMINAL VOLTAGE	660-750 VOLTS D.C.		BRAKE FORCE { % OF LOCO. WEIGHT / IN WORKING ORDER }	85%
TRACTION MOTORS	MAKE & TYPE	ENGLISH ELECTRIC E.E. 519A			
	No.	SIX	SPEED	MAX. PERMITTED SERVICE SPEED	75 M.P.H.
	TYPE OF SUSPENSION	AXLE	CURVE	MIN. RAD. CURVE WITHOUT GAUGE WIDENING	5½ CHAINS
	TYPE OF GEAR DRIVE	SINGLE REDUCTION			
CONTROL SYSTEM	TYPE	BOOSTER			
	MAX. TRACTIVE EFFORT (440 VOLTS PER MOTOR)	45000 LB. AT 20% ADHESION	TRAIN HEATING EQUIPMENT	BOILER MAKE & TYPE	BASTIAN & ALLEN
PERFORMANCE AT 660 VOLTS	CONT. RATING ON WEAKEST FIELD (440 VOLTS PER MOTOR)	6000 LB. TRACTIVE EFFORT / 67·5 M.P.H. / 1630 AMPS. TOTAL TRACTION CURRENT / 1080 RAIL H.P.		STEAMING CAPACITY	1000 LB./HR. AT 380 K.W.
	MAX RAIL H.P. ON WEAKEST MOTOR FIELD (440 VOLTS PER MOTOR)	2200 H.P. AT 35·3 M.P.H.	TANK CAPACITY	BOILER WATER	320 GALLS.

Co-Co electric locomotive 20003 diagram.
BR

SUPPLY SYSTEM	TYPE	THIRD RAIL OR OVERHEAD IN YDS ETC	BRAKING	TYPE { FOR LOCO / FOR TRAIN }	STRAIGHT AIR & AUTOMATIC AIR / AUTOMATIC VACUUM
	NOMINAL VOLTAGE	660-750 VOLTS D.C.		BRAKE FORCE { % OF LOCO. WEIGHT / IN WORKING ORDER }	81%
TRACTION MOTORS	MAKE & TYPE	ENGLISH ELECTRIC E.E. 519/3C			
	No.	SIX	SPEED	MAX. PERMITTED SERVICE SPEED	75 M.P.H.
	TYPE OF SUSPENSION	AXLE	CURVE	MIN. RAD. CURVE WITHOUT GAUGE WIDENING	5½ CHAINS
	TYPE OF GEAR DRIVE	SINGLE REDUCTION			
CONTROL SYSTEM	TYPE	BOOSTER			
	MAX. TRACTIVE EFFORT (440 VOLTS PER MOTOR)	45000 LB AT 19% ADHESION	TRAIN HEATING EQUIPMENT	BOILER MAKE & TYPE	BASTIAN & ALLEN
PERFORMANCE AT 675 VOLTS	CONT. RATING ON WEAKEST FIELD (440 VOLTS PER MOTOR)	6000 LB TRACTIVE EFFORT / 67·5 M.P.H. / 1630 AMPS. TOTAL TRACTION CURRENT / 1080 RAIL H.P.		STEAMING CAPACITY	1000 LB./HR. AT 380 K.W.
	MAX RAIL H.P. ON WEAKEST MOTOR FIELD (440 VOLTS PER MOTOR)	2200 H.P. AT 35·3 M.P.H.	TANK CAPACITY	BOILER WATER	540 GALLS.

Chapter 7
THE Q1 CLASS 0-6-0s

Controversy never seems to be far away when Mr Bulleid is mentioned in railway circles. Some of this surrounds his Class Q1 0-6-0 design. This straightforward 0-6-0 freight engine demonstrated OVB's response to the request that the SR needed a simple, cheap and effective freight hauler that would meet the requirement for war-time austerity at a time when steel supplies were being diverted to the war effort. That the Q1 was a war locomotive goes without saying. That it met its key objectives, effectiveness and austerity, is also true. The controversy erupts when people discuss the Q1 locomotive's appearance. Apparently one either loves it or hates it. There are no half-measures in opinions on the Q1's aesthetics.

In a way, it is ironic that such a locomotive appeared when it did. Other railways were building 2-8-0 freight engines in large numbers, or accepting the new War Department 2-8-0s as an austerity engine with a planned limited life span. It would have been simple for the SR to opt for LMS 8F or WD 2-8-0s rather than introduce a new class of its own. Knowing OVB's initial reaction over the 'unimaginative' Q class 0-6-0, one can only express admiration for his perhaps delayed recognition that the Q was actually a good design that could be developed further and at minimum cost. So, basically, the Q1 was an enlarged Q. It had similar frames, the same wheel size (but Boxpok, of course), the same cylinder dimensions, a higher boiler pressure and a much larger grate area. The Q1 followed the Q class

Austere maybe, distinctly functional certainly, Bulleid Q1 0-6-0 C 8 stands at Feltham depot in west London in Southern Railway days. The steam reverser is clearly visible above the centre coupled wheelset. This angle also shows how practical was the suggestion by the designer that engine crew could stand on the coupling rod to access the inside valve gear for oiling. *W.H.C. Kelland collection, courtesy Bournemouth Railway Club Trust*

precedent in using cylinders with outside steam admission, and thus direct inside exhaust emission. The cylinders exhausted through a Lemaître five-jet blastpipe and a wide, fabricated petticoat and plain chimney. The choice of Stephenson's valve gear was logical, in that the gear was regarded as ideal for the work of pulling slow, heavy freight trains.

The boiler had to be bigger to satisfy OVB's insistence that the boiler is the heart of any steam locomotive, but the SR did not have a suitable one among its various types. What Bulleid did was use the available materials intelligently. The firebox tube plates were made using the pressings for the 'Lord Nelson' class tubeplates, so the Q1 got a large Belpaire firebox but much shorter than a 'Nelson' had, and a necessarily short boiler barrel which was easily rolled from plate in its tapered form. The resulting 27sq ft grate area exceeded the Q class area by 5sq ft, and the short barrel helped to avoid there being too much cold water at the front. The Q1 boiler proved itself in service as a free-steaming, powerful boiler.

To keep down the locomotive weight, the new 0-6-0 was stripped of all 'unnecessary' components and considerable use was made of fabrications rather than steel castings. Among the discarded pieces were running boards and valances, and thus their associated bracketry. Boiler lagging plates

33010 stands ready for action at Hither Green on 16 August 1959, not long after an overhaul. In the background is Drewry 0-6-0 204bhp diesel mechanical shunter DS1173. This was acquired in OVB's time in 1946 for departmental use and so didn't enter capital stock. Nonetheless, the type was later purchased in considerable numbers by British Railways as part of its modernization plan.

were simplified, made of light plate on lightweight frameworks, and shaped partially to match the outline of the locomotive's firebox. Heavy iron castings for the dome and chimney were not used, light steel plating being welded into adequate shapes for these. Drivers were advised that the inside Stephenson's valve gear could be reached easily for oiling by standing on the side coupling rods. Indeed, OVB visited several depots to speak directly to locomotive men and fitters, using the medium of the 'improvement classes' to get his ideas across to interested depot people.

The tender design was similar to that used on his Pacifics but smaller. Both types used a typical Ashford design of frames, wheelsets and axleboxes, with a lightweight structure above making up the coal space and water tank, the sides being curved as with the Pacific tenders. All wheels had B-F-B centres.

The weight of a Q1 locomotive in working order was 51tons 5cwt, less than two tons heavier than a Q 0-6-0. Yet BR measured the power rating of the Q1 as 5F, and it was acknowledged to be the most powerful 0-6-0 in the UK, and maybe also in Europe. The light weight for such a powerful locomotive had one disadvantage, namely the class's ability to stop heavy unbraked goods trains. Train crews had to be careful in handling these in this respect.

Q1 0-6-0 33035 rattles through Knockholt with a southbound unfitted freight. The headcode discs indicate that the train is destined for Folkestone and/or Dover. This route would take the train through Tonbridge, approaching which the crew would need to take care in braking the train on the downgrade owing to the locomotive's relatively light weight which slightly limited its stopping power. *D.C. Ovenden/Colour Rail 18001*

Running into
Bournemouth depot after a loco coal train duty on 24 July 1954 is Q1 33019. Without the cast iron numberplate on the smokebox door, this engine would be almost unidentifiable due to the accumulated dirt!

Otherwise the Q1s proved to be free-running locomotives capable of hauling secondary passenger trains at up to 75mph (post-war when speed limits had been raised) and managing quite heavy goods trains in wartime conditions.

When compared with the haulage capacity of a WD 2-8-0, a Q1 comes out remarkably well. OVB's talk to enginemen at Feltham depot, as reported by his son H.A.V. Bulleid, included a table comparing the two 'austerity' designs and their capabilities. I include an extract from that table here. OVB's comparison showed that a Q1 could haul up a 1 in 200 gradient a train of 101 wagons of 16ton gross weight, and a WD could manage 107 such wagons (110 if one accepts other published versions of WD tractive effort). On steeper gradients, the difference between the haulage capacities was less. As a much cheaper alternative, the SR clearly had a bargain with the Bulleid 0-6-0, particularly when taking into account the Q1's ability to speed along with light passenger trains, something the WD was never intended to do and was not suited to. The comparison between BR's 5F classification of the Q1 and 8F of the WD was peculiar, to say the least!

Forty Q1s were built from 1942. They received only minor modifications during their 25-years life span. One new fitment was a mechanical lubricator mounted on the driver's side (left) of the front running board and driven by a crank from the leading coupled axle end. The last Q1 was withdrawn in 1966. Happily, the first-built Q1 is preserved as part of the national collection. It has performed on the Bluebell Railway as No C 1, and more recently has posed in the National Railway Museum as 33001. Either way, it still attracts controversy!

The Q1 Class 0-6-0s • 77

Comparison, Q1 0-6-0 and WD 2-8-0

		Q1	WD	WD*
Tractive effort lbf		30,000	32,438	34,215*
Weight of engine and tender		89t 5c	125t 3c	125t 3c
Total locomotive resistance (lbf) up	1 in 50 gradient	5,070	7,106	7,106
	1 in 100	3,070	4,305	4,305
	1 in 200	2,070	2,904	2,904
Available tractive effort behind the tender,	1 in 50	24,930	25,332	27,109*
	1 in 100	26,930	28,133	29,910*
	1 in 200	27,930	29,534	31,311*
Equivalent number of 12t wagons at 16t gross,	1 in 50	31	31	32*
	1 in 100	59	62	64*
	1 in 200	101	107	110*

These figures illustrate the effects of engine weights on different track gradients.

* Figures adjusted to later published WD tractive effort.

Class	Q1 0-6-0
Engineer	O.V.S. Bulleid
Built by	SR Brighton (20) and Ashford (20)
BR power class	5F
Number in class	40
Introduced	1942
Cylinders (2 inside)	19in x 26in
Coupled wheels	5ft 1in
Boiler pressure	230lbf/sq in
Grate area	27sq ft
Tractive effort	30,080lbf
Weight in w.o.	51tons 5cwt
SR number series	C 1-C 40
BR number series	33001-33040

On secondary passenger duty, for which the Q1 class seemed quite suited due their free running, 33012 calls at Bramley & Wonersh station, between Guildford and Christ's Hospital, with a stopping train on 26 September 1964. Some examples of this class remained in service until 1966. *Colour-Rail 340087*

78 • OLIVER BULLEID'S LOCOMOTIVES

This rear view of C 1 after preservation shows the total lack of rearwards visibility due to the high sides of the tender. The locomotive was taking water at Sheffield Park on the Bluebell Railway on 6 September 1994.

Q1 locomotive diagram. *SR*

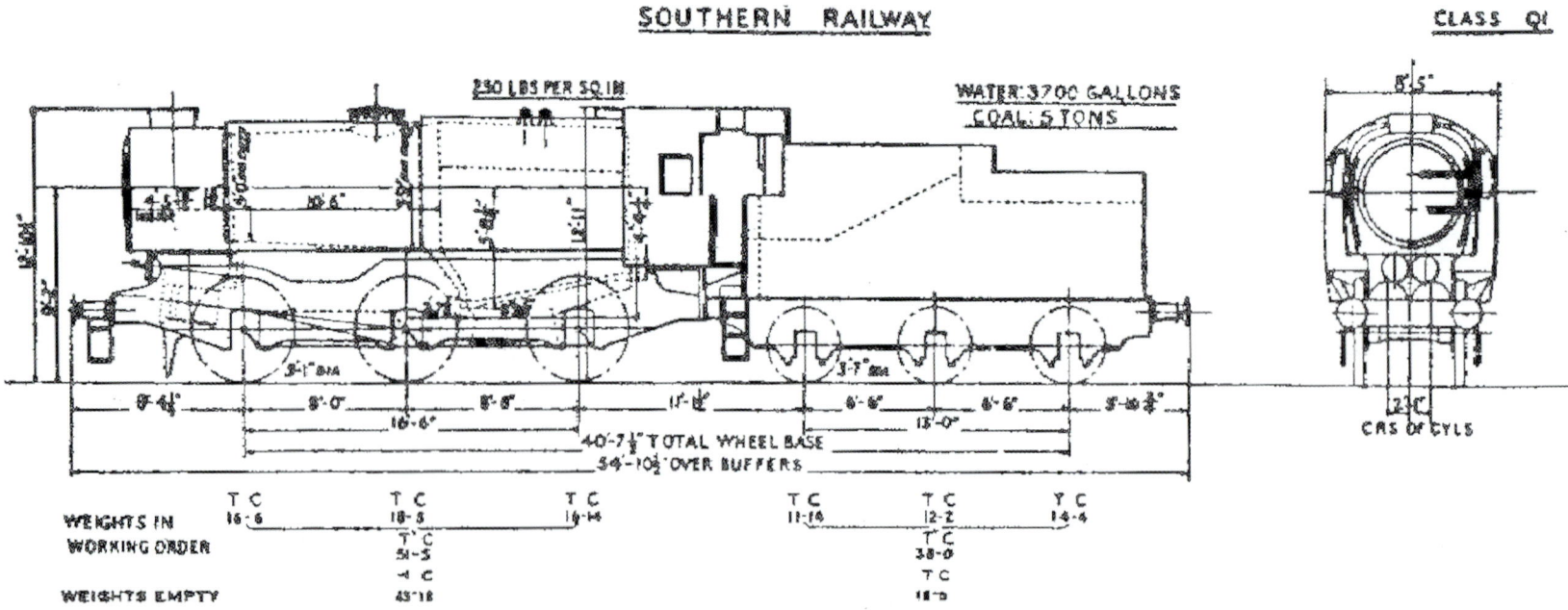

Chapter 8

THE 'WEST COUNTRY' AND 'BATTLE OF BRITAIN' 4-6-2s

During the Second World War, the Southern Railway workshops were deeply engaged in producing equipment for the war effort. This work intensified as preparations were made for the D-Day invasion in May 1944. One can imagine that there was little capacity at this time for new locomotive construction for future post-war needs. As progress of the war began to turn towards favouring the Allies, it became possible once more to look forward to reviving the railway in future years. The SR had taken a severe toll from enemy bombing earlier in the war. Repair work on infrastructure would take several years to overcome the damage, as well as recovering from the reduced maintenance of the war years. Locomotives and rolling stock would need repair, overhaul and replacement. By 1945, the end of the war was in sight, and the SR had already taken its first key steps to order new locomotives.

Posing in original condition, with nameplates in place, is 'West Country' 4-6-2 21C 102 *Salisbury*. In appearance it is like a second batch 'Merchant Navy' but a few inches narrower and a foot or so shorter in length. The tender is a 4,500 gallons version. Note that the cab side sheet merges with the main casing just under six feet from rail level. The livery is malachite green with yellow stripes and a black strip from the top of the wheel space to the bottom of the casings. The nameplate scrolls are red-backed and the city crest sits between the name and the class scrolls. *W.H.C. Kelland collection, courtesy Bournemouth Railway Club Trust*

With the 'Merchant Navy' class established as the railway's front-runner for express passenger work, and the Q1 class still fully intact for general freight, ably supported by the heavier Urie and Maunsell 4-6-0s for the trunk freight trains, the foreseen major requirement on the SR was for mixed traffic locomotives. There was also a niche requirement during high summer for larger locomotives to improve train loads and timings on the West Country routes beyond Exeter. These routes had some severe gradients that challenged the railway's ability to move holiday expresses effectively. Due to axle load limits, the largest locomotives available that could run on the secondary routes west of Exeter were the Maunsell 2-6-0s, rated by BR as 4P 5F; these engines could move quite heavy trains, but not at the useful speeds then envisaged. In his time, R.E.L. Maunsell had drafted a scheme for a three-cylinder 2-6-2, akin to an enlarged U1, which would have been a step in the right direction. OVB's response was bolder.

The need for an axleload no higher than 19 tons was paramount, so a lightweight, high performance locomotive would be ideal. The Chief Civil Engineer was not in favour of leading pony trucks, so a leading bogie was wanted. Obviously aimed at the west-of-Exeter lines, the 'West Country' class design emerged as a smaller version of the 'Merchant Navy'. The comparison between the two classes is interesting. A 'West Country' had the same wheel arrangement, wheel sizes, and Bulleid valve gear, on a wheelbase just 1ft 3in shorter. The cylinders were of smaller diameter, 16⅜in diameter instead of 18in, but the stroke of 24in was maintained, thus enabling the same crank axle design to be used. Boiler pressure was also the same at 280lbf/sq in. The fire grate area was 38.25sq ft, almost 5sq ft more than a 'Lord Nelson' but over 10sq ft less than a 'Merchant Navy'. The 'WC' class boiler barrel was smaller diameter than the 'MN' but pitched higher so that the top of the boiler was at the same height above rail level. The barrel was just 1¼in shorter. It contained four rows of superheater flues, 20 per cent less than a 'Merchant Navy' boiler. The light Pacifics were designed with a maximum width of 8ft 7⅝in so that they could traverse the Hastings line south of Tonbridge; the 'MNs' were the standard 9ft width.

These changes might not appear to use a lot less metal but real life can be deceptive. The 'West Country' class engines each weighed in at 86 tons, some 6 tons 15cwts less than a 'Merchant Navy', or 9 per cent lighter. The maximum axle load of 18 tons 15cwt was usefully less than the 21tons of a 'MN' and ideal for the west-of-Exeter routes. Bulleid had produced Britain's lightest ever 4-6-2 design. Only the BR standard 'Clan' class that appeared in 1952 could approach the low weight of the 'West Country' class, but the 'Clan' was rated by BR as 6P 5F whereas the Bulleid light Pacifics were to be rated 7P 5F. The BR 'Britannias' were 7P 6F but weighed 94 tons, about the same as the 8P 'Merchant Navy' design.

Performance

But how would the lightweight Bulleid Pacifics fare when hauling heavy trains? With their axleload about 11 per cent less than that of the bigger engines, and knowing the propensity of the heavier 'Merchant Navy' type to wheelslip, how would a 'West Country' manage when starting heavy passenger trains? Again, we must compare the larger and smaller Pacifics to understand. We recall that among the earlier trials of the 'MN' Pacifics were runs with up to twenty coaches in tow. After the war, the 'MN's performed daily runs at speed with trains such as the Bournemouth Belle with its heavy twelve-wheeled Pullman cars weighing over 500 tons tare for a twelve-coach train. Allowing for the 11 per cent reduction in adhesion weight, a 'West Country' could thus be expected to start trains of, say, 445 tons. Trains of twelve of the SR's Bulleid and Maunsell stock would rarely exceed 400 tons, so even the thirteen-coach Royal Wessex made up of BR mark 1 stock could be 'West Country' hauled with confidence, as indeed it was diagrammed to be in the Up direction.

In fact, in addition to their ability to do what was needed in Devon and Cornwall, the light Pacifics were well capable of hauling all but the heaviest main line expresses elsewhere on the SR with moderate economy. A 'West Country' could deputise when needed for a 'Merchant Navy', when its performance might be stretched a bit when asked to cover a class 8P diagram, but they could be pushed hard to do this, and were.

During the 1948 locomotive exchanges, the 'West Country' class trio (34004, 34005 and 34006) performed very well in terms of

Already doing work that was rostered for a MN class Pacific, WC 4-6-2 21C 110 *Sidmouth* has at least twelve coaches in tow on the Atlantic Coast Express. Most of the stock is still of Maunsell design, suggesting the picture was taken around 1946 or 1947. *W.H.C. Kelland collection, courtesy Bournemouth Railway Club Trust*

haulage and timekeeping. Indeed, the exploits of 34004 *Yeovil* on the Highland main line are legendary and the legends are happily true. One of the 'lightweights' produced the highest drawbar horse power output of all locomotives tested during the 1948 exchanges, including the locomotives of 8P power class, a credit to Bulleid's design indeed. This was 34006 *Bude* on the Great Central route, which developed a steady 2,010 equivalent drawbar horse power between Leicester and Whetstone. All the Bulleid Pacifics tested in 1948 suffered from higher-than-normal coal and water consumption when compared with other Regions' classes, the 'West Country' class producing the worst figure of all locomotives tested.

Criticism was levelled at the SR for using Pacific locomotives

In 1948 the works around the country were allowed to go on overhauling and painting locomotives in their pre-nationalization liveries until British Railways' new renumbering scheme and new liveries had been approved, which didn't happen until 1949; letters and numbers were changed as seen here, but still in the pre-1948 styles. Thus s21C 116 *Bodmin* was outshopped at Eastleigh still in shiny malachite green, red-backed nameplates, and the full 'Southern' roundel on the smokebox door. *S.C. Townroe/Colour-Rail BRS424*

on surprisingly short trains in the West Country area. This was indeed a fact, but it resulted from the seasonally peak nature of traffic in a major holiday region. During the summer months, most trains were substantially strengthened and 7P motive power was essential. What would have been the alternative? To store the Pacifics for nine months of the year and use Moguls in the low traffic season, and store the 2-6-0s in the summer when the Pacifics were needed? The SR chose to use what they had all the year round, and who can blame them?

One feature that affected the Bulleid Pacifics was their tendency occasionally to catch fire. Oil from the oil bath appeared to have splashed upwards at times, soaking the boiler lagging on the underside of the barrel. The most likely source of ignition would be sparks from the cast iron brake blocks during heavy braking at speed. I witnessed one such fire which mysteriously happened while a Pacific was waiting for coaling at Bournemouth depot. Fortunately, it was standing alongside a water column, so the crew directed the water bag over the top of the locomotive to put out the flames. The visible result was a large rust patch on each side of the air-smoothed casing, which was later painted over with dark green paint, unlined until its next visit to main works.

The 'West Country' and 'Battle of Britain' 4-6-2s • 83

In the far west of England the 'West Country' class engines soon found themselves on short trains when running outside the holiday season. This one has just had the 's' prefix added while the very young British Railways needed time to sort out a comprehensive renumbering scheme. Running as s21C 146, *Braunton* handles a stopping service at Barnstaple made up of a Bulleid two-car set and a Maunsell third class coach.
W.H.C. Kelland collection, courtesy Bournemouth Railway Club Trust

Developments, modifications and adornments

As with the 'Merchant Navy' class, the 'West Country' class locomotives had their cab fronts cut back to enable crews to reach the windscreens for cleaning while standing in the cab and leaning forward from a side window. The majority of the class were built in this condition. Also, from early 1953, light Pacific tenders had their side raves cut down to improve the rearward view. The earlier 4,500 gallon tenders were perhaps less aesthetically satisfactory in this condition than the later 5,500 gallon ones, but eventually all were so modified, the majority (if not all) before the rebuilding of the class began in 1957. Also the plating in front of the cylinders was removed to improve access to the front cylinder covers and relief valves.

From 34071 onwards to 34110, the locomotives were built with cabs at 9ft width; the SR operators had decided not to use the class on the Tonbridge-Hastings

34009 *Lyme Regis* sits at Nine Elms depot in 1959 in its BR condition with revised cab windscreens and the platework removed from in front of the outside cylinders. The livery is BR dark green, often called 'Brunswick green', with just two black stripes edged in orange as lining. The smokebox door's cast iron numberplate replaces the 'Southern' roundel and the gunmetal (brass) nameplates are backed in black, the standard BR adopted from 1949. The yellow solid disc painted on the cabside below the locomotive number indicates that the engine is fitted for briquette feedwater treatment. This caused confusion in the minds of some Western Region folk who thought it meant a severe restriction in route availability, and so the disc was replaced by an inverted solid triangle on all locomotives so equipped.

line after all, and the wider cab improved forward visibility a little.

Because of the success of the light Pacifics, construction continued eventually to reach 110 locomotives. It was deemed that, for regular use on services to the Kent coast, names of obscure West Country towns and villages would not be of much public interest in the south-east corner of England. The idea gained currency of naming almost half the class after people, aircraft, aerodromes and squadrons that had been involved in the Battle of Britain in the skies over Kent early in the war.

The 'West Country' and 'Battle of Britain' 4-6-2s • 85

34011 *Tavistock* is forging ahead through Eastleigh with a Bournemouth West to Waterloo semi-fast in summer 1956. This train was a Nine Elms duty at the time.

The same engine a year later passes the Southern Railway signalbox at Pokesdown in the Bournemouth suburbs as it accelerates downhill, soon to cross the rivers Stour and Avon either side of Christchurch on its way to London Waterloo.

A light Pacific cab photographed in the erecting shop in Eastleigh Locomotive Works shows the similarity to the cab of a 'Merchant Navy'. In this picture the foot pedal to operate the firehole doors is more prominent than in the picture of a 'MN' cab in Chapter 5. Otherwise, the controls are the same. This locomotive's fireman's seat is lowered whereas the driver's is folded up out of view of the camera.

The 'Battle of Britain' class was in fact just another set of names. There was no difference between the two classes mechanically. Both included narrow and wide cabs and both included larger and smaller tenders.

On the Southern Railway, the light Pacifics were placed new into service in malachite green with three longitudinal yellow stripes, as were the 'Merchant Navy' class engines. From 1949, British Railways applied its standard dark green with black-and-orange lining. The first 'WCs' were numbered in the same series as the larger Pacifics, with the 21C prefix and running numbers beginning at 101, the first locomotive, named *Exeter*, being 21C 101. Under British Railways, they occupied the number range 34001 to 34110.

The 'West Country' class nameplates were among the finest on any British locomotives, with the main plate in the shape of a scroll, mounted over a badge or crest appropriate to the place name concerned, with the class name on a smaller scroll underneath the badge. Some less significant place names had no badges, and the locomotives looked a little less grand without them. The Southern Railway painted the nameplate backings bright red. BR changed this to black, which still looked smart but not so striking. Eastleigh Works reverted to painting the nameplates red around 1962. Like all SR nameplates, they were cast in gunmetal (brass) with the lettering an integral part of the casting.

For the 'Battle of Britain' class, a nameplate shaped like an aircraft wing in plan view was placed above an oval-shaped badge which was either that of the body named, or otherwise it showed the Royal Air Force crest. The nameplate backings were painted air-force blue, a colour that was not a good match for malachite green. BR painted them black, which was perhaps better, though from around 1963 they began to appear from works in blue again, this time more effectively standing out from BR's darker green colour. Only 34110 ran without a badge.[9]

BR was interested in making improvements to its steam locomotive fleet in the mid- to late 1950s, witness the application of high temperature superheat on such engines as ex-GWR 'Kings' and 'Castles', and the changes made to Gresley A3 Pacifics. With more modern locomotives such as the Bulleid Pacifics and BR standards, this approach was not available as the locomotives already included these features. One modification that was popular in Austria and in East Germany was the exhaust system devised by the Austrian engineer Dr. Giesl von Gieslingen. The Giesl ejector replaced the traditional blast pipe with a long narrow slot capped by two plates giving seven small exhaust streams in a row. The slot width was experimentally adjustable by dint of moving two plates closer or further apart. The exhaust was directed upwards through a long narrow petticoat and chimney. In older locomotives, it enabled fuel economy to be coupled with better general performance.

BR authorised only two locomotives to test this device, Southern 4-6-2 34064 *Fighter Command*, and BR 9F 2-10-0 92250.[10] On 34064, the Giesl ejector had two key effects. It did indeed help to reduce exhaust back pressure, giving a slight enhancement to the locomotive performance when working hard. It also reduced spark emissions at the same time as raising the exhaust clearer of the cab, thus improving forward view. The degree of improvement was not deemed sufficient to justify the cost of replacing all the Pacifics' Lemaître exhausts and it was not pursued.

End of SR steam, and preservation

The rebuilding of the Bulleid light Pacifics is described in Chapter 23 of this book. It is pertinent to write here that not all the class was rebuilt. Fifty locomotives continued in service in unmodified state until withdrawals began in 1962; some lasted with their normal works overhauls right through to 1967. Indeed, 34023 *Blackmore Vale* and 34102 *Lapford* were in regular service until the end of steam on the Southern Region of BR, being withdrawn in July 1967. Many withdrawn locomotives ended up in Woodham's scrap yard in Barry Island, South Wales, where they remained untouched by the cutter's torch until buyers emerged for them. We are lucky that twenty Bulleid light Pacifics are in existence as I write this book, ten in original form and ten rebuilds. In the twenty-first century, the Giesl-fitted 34092 *City of Wells* and Lemaître-fitted 34067 *Tangmere* have covered themselves in glory with many fine performances out on the main line, justifying several observers' view that the original Bulleid Pacifics were really good engines when assiduously maintained.

Class	WC and BB 4-6-2
Engineer	O.V.S. Bulleid
Built by	SR and BR Brighton*
BR power class	7P 5FA
Number in class	110
Introduced	1945
Cylinders (3)	$16^3/_8$in x 24in
Coupled wheels	6ft 2in
Boiler pressure	280lbf/sq in**
Grate area	38.25sq ft
Tractive effort	31,040lbf
Weight in w.o.	86tons 0cwt
SR number series	21C 101-21C 170
BR number series	34001-34110

* Six locomotives, Nos 34095, 34097, 34099, 34101, 34102 and 34104, were built by BR at Eastleigh, the rest all at Brighton.
** Boiler pressure was reduced in the early 1950s to 250lbf/sq in, giving tractive effort of 27,715lbf.

---

9. In fact, a pair of 'BB' badges with the RAF emblem existed inside Eastleigh Locomotive Works throughout my engineering apprenticeship there in 1954-59; they appeared on display at Works Open Days. Were these the badges intended for 34110?
10. A Giesl ejector was also fitted around this time to Talyllyn Railway 0-4-2ST No 4 *Edward Thomas*. The greatest use of the Giesl ejector in the UK was on locomotives operated by the National Coal Board which chose to fit them to some 'austerity' 0-6-0STs as well as to some Barclay 0-6-0Ts. Interestingly, the preserved 'West Country' 34092 City of Wells has run with a Giesl ejector for many years and has been a good main line performer in that condition.

On cross-country duty, 34047 Callington accelerates out of Southampton Central on 29 November 1955 with the daily through train from Brighton to Cardiff. The locomotive would be replaced at Salisbury by a Western Region 4-6-0, usually a 'Hall', for the run into WR territory, an uneconomic use of motive power if ever there was one!

The 'West Country' and 'Battle of Britain' 4-6-2s • 89

Despite being defined as mixed traffic locomotives, and given the power group 7P 5FA, it was unusual to find 34095 *Brentor* on a freight in the Bournemouth area. The headcode suggests a working from Hamworthy, probably of locomotive or domestic coal. 34095 is crossing the county boundary between Dorset and Hampshire as it enters the Borough of Bournemouth on Coy Pond embankment. As all light Pacifics from 34071 upwards were built to the wider standard SR loading gauge, this shows in this example where the cab side sheets are too wide to blend with the main casing. The tender is a 5,500gallon version.

34105 *Swanage* works an Up express from Weymouth on 16 September 1956. It is on the 1 in 60 of Parkstone bank approaching the station of that name and is banked by another of the same class. The train is a special for the Ian Allan Group and included a Devon Belle observation car.

This evening freight from Southampton Docks to London was often used to return locomotives to their depots after overhaul at Eastleigh Locomotive Works. This sixty-wagons train sometimes had unusual engines at the head as a result (including once a 'Schools' 4-4-0 that must have been stressed!) and on this occasion in 1956 34007 *Wadebridge* was under way heading north through Eastleigh seemingly needing little effort to move the heavy train.

The 'West Country' and 'Battle of Britain' 4-6-2s • 91

For the 1948 locomotive exchanges, 34004 *Yeovil*, 34005 *Barnstaple* and 34006 *Bude*, were fitted with extra-long smoke deflectors, presumably from fears that burning hard and smoky Blidworth coal might hamper the drivers' vision. They remained in this condition until rebuilt or withdrawn. 34005 is seen at Bournemouth depot on 10 October 1954.

Meanwhile, someone on the SR had a different idea and had 34039 *Boscastle*'s smoke deflectors extended forward. The locomotive remained in this state until rebuilt. For many years, 34039 was a Brighton engine and among others worked the daily through trains to Bournemouth, Plymouth and Cardiff, one of which had brought it to Southampton Central where this photograph was taken in November 1955. *Boscastle* was one of the WCs that carried no town crest or badge.

This view of 34006 *Bude* running tender first on an empty stock train into Bournemouth Central on 25 August 1955 illustrates why the SR found it necessary to cut down the side raves on all Bulleid Pacific tenders. To see ahead, the driver has to lean out of the side of the cab; this one is obviously confident that he knows when he must lean out as signals approach, just not at this point!

I sometimes show this photograph at railway enthusiast clubs and ask what is the difference between a 'West Country' and a 'Battle of Britain' 4-6-2, one of each being shown here. The answer is that there is no difference. Both classes embrace the same varieties as each other, narrow cabs and wide cabs in particular. The two locomotives seen at Bournemouth Central on 21 April 1956 are 34105 *Swanage* on the left and 34064 *Fighter Command* in the bay platform.

The 'West Country' and 'Battle of Britain' 4-6-2s • 93

A narrow-cab BB crosses the Taw bridge at Barnstaple with a portion from Ilfracombe that will eventually reach London Waterloo as part of a much longer train. The engine is 34057 *Biggin Hill*, defying completely the original idea that 'Battle of Britain' names should be on locomotives allocated to services to and from Kent!

34057 *Biggin Hill* had been one of the half-dozen Bulleid light Pacifics that spent a year or so working in East Anglia to relieve a motive power shortage there. On 16 August 1951 it arrives at London's Liverpool Street station with a train from Norwich, looking a little out of place perhaps!

One might have expected the operating department to reduce the length of the heavy Bournemouth Belle train when a light Pacific was all they had to haul it. Not so! 34059 *Sir Archibald Sinclair* had the full summer load of twelve heavy Pullmans, most of which were twelve-wheelers and all with plain bearing axleboxes, when seen galloping along Coy Pond embankment near the end of its Down journey on 26 August 1956. This is what these excellent locomotives managed to do – to deputise when needed for their bigger sisters the MN class. Imagine, an 86 ton locomotive with just 56 tons adhesion weight hauling a train of some 525 tons weight. At least rail head conditions were better then than in modern times!

34078 *222 Squadron* awaits its next turn of duty at Exmouth Junction shed, Exeter. This is a wide-cab engine, but the tender is yet to be modified for improved rear view.

34066 *Spitfire* standing at Exmouth Junction with its 4,500 gallon tender looks a little less sleek than before its tender was cut down. The modified tenders were repainted without the black band at the bottom, and with the lining around the tender sides instead of straight back as before; the black-and-orange was spaced out GWR-style, unlike the stripes on the locomotive casing which remained black edged with orange with no gap between the colours. Odd but effective.

The 'West Country' and 'Battle of Britain' 4-6-2s • 97

Experiments to tackle the effects of exhaust drift continued spasmodically. 34035 and 34049 both received different versions of altered front side sheets, and later had smoke deflectors added, all to little avail as the locomotives were returned to normal at their next overhauls. 34049 *Anti-Aircraft Command* is pictured at Eastleigh shed after being so afflicted.

The last-built Bulleid light Pacific, 34110 *66 Squadron*, restarts a Bournemouth to Waterloo service from Eastleigh on 30 May 1955 during the ASLEF strike. The driver was one of the few NUR drivers on the SR books, and was willing to pass through picket lines to continue driving during what, for every railway person, was a difficult time. 34110 was the only BB not to have a badge under its nameplate.

98 • OLIVER BULLEID'S LOCOMOTIVES

This is the last photograph I took of a Bulleid Pacific in unmodified condition working on British Railways before steam finished on the Southern Region. 34102 *Lapford* had two claims to its credit. It was one of the last two unmodified light Pacifics to survive up to the 'end of steam' date, 9 July 1967, and it was the only light Pacific to have been reliably recorded at 100mph (unless any reader knows different). It is seen in June 1967 leaving Wareham on a Weymouth to Bournemouth stopping train.

'West Country' class 4-6-2 diagram. *SR*

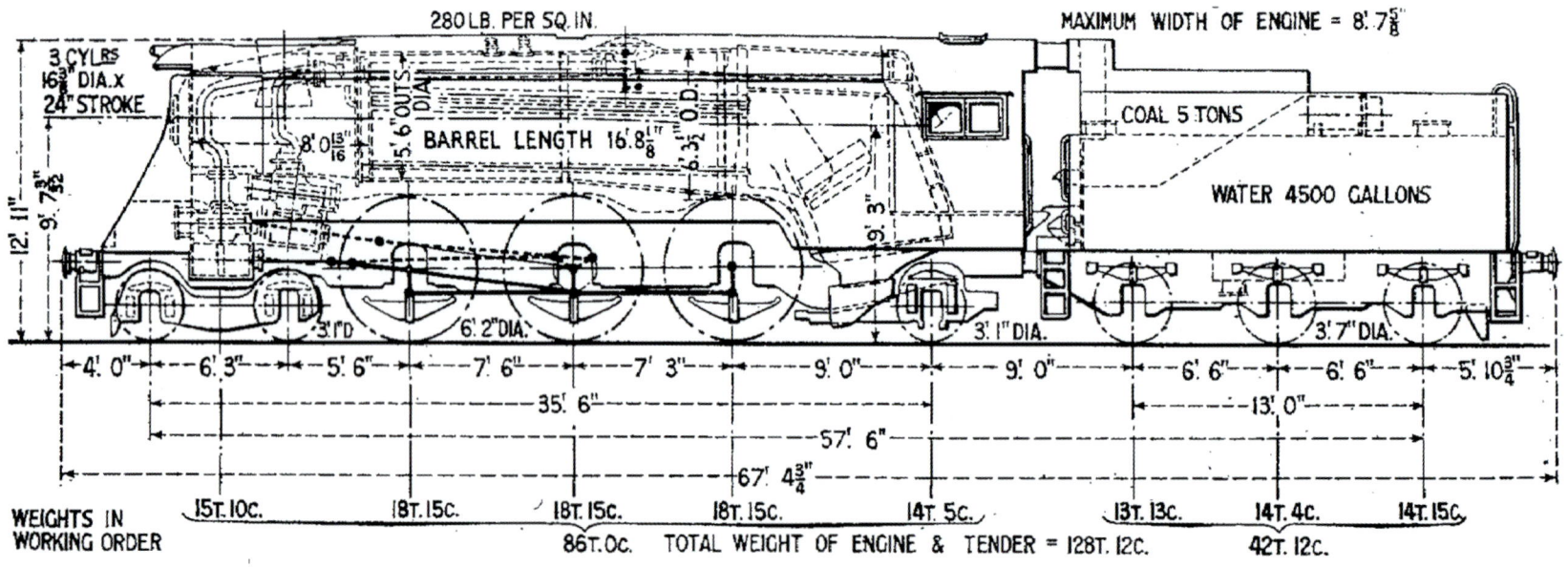

Chapter 9
THE USA CLASS 0-6-0Ts

After the war, the Southern Railway, which owned and operated the large and busy docks at Southampton, was anxious to replace the Class B4 0-4-0T steam shunting locomotives there with something more suited to the heavy traffic the docks were then handling. The need was for a locomotive type with a short wheelbase, of about 50 tons weight and enough power to shunt the trains of up to 60 wagons that had to be formed up or moved around.

Under Oliver Bulleid, some ideas for new 0-6-0 shunting tank locomotives were sketched out in diagram form. Managerially, one might conjecture that the exercise of designing and building a completely new small class of steam tank engines for such a limited potential use could be regarded as costly, however much revenue the docks were bringing in. In the event, other options became available and were pursued.

One option was to buy in enough of the surplus steam tank locomotives that had seen war service in the UK or had been repatriated, and were awaiting disposal by the Ministry of Supply. OVB was presented with two alternative locomotive types that were on offer after the war. The obvious choice was to purchase some of the standard WD 'austerity' 0-6-0ST locomotives that were based on a Hunslet prototype, a simple design with two inside cylinders, many of which were already in service on the LNER as Class J94. But also tempting were the similar-sized 0-6-0 side tank

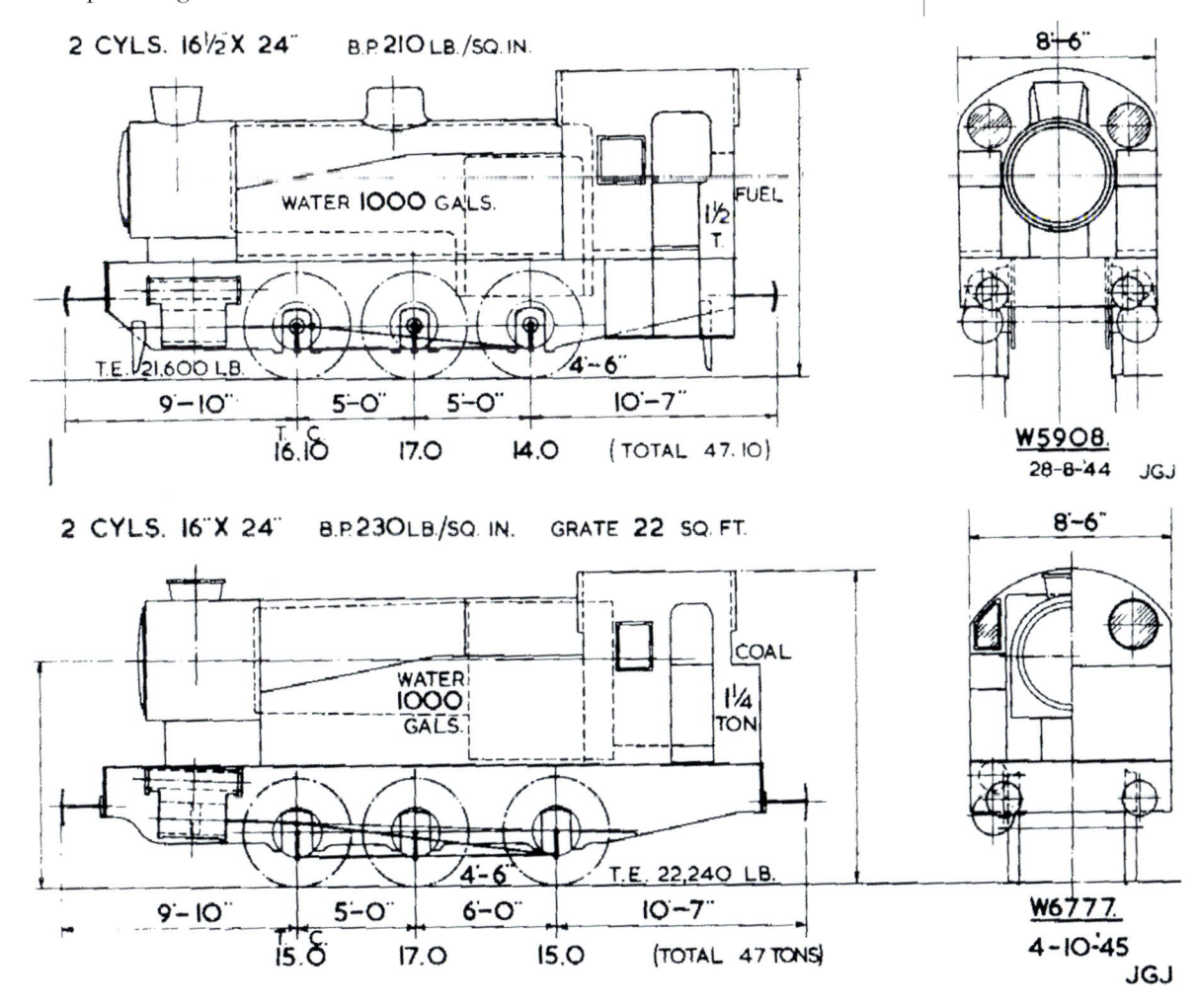

These two diagrams from the Brighton drawing office show attempts to lay out a suitable shunting 0-6-0T for Southampton Docks. *SR*

locomotives that the US Army Transportation Corps had left behind as surplus. These American engines had outside cylinders and outside Walschaerts valve gear and had been designed to fit within the UK loading gauge, even though many saw service on the European continent. Having seen much less active use in the UK, these locomotives were judged to be in better condition than the UK-built saddle tank locomotives, and their components were much more accessible for servicing and maintenance. The SR tried one of the US locomotives from 1946 in Southampton Docks, and it gained favour there. The railway decided to purchase fifteen of the American locomotives to meet its need for fourteen shunters in the docks with one locomotive being retained at Eastleigh Works for spare parts that might otherwise be difficult or expensive to obtain.

For people in the area, the sight of these foreign-looking locomotives transferring wagons through the streets of Southampton was exciting indeed. The Americans had made no attempt to beautify these machines. Their appearance was as functional as it was strange to UK eyes. The SR modified them with vacuum brakes, steam heat equipment, sliding cabside windows, additional hand grabs and radios for crew control. The railway later added hinged footplates below the smokebox fronts so that shed staff could stand on them to clean out the smokeboxes more safely. They also received enlarged bunkers to increase their coal capacity. They spent most of their UK working lives based at the small depot

It was Mr Bulleid who chose to buy fifteen USA Transportation Corps surplus 0-6-0Ts for use in Southampton Docks, rather than the British Hunslet type 0-6-0STs that were surplus from the Ministry of Supply. The simplicity of the American design was useful, and it was possible to select fifteen locomotives in better condition than most of the British ones. By 14 May 1955 these two engines, 30065 and 30068, looked well settled into their work in the Old Docks (later known as the Eastern Docks). Each locomotive crew had a radio through which they received their orders for activity in the extensive docks areas.

The USA Class 0-6-0Ts • 101

30063 poses between bouts of shunting in the Old Docks at Southampton in May 1955.

The fourteen USA 0-6-0Ts were allocated to the small depot within the Eastern Docks ('old' docks) at Southampton. Facing outwards on 9 July 1958 are 30069 and 30062. 30062 (right) has its hinged front footplate clipped in the raised position, whereas 30069's is resting on the front buffer beam.

located within Southampton's Eastern Docks, trundling the six miles to and from Eastleigh only for occasional works repairs or overhauls.

By 1962, the USA tanks were due to be replaced by diesel shunting locomotives. A variant of an established Ruston-Paxman industrial design was chosen as ideal for this location. But the usefulness of the USAs had not been lost on Southern management. At least nine of the fourteen survived to take on other work. Six found themselves being adapted for the role of works shunters, some being allocated to departmental stock for this purpose, notably the two pairs at Lancing and Ashford Works. Other departmental USA tanks went to shunt at Meldon quarry and Redbridge civil engineering depot, Southampton. Three remained in operational stock, 30064 and 30073 being used as works shunters at Eastleigh and 30072 shunted the depot at Guildford. The designated works shunters were repainted in SR carriage stock green, which suited them well. Because of the need to improve the drivers' sighting round a left hand curve, those at Lancing had to be converted from right hand drive to left hand drive, an operation that was very straightforward due to the 'Meccano' style in which the reversing and valve gear components could be reassembled. The Ashford pair received the names *Wainwright* and *Maunsell*, commemorating the last two CMEs who had been based there. The only significant problem associated with the USA locomotives in their latter years on BR was the tendency for axlebox bearings to run hot while on long transit moves.[11]

---

11 The first of the fourteen Ruston diesel locomotives that replaced the USA 0-6-0Ts also ran hot on its delivery run. The rest were delivered from Lincoln to Hampshire by road; but that is another story.

In 1960, 30073 was trialled at Lancing Carriage Works to see if it was suitable for working there so as to replace the ancient A1X class. 30073 rests after duty with 32636 (right) which was at that time BR's oldest locomotive, dating from 1872. Unfortunately, the USA engine had to face away from the carriage repair shops because it was built as a right-hand-drive engine and the tracks curved to the left. The driver claimed it was not safe for him to drive it that way round.

The solution for Lancing Works was for a pair of USA tanks to be converted to left-hand-drive, the first of which was renumbered DS236 and specially painted in BR/SR carriage stock green. The green was lined out Bulleid-style in black-and-cream. Several other USA 0-6-0Ts found their way into departmental stock after being displaced at Southampton by Ruston diesels.

After final withdrawal, USA tanks have appeared in preservation on the Bluebell Railway (30064), the Kent & East Sussex Railway (*Wainwright* and *Maunsell*) and on the Keighley & Worth Valley Railway in West Yorkshire. The latter railway solved the hot axlebox problem for good by fitting No 72 with a mechanical lubricator; a similar modification was applied later to the pair on the Kent & East Sussex Railway

Those readers who have seen preserved 0-6-0Ts in the UK carrying numbers such as 30075 may be aware that other USA 0-6-0Ts continued to be used by a few overseas railways after the war. I have seen them in France, Austria and China. Others went to Yugoslavia, which went on to build many more to a slightly different design. Two at least of these latter have been imported to the UK in recent decades, and one has been painted to look like one of the US-built machines. As far as I am aware, apart from the ex-Southampton Docks engines there are no other genuine ex-USTC 0-6-0Ts in the UK.

Class	USA 0-6-0T
Engineer	O.V.S. Bulleid*
Designed for	US Army Transportation Corps
Built by	Porter (61 and WD1261), Vulcan (USA) (62-74)
BR power class	3F
Number built	15**
Introduced	1942
Cylinders (2 outside)	16½in x 24in
Coupled wheels	4ft 6in
Boiler pressure	210lbf/sq in
Grate area	20sq ft
Tractive effort	21,600lbf
Weight in w.o.	46tons 10cwt
SR number series***	61-73, WD4326
BR number series***	30061-30074

* Responsible for the purchase and modification of the Class USA.
** 15 purchased by SR in 1946/47, including WD1261 kept for spares. The USA originally built 382 of this type.
*** See separate table for locomotive numbers.

Class USA 0-6-0T: numbers and names

WD Nos	SR Nos	BR Nos	Deptl Nos and names
1264	61	30061	DS233
1277	62	30062	DS234
1284	63	30063	
1959	64	s64 / 30064	
1968	65	30065	DS237 *Maunsell*
1279	66	30066	DS235
1282	67	30067	
1971	68	30068	
1952	69	30069	
1960	70	30070	DS238 *Wainwright*
1966	71	30071	
1973	72	30072	
1974	73	s73 / 30073	
4326		30074	DS236
1261*			

* Not taken into SR or BR stock but used for spares.

At least four USA 0-6-0Ts are preserved in the UK plus one of the Yugoslav modified design engines. Former Guildford depot shunter, now No 72 of the Keighley & Worth Valley Railway, makes a spirited departure up the grade out of Keighley in 1972 with a four-coach train. The railway painted it in a typical American livery of silver smokebox and buff-coloured tanks and cab, nicely lined out.

One of the Yugoslav imports has been painted to match the Southampton Docks engines as 30075, seen in Barrow Hill Roundhouse on 22 September 2012.

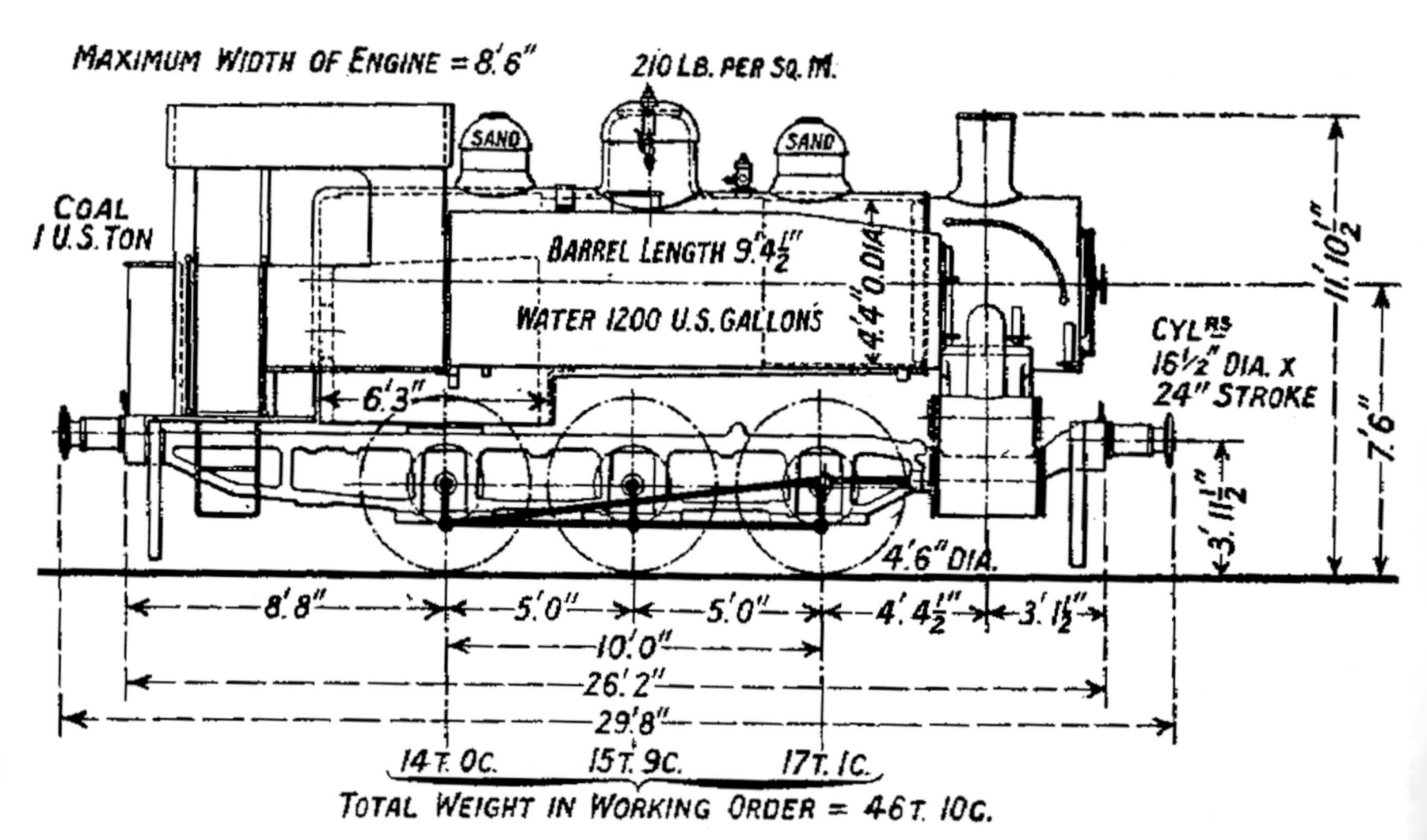

USA 0-6-0T diagram. *Possibly MoS*

Chapter 10

THE BULLEID/ENGLISH ELECTRIC DIESEL SHUNTERS

I was fortunate when, as an eleven-year-old, I was able to travel with the Bournemouth Junior Railway Club to visit Ashford Locomotive Works and the nearby depot in 1949. I still remember vividly the two locomotives there that impressed me the most. Both were standing on the track outside the erecting shop. One was an overhauled WD 2-10-0, freshly painted black with a number in the 7xxxx series. The other was brand new diesel shunter 15214 that had just been outshopped. Neither number was in my copy of an Ian Allan *ABC*.

15214 was the fourth of a batch of twenty-six 0-6-0 350bhp diesel electric shunting locomotives that were being built at Ashford. This was the SR's first significant move towards eliminating some of the shunting tank engines that performed at stations and yards around the Region. The Southern Railway had built no shunting locomotives in its time other than the eight Z class

Shunting quietly at Eastleigh on 22 May 1955 is 350bhp 0-6-0 diesel electric shunting locomotive 15235, its Bulleid-inspired Boxpok wheels lit up by the evening sun. The 15xxx series of locomotive numbers was for the various regional builds of 350bhp shunters, most of which had English Electric equipment.

0-8-0Ts and the three 1937-built 350bhp diesels already described, so nearly all its dedicated shunting engines were either old, small or becoming unsuitable for modern conditions. The choice of what in effect was a standard English Electric diesel shunting design was logical. The type had been in production since just before the Second World War, with significant numbers being delivered to the LMS and to the War Department.

The new diesel electrics were an update on the three delivered to the SR before the war, and with two major differences. The traction motors drove the axles of the outer wheelsets as before, but through double-reduction gearing enabling smaller motors to be used, giving the locomotives a slightly lower top speed of 27½mph. This compared with 20mph for the similar locomotives being supplied to the other Regions. The new Ashford-built locomotives were lighter than the older three SR ones. The other difference from the LMS and other locomotives was the provision of B-F-B wheel centres on these otherwise standard locomotives, their only obvious Bulleid feature.

Compared with modern, late-twentieth century shunting locomotives, the EE 350bhp shunters now appear distinctly over-engineered. Their type 6KT six-cylinder in-line diesel engines were naturally aspirated, that is they used air at atmospheric pressure; they were not turbo-charged. The engines were heavy in relation to their power output. But for their planned duties, this

Stabled at Ashford on 28 September 1970 is 15232 showing off its later BR dark green livery. *Colour-Rail 200490*

was not a problem. High tractive effort at low speeds does not need high power output to shift quite substantial loads. The heavy weight of the medium-speed diesel engines located on heavy locomotive frames enabled the total locomotive weight to be sufficient for traction without the need for excess ballasting. The vintage diesel engine design was also rugged and very reliable, easy to maintain and repair, and capable of lasting as many decades in service as owning railways might wish, as has happened to BR's class 08 type which was a more recent example of the same basic design (introduced in 1953).

The twenty-six locomotives of this SR built class were scattered throughout the Southern Region of BR to places that had significant freight yards. They replaced steam locomotives on hump shunts including the Class G16 4-8-0Ts and Z 0-8-0Ts, and many older tank locomotives at other locations. However, being non-standard in certain components, the SR-built diesel shunters later became superseded by more recently-built BR Class 08s and the higher-speed 09s in the 1960s. Three of the SR locomotives were sold to industrial owners, but only one of these survives today, 15224 which is on the Spa Valley Railway in Kent at the time of writing. It had worked at the nearby Snowdown colliery between 1970 and 1983.

Class	0-6-0 diesel electric
Engineer	O.V.S. Bulleid / English Electric Co
Builder	BR Ashford Works
Number in class	26
Introduced	1949
Diesel engine	English Electric 6-cylinder 6KT
Diesel engine rating	350bhp
Traction generator (dc)	EE 801/7D
Traction motors (dc)	EE506A (2) with double-reduction gears
Driving wheels diameter	4ft 6in
Tractive effort	24,000lbf
Maximum speed	27½mph
Train heat	None
Weight in w.o.	49tons
Number series	15211-15236*

* NB: BR allocated the Class number 12 to this type, but none survived long enough to carry a 12 001 series number.

Chapter 11
THE PAXMAN 0-6-0 DIESEL SHUNTER

An odd locomotive that later seemed to spend much of its time in a siding alongside Ashford Works was the Paxman 500bhp diesel mechanical shunting locomotive 11001. The SR, having found that its first three diesel electric locomotives 1, 2 and 3 were less suited for inter-yard freight transfer work than first thought, persisted in the idea with this larger machine that had more power and a higher top speed. 11001 was introduced in 1949 and intended to be allocated to Norwood Junction for freight moves around the area.

The 12-cylinder Paxman diesel engine drove an hydraulic coupling, otherwise called a fluid flywheel, which drove the input end of the mechanical gearbox. The gearbox had three forward and three reverse gears. Third gear gave the locomotive a top speed of 36mph. The output shaft from the gearbox

The BR official picture of the 500bhp Paxman 0-6-0 diesel mechanical shunting locomotive 11001 shows clearly the jackshaft drive from the gearbox under the cab, driving the centre coupled wheels through a substantial connecting rod each side. This was the SR's second attempt at developing a diesel 0-6-0 that could act as a freight transfer machine as well as a large yard shunter. Its unreliability became legendary. *BR*

drove a jackshaft, the ends of which drove a heavy connecting rod which was connected to the centre wheels crank pin. The wheels were coupled with normal coupling rods which transferred the drive to the outer wheels. These were of the B-F-B patent type. Braking was by air, but it had no train brake so could only work unfitted trains on main lines.

The locomotive had a tall cab with high roof. The engine and drive were under a long bonnet which was low enough in height to enable good forward vision from the cab. At the front, under the bonnet, was the fuel tank, then the cooler group with side radiators, then the engine and drive.

11001 was allocated to Norwood Junction and did indeed carry out the duties for which it was designed. It also spent time in 1952 on trial at Stourton marshalling yard in Leeds. Unfortunately, it proved to be a particularly unreliable locomotive. After a gearbox failure in 1958, it waited hopefully at Ashford in partially dismantled state, but was withdrawn from stock in 1959.

Class	0-6-0 diesel mechanical
Engineer	O.V.S. Bulleid
Builder	BR Ashford Works
Number in class	1
Introduced	1949
Diesel engine	Davey Paxman 12-cylinder RPH Series 1
Diesel engine rating	500bhp
Fluid coupling	Vulcan Sinclair
Gearbox	SSS Powerflow 3-speed with reverse
Driving wheels diameter	4ft 6in
Tractive effort	33,500lbf
Maximum speed	36mph*
Train heat	None
Weight in w.o.	49tons 9cwt
Number series	11001

* Some sources show the design speed as 45mph.

11001 trundles through Norwood Junction station with a short transfer goods train. *Internet*

112 • OLIVER BULLEID'S LOCOMOTIVES

11001 went to Leeds for a time in July 1952 and was used to shunt the freight yard at Stourton. It soon returned to the Southern Region. *Yorkshire Post/David Heys collection*

11001 0-6-0 diagram. *SR*

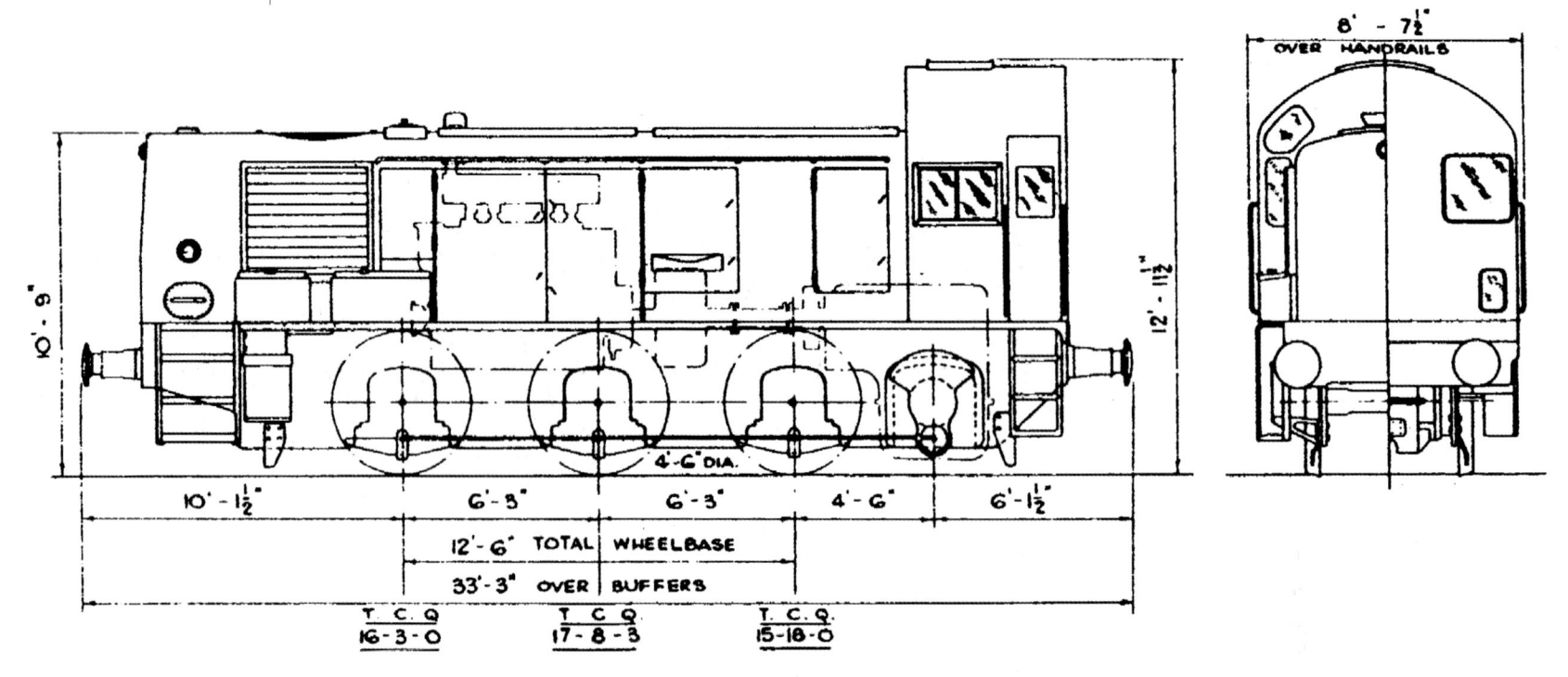

Chapter 12
THE 'LEADER' CLASS 0-6-6-0Ts

The 'Leader' class project is a classic example of what can happen when a management team loses sight of the original objective of a project and finds itself led into a situation that has taken on a life of its own, growing away from what was really wanted as it proceeds.

It all started with the Southern Railway operating department's declaration that it needed some new, modern tank locomotives to replace aged passenger locomotives that had survived well beyond their normal life spans. The Southern Railway had built no tank locomotives for secondary passenger services, many of which were relying largely on pre-grouping 4-4-2Ts or 0-4-4Ts. A lot of these locomotives dated from the latter years of the nineteenth century. On the South Eastern Section, 0-4-4Ts from both the South Eastern Railway and London Chatham & Dover Railway were still in use on branch lines, though electrification was reducing the need for larger engines on secondary main line stopping trains. On the Central Section, a host of old 4-4-2Ts from the

The 'Leader' story begins with the need to replace the aged ex-London & South Western Railway Drummond M7 0-4-4Ts on London Waterloo to Clapham Junction sidings empty carriage workings. Typically, 30320 struggles to start a train of at least ten main line coaches out of the terminus on 7 April 1957, though it is almost certainly getting a helpful preliminary push by the train engine at the buffer stops. Once out on the main line, however, 30320 will be on its own with this heavy load.
D.C. Ovenden/Colour-Rail 18012

This diagram numbered in the 'Waterloo' series, though probably drawn at Brighton, was one of many that were discussed during the creation phase of the 'Leader' project. It shows a 0-4-4-0T locomotive based on a strong girder frame with a central well, running on two bogies each with three cylinders almost certainly intended to use sleeve valves. These would be fed from a wide firebox boiler with the high pressure of 350lb/sq in. As a concept, if the weight could have been brought down to below 80tons, this might have been a viable option for the task of replacing tank locomotives on outer suburban trains and empty stock workings.
Southern Railway

London, Brighton & South Coast Railway struggled with the Oxted group of quite heavy commuter-type trains on hilly routes that were not that easy to operate. Out of London's busy Waterloo station the venerable Drummond M7 0-4-4Ts were still expected to shuttle empty trains of up to thirteen main line corridor coaches to and from the carriage sidings at Clapham Junction, a duty on which they were clearly overloaded.

It was a characteristic of the Big Four railways that they carried on by and large the tradition of designing their own locomotives rather than buying something that the private manufacturers or other railways might have had available that was suitable. Thus, the SR began sketching diagrams of ideas as they came forward, and with O.V. Bulleid's agile mind the ideas came with some variety, though they did follow a pattern of progressive thought.

Initial thoughts focussed on the Q1 0-6-0. Could this be used without significant change? For example, could a Q1 be used running tender-first, and also in push-pull mode, at speeds up to 75mph, the SR's maximum speed on many secondary routes? Tests showed that the locomotive and tender did indeed ride sufficiently well in both directions for this option to be considered seriously. But a major issue was the restricted view past the Q1 tender when running in reverse. Indeed, a diagram was produced which showed a modified Q1 with tender raves cut back to improve the rearward view, the locomotive part being blessed with a 'West Country'-style casing and smokebox front with smoke deflectors. But opinions were already forming that a tank engine design would be better, and a 0-6-4T version of the Q1 had already been laid out in a diagram. However, a wish emerged of having carrying wheels to guide the locomotive into curves in either direction, so the next diagram showed a 4-6-4T version that took account of the CCE's objection to pony trucks. While several schemes were tried around the 4-6-4T frame, including one with an enclosed body with a driving cab at each end and a tiny cab for the fireman, Bulleid eventually objected to the obvious waste of potential adhesion weight with only three out of seven axles powered. This sowed the seed for thinking about an all-adhesion locomotive wherein the total locomotive weight was available for adhesion – like a diesel locomotive but using steam technology.

Thoughts then centred on a double-bogie locomotive with two four-wheeled bogies. This would need to weigh no more than 80 tons to keep within the civil engineer's axleload limit on secondary routes. Drawing office engineers developed a diagram that showed a locomotive of B-B configuration. OVB's influence is very clear in this layout which had several unusual features. The boiler was necessarily short, and to produce the required power within the weight limitation it would need to be pressed at 350lb/sq in. Only Oliver Bulleid would have required each bogie to be powered by *three* cylinders when two each would have been enough for the duties envisaged. On the heavy dipped girder frame, the rest of the locomotive was laid out in conventional sequence. Allowing spaces for water and coal storage, the locomotive would have had a front end appearance like a 'West Country', a well-laid-out cab for the crew, and a bunker shaped to facilitate good rearwards vision.

It seems that a lot of effort went into this proposal, which might well have produced an exciting locomotive that would have met all expectations, that is if its maintenance and reliability were not adversely affected by possible mechanical complications.

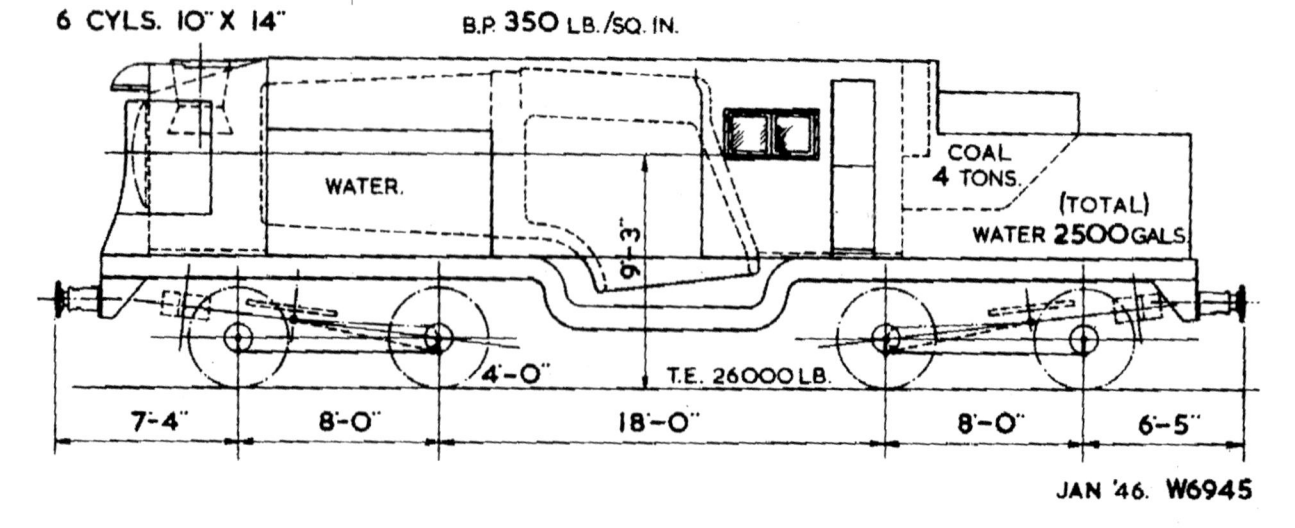

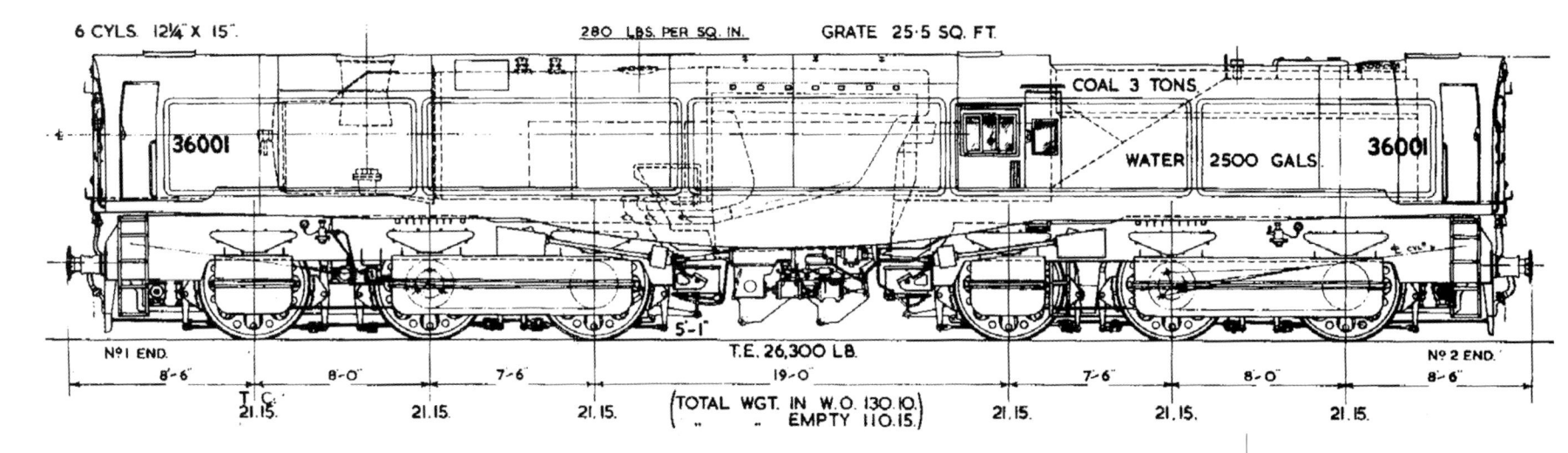

Regrettably, try as they may, the engineers in Brighton drawing office could not bring the design's weight calculations down to the essential 80 tons.

So Mr Bulleid went back to the SR Board and the CCE with a request that the new locomotive should have six axles rather than four. At some time in this process, OVB advanced the idea that such a configuration would give scope for the specification for this 'new tank engine' to be expanded. He was now offering to produce on six axles a bogie steam locomotive that could haul 500 tons at 90mph or pull freight trains as heavy as the Co-Co electric locomotives could. Faced with the ever-persuasive personality of Mr Bulleid, the Board agreed to this. The 'Leader' concept took another step forward, but it was a step further away from what had been the original objective of the project, to replace old tank locomotives on outer suburban trains and empty stock workings with modern locomotives designed to do the same work. An order was later placed for five locomotives, recognising that there was a degree of innovation that needed to be proven in traffic (possibly an understatement) before series production could progress.

Several more diagrams came out of the drawing office before the concept began to coalesce into a form ready for detail design to begin. The influence of the Q1 design was still there in that the wheel diameter was the same 5ft 1in. Each bogie had three axles which were coupled by chains linking sprockets on the axle ends. Each bogie had deep plate side frames and each had a three-cylinder engine between the frames at its outer end, driving the crank axle. Three sets of a more compact version of Bulleid valve gear, located between the crank and inner axles, were driven by three cranks set at 120° in a lay shaft, the shaft itself being chain driven from the centre crank axle with an intermediate sprocket to facilitate chain tensioning. Bulleid's friend Ricardo had persuaded him to fit sleeve valves in which the valves had the form of a hollow cylinder that enveloped the drive cylinder, an idea that came from the automotive industry, and that quite clearly required further development even there.

Accordingly, OVB obtained Brighton Class H1 Atlantic 2039 *Hartland Point* for experimental fitting with sleeve valves. This locomotive showed the potential for unreliable operation of these valves. It had a rostered duty for some time, namely hauling carriage stock between the works at Lancing and Eastleigh for repair. Presumably, the unreliability it demonstrated was assumed to be teething troubles rather than fundamental to the type, because OVB persisted with sleeve valves on the 'Leader' design. An addition, again suggested by Mr Ricardo, was for the valves on the 'Leader' type to twist as well as move fore-and-aft, adding further mechanical complication to an already adventurous design, supposedly with the aim of improving lubrication. Because it caused several locomotive failures, this rotation feature was disconnected early in the 'Leader' trials.

The final version ended up as a six-axle locomotive of higher power than needed for its original task and of excessive weight. Some observers would add excessive complication as a significant attribute. BR

116 • OLIVER BULLEID'S LOCOMOTIVES

Early experiments to check the validity of OVB's wish to use sleeve valves on the 'Leader' class were conducted by fitting sleeve valves to Class H1 4-4-2 2039 *Hartland Point*. The locomotive was further altered in the new blastpipe and chimney, and in the removal of running boards and valances from just behind the cylinders to make room for equipment.
John Click, courtesy National Railway Museum

The 'Leader' Class 0-6-6-0Ts • 117

This closer view of a cylinder on 2039 shows the steam pipe leading to the middle of the steam chest which surrounds the cylinder, and the elongated exhaust outlets at either end. *John Click, courtesy National Railway Museum*

Carried by the bogies was a long, heavy underframe that supported a lightly-constructed body embracing the rest of the locomotive. With the exception of the cabs, the locomotive above the frame was laid out in conventional sequence, the boiler leading and the coal and water spaces at the rear. The firebox was unusual in that OVB dispensed with the traditional water-jacketed firebox, leaving the firebox sides and back to be contained by steel plating lined with fire bricks. The boiler had four thermic syphons supporting the firebox crown. Pressed at 280lb/sq in, the boiler turned out to be a good producer of steam, in true Bulleid tradition. It was of all-welded construction, possibly the first such boiler in a main-line British locomotive.

Among all the innovations was one that Bulleid believed would 'sell' the locomotive to operators, namely that there was a driving cab at each end. It followed that the fireman would need his own space, just behind the boiler from where he could attend to the fire and handle boiler management. The layout of three separate cabs was the innovation that, in hindsight, sounded the death knell of the 'Leader' design. Many changes proved necessary to the locomotive purely to deal with the adverse effects that these three cabs produced.

The first issue was communication between the fireman and the driver, deemed an essential feature by some observers, though others would point to the enforced separation of driver and fireman already in use when driving a push-pull train from the carriage end. To accommodate a

A 'Leader' class boiler stands after delivery in Brighton Works erecting shop. It shows provision for a four-row superheater, and the unusual shape of the firebox, which had no conventional back plate. The boiler's all-welded construction is evident. It makes an interesting comparison with the 'West Country' class boiler behind it. The cylinder casting in front is for a 'West Country' a class that was being built at Brighton at the time.
John Click, courtesy National Railway Museum

There was originality in the neat arrangement of the Bulleid valve gear for the 'Leader' locomotives, as seen in this diagram. However, the sleeve valves were a constant source of trouble, and possibly one reason for the steam consumption being so high when 36001 was running on trials. Also, the high number of links in the valve gear drive to the valves would have reduced accuracy of cut-off and increased the potential for unreliable valve events.

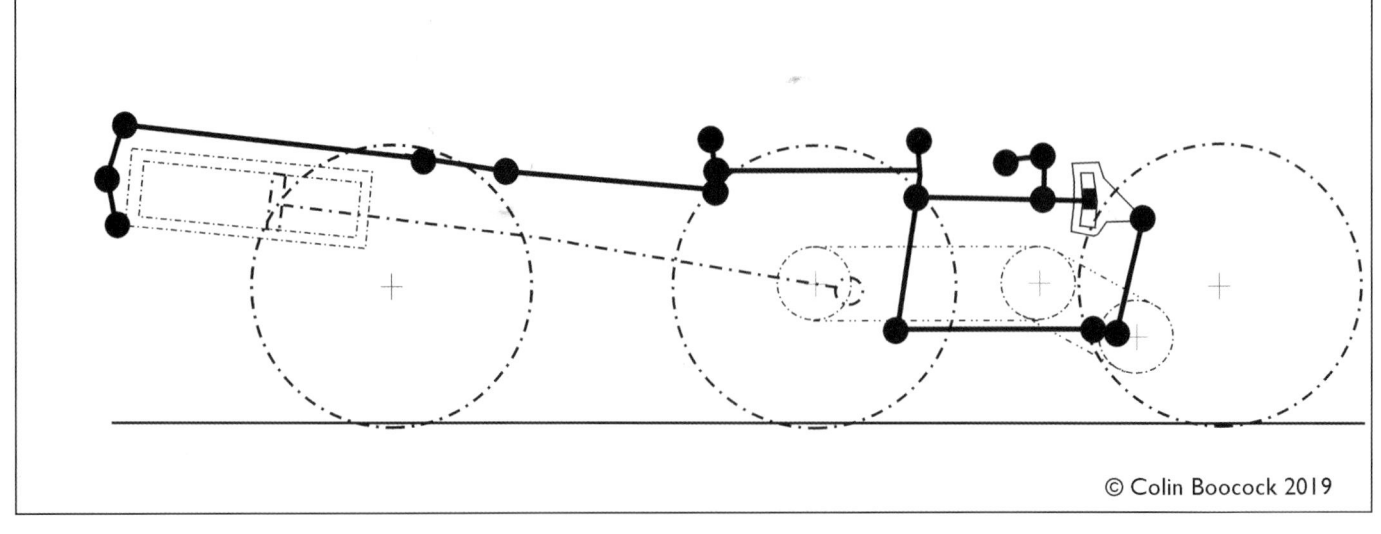

side corridor past the boiler so that the leading driving cab was linked to the fireman's cab, the 'Leader' boiler was placed offset from the centreline of the locomotive. That had consequences.

Any thoughts that this lateral imbalance could be dealt with by adjustments to the leaf springs on either side of the locomotive bogie frames were soon dispelled. The locomotive was too heavy on one side compared with the other. To correct this, heavy weights were laid on the corridor floor to counterbalance the weight of the boiler. This also had a consequence, making the corridor less than suitable for its purpose. The extra weights were only part of the overall locomotive weight problem. When 36001 was weighed, the official weight was declared as being 130 tons, well over the formerly-stipulated 20 ton axleload.

In service, the cab arrangement led to complaints that the fireman was in too hot an environment. The small cab only had one door on one side of the locomotive. There was very little natural draught for fresh air, and hot steam pipes as well as the steel firebox backplate raised the temperature in the cab to close to unbearable. The leading driving cab was also declared as being uncomfortably hot; to alleviate this, during trials, the crews adopted the practice of turning the locomotive at each end of a journey so that they could drive from the bunker-end cab. Following early trial running, the heat generated in the fireman's cab was alleviated a bit by a decision to fix an extra layer of firebricks around the firebox walls. This had an adverse consequence that affected the locomotive's performance potential, namely the grate area, originally set at 33sq ft, was reduced to 27sq ft, not much more than a Maunsell 2-6-0.

Unreliable trial running out of Brighton Works, together with the frequency in which 36001 required works fitters' attention, and indeed the many unplanned visits into the erecting shop, would have been disruptive to the normal operation of the works which was still building light Pacifics as well as overhauling traffic locomotives. Six light Pacifics were built at Eastleigh, apparently to alleviate the stress on Brighton Works. The 'Leader' became a major irritation at Brighton; it was possibly this that led eventually to the locomotive's transfer to Eastleigh for its formal load tests and runs with the former LNER dynamometer car.

Comparative trials were run with increasing loads on the London to Southampton main line between Eastleigh and Basingstoke or Woking. The comparison locomotive was a Maunsell U class 2-6-0, a successful mixed traffic design from the 1910s that had a grate area of 25sq ft, and thus theoretically almost able to match the 'Leader' for power output. The trial results emerged to be firmly in favour of the simple two-cylinder engine which produced considerably better efficiency figures when handling the same loads in the same timings as did the 0-6-6-0T.

After the dynamometer car had left the SR, the Eastleigh team took 36001 out for one last trial run with a fifteen-coach load to and from Woking. On this occasion, the 'Leader' met the load and timing specification faultlessly, keeping to the 50mph speed limit imposed on it. Regrettably, BR management had by then turned their backs on the project. 36001 had made one

While no 'Leader' class 0-6-6-0T entered revenue service, 36001 underwent a long series of trials aimed firstly at improving its reliability. These early trials were based at Brighton. Later trials to test its thermal and traction performance were based at Eastleigh. These included main line trials with the ex-LNER dynamometer car, with a U class 2-6-0 being tested separately as a comparison. One of the trials is ready to leave the east yard at Eastleigh. *John Click/ G. Beesley collection*

On one of these dynamometer car trials, 36001 is seen on the four-track section north of Eastleigh, between Allbrook and Shawford, heading probably for Woking. *S.C. Townroe/Internet*

last attempt to impress, which it had done.

So, 36001 was less efficient than a standard engine, too heavy for the track, too hot for its crew, and too unreliable for regular service. There was also the fact that having only one exterior door in the fireman's cab was a potentially unsafe situation; if in an accident the locomotive turned over on to the side with the fireman's door, there would be no quick way for the fireman to escape. All of these things were such a pity because, had the innovations been minimised during the design phase so that 'Leader's' engineering could have been more practical, it would have worked. A central cab with reasonable fore and aft views would have eliminated the complication of three cabs, and piston valves for two cylinders on each bogie would have met the traffic need.

The 'Leader' Class 0-6-6-0Ts • 121

The idea of a total-adhesion large steam locomotive was not a new one. Elsewhere in the world, indeed in Europe, there were examples of Mallet 0-6-6-0Ts with one cab, two power bogies and two pairs of cylinders arranged for compound working. It was perhaps typical of OVB that he either ignored or failed to recognise the existence of such locomotives, a modern development of which might well have been a better option.

36001 was built at Brighton Works and completed soon after British Railways was born. The Railway Executive's member for mechanical engineering was Robert Riddles. He gave OVB sufficient time and support to pursue trials with 36001 to see what real potential for further production the design had. After Oliver Bulleid retired from BR in 1949, Riddles set Ron Jarvis, then Chief Technical Assistant at Brighton, to report on the project's prospects. Ron wrote that, while it was potentially possible to make the 'Leader' concept work, it would require a major redesign of the locomotive and the construction of a new prototype. BR decided that there were not sufficient resources to devote

36001 stabled at Eastleigh during or after its series of trials in 1950. This shows the fireman's cab door; on the other side of the locomotive the fireman had no door, a situation that gave rise to lack of ventilation in a very hot location.
W.H.C. Kelland collection, courtesy Bournemouth Railway Club Trust

to such a demanding project, particularly when the perceived traffic need could be met by other means. The project was stopped in 1951, and all five locomotives were scrapped, 36002 (complete) to 36005 (early stages) in their various states of construction being brought out of storage for this purpose.

A codicil to this sad story is that by 1950, BR had arranged for Brighton Works to build LMS-type Fairburn 2-6-4Ts, and from 1951 BR Class 4 2-6-4Ts, in quantity for the Southern Region outer suburban lines that needed newer steam traction. These all had leading pony trucks, but under BR's management the perceived problem on the SR of two-wheeled leading trucks had suddenly disappeared. The ancient M7 0-4-4Ts working the Clapham empty stock trains handed the job over to surplus ex-Western Region 0-6-0 pannier tanks, which in turn gave way to Ivatt 2-6-2Ts of LMS design. So in the end, the need for 'new tank engines' was met mainly with two-cylinder simple locomotives with three out of five or six axles powered, not a far cry from the Bulleid 0-6-4T and 4-6-4T ideas which would have saved everyone a lot of trouble!

Class	Leader C-C
Engineer	O.V.S. Bulleid
Built by	SR and BR Brighton
BR power class	unclassified
Number in class	5*
Introduced	1949
Cylinders (6 inside)	12¼in x 15in
Coupled wheels	5ft 1in
Boiler pressure	280lbf/sq in
Grate area	25.5sq ft
Tractive effort	26,350lbf
Weight in w.o.	130tons 10cwt
BR number series	36001-36005

* Only two locomotives, 36001 and 36002, were fully completed. None entered revenue service.

Answers to the Southern Railway's motive power needs already existed on other railways in the UK, but internal pride always went for the home-produced designs. It was only when British Railways began to take control of the Regional power policies that the Southern gratefully received from 1950 a batch of Brighton-built Fairburn 2-6-4Ts of LMS design for the outer-suburban duties for which the 'Leader' class locomotive were intended. One of these, 42096, is seen leaving Bournemouth Central with a stopping train heading for Bournemouth West on 11 April 1955.

The Southern Region's Fairburn tanks were quickly followed by a large group of BR standard 2-6-4Ts, designed and built at Brighton. One of these, 80016, was unusually employed cross-country on the daily Brighton to Cardiff train, seen leaving Southampton Central on 1 March 1955 competently deputizing for a 'West Country' Pacific. The BR 2-6-4Ts' more usual haunts were on the Central and Eastern Sections of the SR.

Chapter 13
THE 1CO-CO1 DIESEL ELECTRICS

A reliable source suggests that back in 1946, even before the LMS began planning for the new diesels 10000 and 10001, the Southern Railway was foreseeing its need for some prototype main line diesels.

As it happened, the SR took much longer in this process, presumably because the end of the 1940s was an exceptionally challenging period, what with construction of the 110 light Pacifics and the third batch of 'Merchant Navy' class engines proceeding apace, as well as the work on the 'Leaders', early diesel shunters and the double-deck electric sets demanding detailed attention.

The SR was looking ahead to the eventual elimination of steam traction on its main lines. One option being considered was that,

The new 10201 did some brief test running on the Midland Main Line, as seen here during a stop at Loughborough, but it spent most of the summer of 1951 in the Festival of Britain exhibition in London.
W.H.C. Kelland collection/Bournemouth Railway Club Trust

on the Western Section, third rail electrification might be extended to the Bournemouth and Salisbury main lines, but the latter would probably not go any further west. There was a clearly perceived future need for diesel locomotives to take over expresses bound for beyond Salisbury, for which a powerful diesel type would be needed that could replace the 'Merchant Navy' locomotives when their time came. Construction of steam Pacifics continued on the SR until the last 'Battle of Britain' 4-6-2 emerged in 1951. It was timely, therefore, that the first prototype SR main line diesel was outshopped immediately before that same year.

10201 and 10202 were built at Ashford as a pair with potential for working in multiple. In the event, after trials on the LM Region, 10201 spent the summer of 1951 as a star exhibit on the Festival of Britain site near London Waterloo, while 10202 began trials and then express passenger train working on the London-Weymouth and Exeter main lines. The slightly more powerful 10203 began its life in 1954. These were heavy locomotives but had high tractive effort and good adhesion, enabling them to start heavy express trains swiftly, even if they took their time to reach balancing speed. Their maximum rated running speed was 90mph, enabling them to cope with the SR's main line speed limit of 85mph without stress.

The equipment and layout of these locomotives was entirely conventional except for the bogies. The English Electric Company designed and supplied the 1,750bhp 16-cylinder 16SVT (supercharged Vee type) four-stroke diesel power unit with its dc generator, the traction control equipment and the six traction motors. The SR's drawing office at Brighton worked out and designed the physical layout of the locomotive. Subjected to the CCE's strictures about axle loads, OVB acknowledged the need for an additional axle on each bogie. This carrying axle was located at the outer ends of the locomotive bogies.

The plate frame bogies were straightforward to manufacture and followed the pattern set by the three Co Co electric locomotives with leaf side springs and a pivotless

In 1952 the 'Southern twins' 10201 and 10202 settled down separately to working diagrams on the Bournemouth and West of England main lines. At 1,750bhp their performance was a reasonable match to a Bulleid light Pacific, and they could manage most 'Merchant Navy' diagrams when conditions were favourable. 10201 was working the Up Bournemouth Belle when photographed leaving Bournemouth Central on 6 July 1952.

10201 sweeps into Bournemouth Central with the 2.30pm from Bournemouth West to London Waterloo on 17 May 1953. The train is formed fully of matching Bulleid stock in BR's cheerful carmine red-and-cream livery.

centre on which the locomotive underframe rested on sector plates centred by springs. The carrying axle was held in a pony truck pivoted off the bogie frame by a neat arrangement of guiding arms. While undoubtedly heavy to modern eyes, this bogie design rode well and was adopted for British Railways' future requirements for Type 4 diesel electrics produced by both English Electric and BR's own workshops, eventually supporting a total of 399 locomotives.

The locomotive body was built up on a strong girder underframe. The body design was simple, with curved sides, spaces for radiator and ventilation grilles, and a slightly rounded front plan that actually looked quite smart.

The curved sides matched the curve of SR standard Bulleid coaching stock. End gangways enabled the crews of locomotives coupled in multiple to pass between the two. Six folding headcode discs on the cab fronts each revealed a marker lamp and a white disc shape when opened up; when folded down they became visually insignificant. This headcode display feature was to become standard on early BR-specified diesel locomotives. Train heat was by oil-fire steam generator, and a useful facility for the crew was a small lavatory within the locomotive.

By the time 10201 emerged from Ashford Works, BR had standardised on the livery first introduced by the LMS on 10000. This had a black body with silver-grey roof surrounds, a stainless metal mid-body lining band, as well as silver-grey side and bogie frames. The locomotive numbers were in raised stainless metal in standard BR Gill Sans style.

The third locomotive, 10203, had the engine speed raised from the 750rpm of the earlier two to 850rpm and was rated at 2,000bhp. 10203 was outshopped from Brighton Works early in 1954 and spent its first year on services on the West of England Main Line. In effect, this locomotive was the prototype for the future English Electric Type 4 design, which deviated from it only by dint of a different body shape and layout of auxiliary equipment.

10203 was the third of the trio, uprated to 2,000bhp, thus forming the technical prototype for the English Electric Type 4s. It is seen at Eastleigh in 1954 when in nearly-new condition. *B.J. Swain/Colour-Rail DE1512*

Diesel locomotive failures did occur from time to time, and steam had to come to the rescue. On 23 May 1953, 10203 had to be helped from somewhere east of Weymouth with an express for London Waterloo. Maunsell class U 2-6-0 31625 did the honours, seen on arrival at Bournemouth Central where both locomotives were removed from the train. One can only admire the strength of the medium-sized Mogul having had to shift that lot up the 1 in 60/50 of the bank out of Poole!

All three SR locomotives were transferred together with 10000 and 10001 to the London Midland Region in 1954/55 and worked on the West Coast Main Line variously on express and suburban trains, plus some freight. 10201 and 10202 were often employed in multiple on such prestige trains as the Royal Scot, 10203 being used singly on this train on occasions, coping due to its higher horsepower.

The LMR repainted them in BR dark green with orange-and-black lining along the body mid-strip, a style that didn't really suit them. The arrival of large numbers of BR-inspired diesels, and the first phase of WCML electrification, rendered them surplus in the eyes of LM Region management who withdrew them from traffic in 1963. They languished for a while at Derby, but eventually were scrapped. None of these, nor either of 10000 and 10001, were held for preservation despite their pioneering contribution to the UK's development of diesel locomotives.

Class	1Co-Co1 diesel electric
Engineers	O.V.S. Bulleid/ C.S. Cocks
Builder	BR Ashford Works/ Brighton Works*
BR power class	5P 5F/6P 6F*
Number in class	3
Introduced	1950/1954*
Diesel engine	English Electric 16SVT
Diesel engine rating	1,750bhp/2,000bhp*
Electric traction equipt.	English Electric Co.
Traction motors (6 dc)	EE 526A
Driving wheels diameter	3ft 7in
Tractive effort	48,000lbf/50,000lbf*
Maximum speed	90mph
Train heat	Oil-fired steam generator
Weight in w.o.	135tons/132tons*
Number series	10201, 10202, 10203*

* Details refer to 10203.

In late 1954, all three Southern main line diesels, together with the LM pair 10000 and 10001, were transferred permanently from the SR to the London Midland Region. They were used principally on the West Coast Main Line. On 13 July 1955, 10201 was ready to leave Birmingham New Street with an express to London Euston.

The 1Co-Co1 Diesel Electrics • 129

Two years later BR had decreed that main line diesels be painted in lined-out dark green, the same colours as express steam locomotives. 10201 and 10202 in multiple snake their way into Crewe station with the Royal Scot service on 3 August 1957. Only 10203 was permitted to haul this prestige train single-handedly. *W.H.C. Kelland collection, courtesy Bournemouth Railway Club Trust*

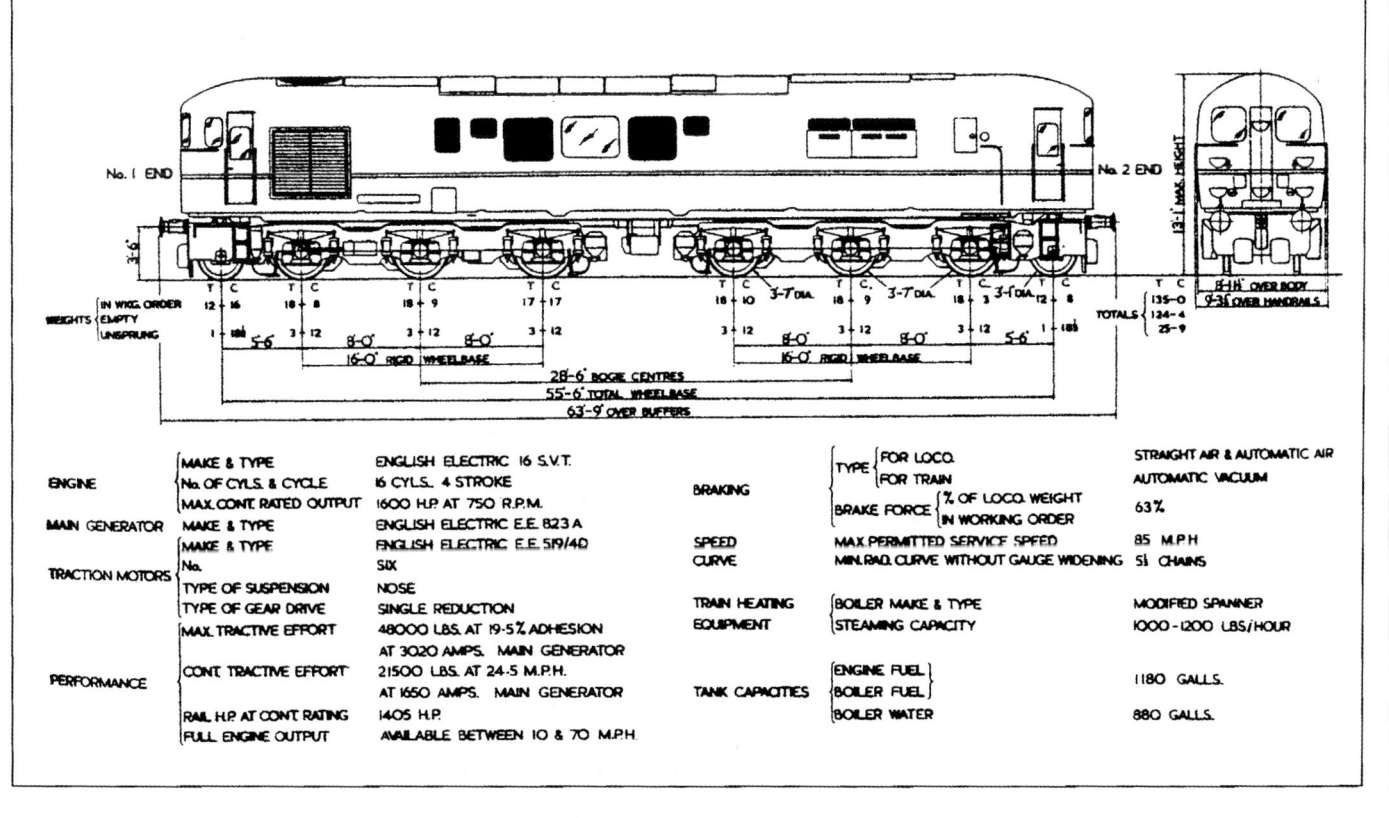

ENGINE	MAKE & TYPE	ENGLISH ELECTRIC 16 S.V.T.	**BRAKING**	TYPE { FOR LOCO. / FOR TRAIN	STRAIGHT AIR & AUTOMATIC AIR / AUTOMATIC VACUUM
	No. OF CYLS. & CYCLE	16 CYLS. 4 STROKE			
	MAX. CONT. RATED OUTPUT	1600 H.P. AT 750 R.P.M.		BRAKE FORCE { % OF LOCO. WEIGHT IN WORKING ORDER	63%
MAIN GENERATOR	MAKE & TYPE	ENGLISH ELECTRIC E.E. 823 A	**SPEED**	MAX. PERMITTED SERVICE SPEED	85 M.P.H
TRACTION MOTORS	MAKE & TYPE	ENGLISH ELECTRIC E.E. 519/4D	**CURVE**	MIN. RAD. CURVE WITHOUT GAUGE WIDENING	5¼ CHAINS
	No.	SIX			
	TYPE OF SUSPENSION	NOSE	**TRAIN HEATING EQUIPMENT**	BOILER MAKE & TYPE	MODIFIED SPANNER
	TYPE OF GEAR DRIVE	SINGLE REDUCTION		STEAMING CAPACITY	1000-1200 LBS/HOUR
PERFORMANCE	MAX. TRACTIVE EFFORT	48000 LBS. AT 19.5% ADHESION AT 3020 AMPS. MAIN GENERATOR		ENGINE FUEL	
	CONT. TRACTIVE EFFORT	21500 LBS. AT 24.5 M.P.H. AT 1650 AMPS. MAIN GENERATOR	**TANK CAPACITIES**	BOILER FUEL	1180 GALLS.
	RAIL H.P. AT CONT. RATING	1405 H.P.		BOILER WATER	880 GALLS.
	FULL ENGINE OUTPUT	AVAILABLE BETWEEN 10 & 70 M.P.H.			

1Co-Co1 locomotive 10201 and 10202 diagram. *BR*

Chapter 14
THE IRISH INHERITANCE

When O.V.S. Bulleid arrived in Ireland in October 1949, the railways that were the responsibility of the transport company Córas Iompair Éireann were showing significant signs of lack of investment. Of the 5ft 3in gauge network, the main line from Dublin North Wall and Kingsbridge to Cork and Limerick (via Limerick Junction) was cleared for 21 ton axle load. A considerable part of this main line was laid on 60ft lengths 85lb/yard bullhead rail. However, the former MGWR routes were laid on 60lb/yard flat-bottom rails on wooden sleepers. Some of the light branches had 45lb/yard rails. The ruling axleload for system-wide route availability was 14.5 tons. All routes were single track except the Cork main line and the Bray commuter routes. Stations were in need of repairs. Signalling was largely semaphore and closely akin to the original set-up in each area, though colour light signals were appearing around Dublin. There were large numbers of level crossings, many of them manned by permanently resident crossing keepers.

When O.V.S. Bulleid arrived in Ireland in 1949, the largest locomotives there were the three B1a class 4-6-0s designed by E.C. Bredin and introduced in 1939. These were used solely on the Dublin – Cork main line. No 800 *Maeve* was photographed at Cork depot in July 1957.

The broad gauge steam locomotive fleet of 450 locomotives was made up of sixty-eight different classes, an average of less than seven locomotives per class. Many classes consisted of just one locomotive. The largest class numerically had been the J15 0-6-0 of which 110 were built between 1866 and 1910, but this was not typical. Equally alarming was the age of the fleet, there having been little investment in locomotive building since the country had split in two in 1922. Many locomotives were already over fifty years old; the fleet was visibly lacking in quality maintenance. OVB had recommended thinning out the number of types and reducing the fleet size when he was contributing towards the Milne Commission's report. He now arrived with a mandate to carry this out, but was faced with the CIÉ Board's decision to proceed with dieselising the railways and eliminating steam altogether.

In 1947-48, Inchicore Works in Dublin had built a small class of five 487bhp 0-6-0 diesel electric shunting locomotives using Mirrlees engines and Brush electric traction equipment, and these were proving successful. This was being followed up with a plan to build a pair of medium-powered Bo-Bo main line diesel electrics using Sulzer engines with Metro-Vick traction equipment; these were introduced in 1950 soon after OVB had taken up his post of CME. The next project was for six large Co-Co locomotives each carrying a pair of the same Sulzer/Metro-Vick power units; these were intended for heavy passenger and freight trains on the Cork main line. The twelve power units that had been ordered for the Co-Co locomotives were delivered and were stored in the old tram shed at Dalkey together with the generators and traction motors, the project having been cancelled

A fleet of twenty-six 2-6-0s had been introduced by the Midland Great Western Railway and Great Southern Railways in the 1920s. These were actually N and U class engines as designed by the South Eastern & Chatham Railway and were in concept the most modern mixed traffic engines available on CIÉ at the time of Bulleid's arrival. They had been supplied by Woolwich Arsenal and assembled in Broadstone and Inchicore Works.

Dublin suburban in 1957 - among the oldest engines in Ireland were some ancient 4-4-0s from the nineteenth century such as D14 4-4-0 No 89 seen calling at Dublin Westland Row station with a train from Dublin Amiens Street to Bray in July 1957. This was a class designed by J.A.F. Aspinall for the Great Southern & Western Railway before he moved to the Lancashire & Yorkshire Railway; many of his old Irish express passenger engines outlived his L&YR ones by two decades! The unpainted aluminium-clad vehicle in the bay platform (left) is one of Mr Bulleid's four-wheeled train heating vans.

The Irish Inheritance • 133

Irish goods engines were very largely 0-6-0s of several different classes including the former Midland Great Western engines by Atock. No 593 was on branch line duty when seen at Claremorris in July 1957.

Peripheral railways in Ireland often hung on to odd locomotive types in the 'horses for courses' tradition. This 4-6-0T was one of eight built by Beyer Peacock for the Cork, Bandon & South Coast Railway's main line mixed traffic services from Cork to Bantry. The class was eventually displaced by diesel railcars and C class diesel locomotives, not so long before the railway closed altogether. OVB's input to the Milne Commission included a requirement to reduce the multiplicity of steam locomotive types at the earliest opportunity.

following a recommendation by the Milne Commission. The CIÉ Board now developed a forward strategy for modernising the railway based on dieselisation where this made economic and strategic sense.

CIÉ had become aware of the success of the twenty AEC/Park Royal diesel railcars that the Great Northern Railway (Ireland) had introduced from 1950. The new traction strategy was based on using similar railcars but capable of running as multiple sets. These would be purchased in as large a number as could be fully utilised on daily passenger services on main lines and on secondary routes. Less frequent and seasonal passenger trains would be handled by diesel locomotives, which would be of mixed traffic type and so able also to haul freight and mixed trains. The two orders totalling sixty diesel railcars were specifically for cars identical to the Great Northern Railway (Ireland) vehicles but equipped for multiple working of up to four power cars.

At that time, Ireland was still somewhat uncertain of the reliability of the supply of diesel fuel. Some steam locomotives would need to form a reserve fleet that would be capable of deputising for diesels in an emergency. These would otherwise be available to handle seasonal goods workings such as the transport of sugar beet,

The Irish Inheritance • 135

Before OVB arrived to take up his consultant engineer post on CIÉ, Inchicore Works had outshopped the five 487bhp 0-6-0 diesel electric shunting locomotives that later became the D class. These were fitted with Mirrlees engines and Brush electrical equipment. D303 was photographed outside Inchicore Works in 1958, painted in mid-green.
W.H.C. Kelland collection, courtesy Bournemouth Railway Club Trust

The influx of 60 diesel railcars ordered in two batches from ACV (Park Royal/AEC) began in 1952 and was completed by September 1954. With car 2657 leading, a suburban service from Cork approaches the port of Cobh, formerly Queenstown, in July 1957.

Also delivered in 1952 were the four three-feet gauge diesel mechanical railcars for the West Clare section of CIÉ. One was pictured calling at Corofin station in July 1957 with a working from Ennis to Kilrush. The signalman walking away on the platform has just exchanged the single line tablets with the driver so that the railcar can traverse the next section of single track, and will shortly enable the diesel-hauled freight train on the other loop track to proceed in the Up direction.

of which Ireland was a strong producer at that period, and they would be on hand for infrastructure trains, too. In an oil crisis, the steam locomotives would be required to burn the locally-produced peat which the Irish call 'turf'. Before the Board could proceed to enact any stage of this strategy, CIÉ had to request and obtain agreement by the government for the strategy and its funding.

Oliver Bulleid was initially appointed as Consulting Mechanical Engineer. CIÉ was nationalised in June 1950 and OVB given his substantive post of Chief Mechanical Engineer on 1 February 1951. As CME, Oliver Bulleid was managerially responsible for overseeing the preparation of the specifications that would go out to manufacturers expected to be tendering for construction of these diesel locomotives. It is clear that he was able to delegate much of the specification work to make use of the available talent and experience among senior engineers within his organisation. Much of this work appears to have fallen on Assistant Chief Mechanical Engineer J.J. Johnston, with Lucas Collins, also an Assistant Chief Mechanical Engineer, being deeply involved in the tender evaluation process. Suffice it to say that, when the orders went out for the new diesel locomotive fleet, many observers were surprised at the large numbers being ordered without any provision for testing and running prototypes. Others were surprised that the prevailing preference among Inchicore engineers for buying proven engines and equipment from General Motors of the USA was not followed through at this time.

On 25 January 1956, by which time the A class were being delivered, Lucas Collins's position was re-designated Deputy Chief Engineer (Mechanical) with a reporting line to Dan Herlihy who was Chief Engineer, a post initially announced as covering civil engineering. The same regrouping re-designated J.J. Johnston as Assistant Chief Mechanical Engineer (Technical). This effectively side-lined OVB, who was encouraged to concentrate on bringing the turf-burner project to fruition.

Each new locomotive class is described in the following chapters. They cover the sixty 1,200bhp Co-Cos and thirty-four 550bhp Bo-Bos ordered from Metropolitan-Vickers, the twelve 960bhp A1A-A1A locomotives from the Birmingham Railway Carriage & Wagon Company (these created a future for the twelve Sulzer power units stored at Dalkey), and the two classes of diesel shunting locomotives, one of which was designed and built at Inchicore. One chapter in this book highlights the bold experiment to dieselise the narrow-gauge West Clare Railway.

The steam locomotive proposal was clearly the one which exercised Bulleid's mind the most. In this case, the ability to burn turf economically in a steam locomotive was as yet unproven. Through necessity, attempts had been made to burn turf briquettes in locomotives during what the Irish knew as 'the Emergency', which others named the Second World War. In those years of austerity, supplies of British steel and coal were in great demand for the war effort and the UK had restricted the quantities it could export to Ireland. Burning turf in existing steam locomotive fireboxes had enabled some trains to run, but with many failures to complete journeys due mainly to the much lower specific energy content of turf compared with coal which necessitated up to three times more turf being needed by volume. To produce a locomotive type that could burn oil in good times and turf in lean times was a challenge. OVB quite rightly insisted on experimental prototypes, which are discussed in some detail in Chapter 22.

When Oliver Bulleid retired in 1958, he had completed what he had been required to do. The diesel railcar fleet had been launched in 1953. In the three years from 1955 to 1957 inclusive, CIÉ had introduced all its new diesel classes, and put the prototype turf-burning steam locomotive on the rails. By 1958, CIÉ was already running more of its trains with diesels than with steam; unwanted steam locomotives were gathering at depots and eventually heading for the scrap yards. His turf burning locomotive experiments were coming good. The diesel locomotives in particular had their trials and tribulations, which are covered in the relevant chapters in this book, but they were quite clearly in charge.

It wasn't OVB's fault that oil supplies became so reliable that CIÉ management decided to abandon steam altogether. The pending bankruptcy of the Great Northern Railway Board's railways in 1958, and the division of its assets between CIÉ and the Ulster Transport Authority across the border, forced an unwanted temporary upsurge in steam traction on CIÉ, thus thwarting any plans for steam to have gone by the end of the 1950s. The GNRB inheritance also added extra urgency to CIÉ's need to look to America for some new diesel locomotives, a move already underway once the unreliability of the Metro-Vick locomotives was proved to be fundamental to the type. Buying locomotives from the USA had been something that Lucas Collins had recommended when the diesel programme was first being developed. The success of the first class of General Motors locomotives on CIÉ, the Class 121 Bo-Bos, led to it becoming the basis for future purchases in view of their reliability. By the end of March 1963, CIÉ was able to claim that its use of steam traction had finished. In that year, I visited the scrap sidings at the back of Inchicore Works. The turf-burning CC 1 was there among redundant locomotives from all over the republic, all being set up for the cutters' torches. The Republic of Ireland had managed to be five years ahead of British Railways in eliminating steam traction.

The chapters which follow are ordered in the sequence of delivery of the first unit in each class, not in alphabetical order nor in the sequence in which they were ordered. Thus, although the B class locomotives were ordered before the F class locomotives, the latter were delivered before the former were completed; also while the E class equipment was ordered before the G class locomotives, the first of the latter class was the earliest in traffic.

Just after OVB retired, CIÉ was gifted with half the assets of the Great Northern Railway Board when that organisation was declared imminently bankrupt in September 1958. This Class S1 4-4-0 No 171, now preserved with its GNR(I) name *Slieve Gullion*, became part of CIÉ stock as seen in 1963 by the initials stencilled on its buffer beam. This unplanned influx of steam locomotives into CIÉ's fleet gave additional urgency to the need for more new diesel locomotives beyond those ordered during the Bulleid era.

Chapter 15

THE PROTOTYPE BO-BO DIESEL ELECTRICS

It was as early as 1945 that CIÉ decided to probe dieselisation by ordering prototypes. Two types were envisaged initially, a general shunting locomotive and a medium-sized mixed traffic type of around 900bhp capable of running in multiple, and equipment for these was ordered in 1945. Orders for equipment for six examples of a larger 1,800bhp Co-Co for heavier main line passenger and freight trains were placed in 1948. Post-war restrictions on availability of steel and an alleged shortage of engineering knowledge of diesel traction in Ireland and the UK led to delays. In the event, escalating costs and the likelihood that electrical equipment might need to be sourced from the European continent led CIÉ to decide to design and build the prototype locomotives 'in house' at its Inchicore Works in Dublin. The five diesel shunters were conventional, conceptually based on the format used by English Electric but in this case using more powerful engines from Mirrlees and electric traction equipment from Brush. These locomotives were already in service

When new in 1950, prototype diesel electric Bo-Bo 1100 stands outside Inchicore Works in plain dark green livery. Note the row of four multiple working connections above the buffer beam. *W.H.C. Kelland collection, courtesy Bournemouth Railway Club Trust*

before Oliver Bulleid arrived at Inchicore in 1949.

The two mixed traffic main line diesel prototypes emerged from Inchicore Works in January 1950 and April 1951. Their rather cautious specification had required them individually to be capable of hauling a 360 tons freight train at 40mph or a 120 tons passenger train at 55mph. They were of Bo-Bo layout with wide bodies and end cabs, using 915bhp Sulzer six-cylinder in-line engines and Metro-Vick electric traction generators, traction motors and control equipment. On early trials, No 1100 unsurprisingly outperformed its specification, for example proving itself able to haul a 350 tons eleven-coach train from Dublin to Cork non-stop in four hours ten minutes at an average speed of 40.3mph. A test freight train of 700 tons gave the multiple pair a chance to show off their heavy haulage capacity, aided no doubt by the rugged nature of the Metro-Vick electric equipment.

1100's bogies used only primary springing of the leaf type with small coil auxiliary springs, and were responsible for giving the crew a notably rough ride at speed. For 1101, swing link secondary suspension was fitted, though this allegedly made little improvement. The driving cabs were spartan, the seats for the driver and assistant being hinged off the back wall of each cab. The driving desk design was quite deep, but without adequate space underneath for the driver's legs and feet, so driving these locomotives was not a totally comfortable experience. A positive change, in 1956, was upgrading their Sulzer engines from 915bhp to 960bhp. At the same time they were renumbered from 1100 and 1101 to B113 and B114, following on from the B101 series (see Chapter 18).

These two locomotives had an axleload of 21 tons. This restricted their field of operation severely, to just the Dublin to Cork main line and the North Wall branch

No 1100 accelerates with a Down train on the Cork main line in 1957. The coaches include Bulleid, Park Royal and earlier vehicles. *C.L. Fry*

In 1963 B113, the former 1100, is nearing completion of an overhaul in the diesel erecting shop at Inchicore. The multiple connections have been blanked off. Behind B113 is one of the B121 series of General Motors Bo-Bos, the success of which convinced CIÉ to continue to buy diesels from GM.

in Dublin. Most other main lines and all secondary routes in the republic required locomotives of lower axleloads, a feature that future builds of production locomotives would meet. The prototype Bo-Bos' maximum speed of 55mph was also lower than was being specified for speeds of future express passenger trains, for which the originally planned six Co-Cos were envisaged. Being too heavy for secondary main lines, and too slow for the principal main lines, 1100 and 1101 had already taught CIÉ's operating department to aim for lower axleloads and higher speed capability for future main line diesel builds.

It is certain that Oliver Bulleid did not influence the progress of these two prototypes as they were already well advanced when he first arrived at Inchicore. Rather like the Southern Railway Q class, 1100 and 1101 were allowed to follow their own path, though quite clearly CIÉ made good use of the experience with them when placing orders for the large batches of new diesel locomotives that were to follow. OVB may well have been behind the cancellation of the Co-Co project, however.

After many years of regular main line work, their steam heat boilers and water tanks were removed as part of CIÉ's new policy of including separate heating vans in hauled passenger trains (a way of keeping future locomotive axleloads within bounds). Running as local freight locomotives, the two Bo-Bos remained in traffic for their final decade until a persistent but intermittent brake fault caused them to be sidelined. Until then, engineers had been unable to determine exactly why either locomotive would occasionally lose its brake air; on some occasions they had run away, with or without wagons attached. A modification in the early 1970s in which chokes were fitted to the air pipes leading to the brake cylinders was supposed to cure this, but the two locomotives were finally withdrawn from service in 1975. CIÉ had briefly considered re-engining them with General Motors 8-645-E engines for the Tara Mines traffic but this was not pursued. Nevertheless, to sustain a twenty-five years life for what were ostensibly prototypes was quite a creditable performance.

During their early lives, the pair were painted dark green. They were repainted mid-green in 1956 at the time of their engine uprating. I saw B113 and B114 during and after overhaul in 1963 dressed in their more 'modern' colours of black, white and tan. Following complaints about workshop and locomotive noise from people living in a neighbouring estate opposite Inchicore Works, a 'sound barrier' of withdrawn diesel locomotives was shunted into a siding on the north side of the main line; for a time, these two machines became a static part of that.

No B113, the former 1100, is preserved in the National Folk and Transport Museum at Cultra near Belfast, and is thus the oldest surviving main line diesel locomotive in the British Isles.

Class	C2a Bo-Bo
Builder	CIÉ Inchicore works
CIÉ later classification	B113
Number in class	2
Introduced	1950
Diesel engine	Sulzer 6LDA28 915hp*
Electric traction equipt.	Metropolitan-Vickers
Traction motors (4 dc)	MV137CW
Maximum speed	55mph
Weight in w.o.	84tons**
Original number series	1100, 1101
Later number series	B113, B114

* Uprated in 1956 to 960bhp.
** 80tons after removal of the steam heat boiler and water tanks.

After overhaul at Inchicore in 1963 stands Bo-Bo B114, the former 1101. Painted in the current 'modern' style of black, white and tan, B114 is flanked by locomotives in the previous two colours. On the left is an A class Co-Co showing how the original silver livery so seriously discoloured over time, in this case over about eight years from new; on the right is a C class Bo-Bo carrying the mid-green style.

Chapter 16
THE F CLASS B-B DIESEL MECHANICALS

When Córas Iompair Éireann took over the railways formerly known as the Great Southern Railways in 1924-25, included in the mix were some minor railways of three feet gauge. Of these, the Tralee & Dingle Railway was heading for imminent closure, running just one day a month for cattle movements; the Cavan & Leitrim Railway was active in its area, serving Ireland's only significant coal mines at Arigna as well as moving cattle to market; and the West Clare Railway was staggering along serving an economically weak area of western Ireland. As a general carrier with no dominant major traffic flow, the relatively short WCR was selected as a trial for total dieselisation, to determine whether dieselisation could save such a railway from early closure. The West Clare connected with the CIÉ secondary line from Limerick to Galway at Ennis and meandered round County Clare, reaching the west coast before heading south through sparsely populated and agriculturally poor land; it reached a small port on the Shannon estuary at Kilrush, and branched off just before there to the tiny Atlantic seaside resort of Kilkee. Even in the first decade of the twentieth century, the West Clare Railway had been publicly known to be decrepit and unreliable.

The County Donegal Railway had successfully dieselised its regular passenger trains using railcars from the UK firm Walkers of Wigan. The success of these prompted CIÉ to follow the same pattern. By 1952, four articulated, unidirectional diesel railcars were being introduced that were identical to the last two that the same firm had delivered to the CDR. They weighed 11tons, had 102bhp Gardner 6LW diesel engines driving through mechanical gearboxes, were unidirectional and had a top speed of 38.5mph.

In 1955, Walkers delivered three diesel mechanical locomotives to the WCR section for freight services. These locomotives were of B-B wheel arrangement, being basically a pair of standard railcar bogies complete with engines and transmissions carrying a frame with a central cab; this configuration produced a 214bhp freight diesel locomotive with almost all components already familiar to drivers and maintenance staff. Like the railcars, they had mechanical drive to one axle on each bogie, the adjacent wheelsets being driven by side coupling rods. In normal freight service, these locomotives were driven with the first four gears operable, giving a top speed of 25mph. If called upon for passenger work, the driver could unlock a fifth gear, raising the top speed to 32.5mph.

At that time, WCR freight trains were quite lengthy, and these locomotives were clearly better haulage machines than the steam locomotives they replaced, even allowing for the pauses for gear changes. The railcars and the three diesel locomotives were painted in CIÉ's plain dark green, later revised to mid-green, unlined.

With three railcars operating each day, the WCR was able to provide a more frequent and comprehensive passenger train service than had been the case in steam days, each railcar from Ennis connecting into another at

The F Class B-B Diesel Mechanicals • 143

In April 1957, three-feet gauge diesel mechanical B-B F501 was working freight at Doonbeg and looking well-kept, or indeed recently overhauled. At least the first five vehicles are cattle vans, though the leading one appears to have a tarpaulin loosely stretched over the body in place of a firm roof. *K. Cooper/Colour-Rail NG206*

Class	F B-B
Builder	Walker Brothers, Wigan
Number in class	3
Introduced	1955
Diesel engine	Gardner 6LW
Engine power	107bhp (x 2)
Hydraulic transmission	Wilson five-speed gearbox
Maximum speed	25mph*
Weight in w.o.	23tons 0cwt
Original numbers	C31-C33**
Second number series	F501-F503**

*   32.5mph in 5th gear
** Until the end of steam working, C series numbers indicated locomotives allocated to the West Clare section. Renumbering the three diesel locomotives into the F series as they went into service brought the locomotives in line with the new numbering for the other diesel classes being introduced on CIÉ at that time. (The new C series of numbers was for 5ft 3in gauge Bo-Bos.)

the southern junction at Moyasta. Nonetheless, the savings in train crews and any increase in patronage were not matched by economies in other operating methods. By 1960, the West Clare system was the last surviving narrow gauge railway in the whole of Ireland. The WCR was economically not viable and it closed in 1961. The three diesel locomotives ended up in the scrap yard at the back of Inchicore Works, and before the end of 1963 they had been dismantled.

F503's driver checks inside one engine compartment while his freight train from Ennis is looped at Milltown Malbay to allow a railcar and trailers to call in the opposite direction. The coupling rod drives between the wheels on the bogies are clearly visible. Each bogie is driven by one Gardner engine through an hydraulic coupling and five-speed gearbox, the fifth gear being switched out when on freight work.

After closure of the West Clare Railway in 1961, the three locomotives went to Inchicore for storage and possible sale, something that didn't happen. F501 and F502 stand awaiting the cutter's torch in 1963 in the company of former CIÉ and GNRB steam locomotives.

Chapter 17
THE A CLASS CO-CO DIESEL ELECTRICS

It was a very bold step in the early 1950s for CIÉ to order 94 new diesel locomotives at once from one manufacturer in the UK. Metro-Vick was not the preferred choice of CIÉ's engineers who had lobbied hard for the Board to buy from America, preferably from General Motors.

Tenders had in fact gone out to no less than forty-one suppliers around the world, of whom twenty-two replied (see Appendix 1). The choice in the end resolved itself to a small number of firms in the sterling area, partly because other currencies were in short supply, but also because of a need to resolve

a key trade arrangement between the Irish and UK governments. It is interesting that two designs were chosen in which almost all components, including the diesel engines, were of British design and manufacture. The choice of Metropolitan-Vickers as the main supplier would have been

In July 1956, brand new Co-Co No A51 arrives at Dromod with a Dublin Westland Row to Sligo train formed of modern Commonwealth-bogied stock. At Dromod, a connection was made with the morning narrow gauge steam train to Ballinamore and Belturbet on the Cavan & Leitrim section, though very few passengers actually made the transfer to the small station behind the building on the left.

influenced by CIÉ's satisfactory experience with the electric traction equipment in 1100 and 1101, the two Sulzer prototypes. A British alternative design with Sulzer traction power was also on offer but was more expensive.

The larger of the two new classes, both in power and numerically, was the A class Co-Co design, a relatively lightweight machine capable of exerting 1,200bhp at the crankshaft. Sixty of these potentially useful locomotives were ordered, designed for a top speed of 75mph and intended for both express passenger trains and heavy freight.

In all but one respect, they were conventional machines. Riding on two three-axle Commonwealth type bogies, each with compensated primary coil springing and three axle-mounted traction motors, the locomotive body was of modest length. Their weight of 85.3 tons enabled them to comply with the general axleload restriction of 14½ tons across most routes on CIÉ.

There were two full-width end driving cabs and relatively few bodyside ventilation grilles, giving them a neat external appearance. Inside, the power unit sat centrally, with its cooling unit at one end of the body and equipment compartments at the other. There was no train heat boiler, CIÉ having decided to include independent train heat vehicles in its passenger trains.

The Metro-Vick dc generator was driven by an eight-cylinder Crossley two-stroke diesel engine. The engine design included a Crossley patent which used ports in the cylinders to duct the pressure pulse of an exhausting cylinder towards the intake air of an adjacent cylinder, thus providing a form of pressure-charging without using an expensive turbocharger; the scheme also eliminated valves in the cylinder head. So, ostensibly,

Co-Co A10 was being serviced at Limerick when seen in summer 1957. Note the apparatus on the cabsides for exchanging the single line tablets at crossing point and loops (the apparatus is swung upwards out of immediate use). Most CIÉ main lines are single track.

here was a simple design of engine with fewer mechanical complications when compared with more conventional diesel engines. Mr Bulleid was said to be quite excited about this.

This was an interesting choice of engine. A fleet of similar locomotives had very recently been ordered by the Western Australian Government Railways, but other railway experience with this make of engine at that time was nil. There was a view that the same engine had performed well when used in submarines, but history tells otherwise, particularly that the tell-tale heavy exhaust smoke was a major give-away out at sea; in any case, one can be assured that conditions at sea for mechanical equipment are quite different from conditions on a railway.

All other engine choices available from the UK were four-stroke types, the four piston strokes in sequence being intake (down stroke), compression, power and exhaust; in a four-stroke engine the air intake and exhaust are through valves in the cylinder head that are usually mechanically actuated to open by a camshaft; they are otherwise held shut by strong springs. In a two-stroke engine, the downward piston stroke starts with the cylinder air fully compressed. Ignition takes place, producing power. The air is exhausted through ports in the cylinder wall uncovered by the piston near the bottom of the stroke, and intake air is forced in as the piston begins its upward stroke, covering up the intake and exhaust ports and beginning the compression process. General Motors in North America had developed a blower-charged two-stroke engine principle that worked well, albeit a little less efficiently than a conventional four-stroke engine.

During Mr Bulleid's tenure at Inchicore, CIÉ continued to rely on the vacuum brake for all trains requiring continuous brakes. Most passenger trains were marshalled with old and new vehicles mixed, so this was a sensible decision at the time. In the British Isles as a whole, the concept of making up passenger trains into fixed sets was mainly limited to Southern Railway practice, so Ireland was unexceptional in this. It was not until the 1970s that Ireland began to lead the way by eliminating most loose-coupled mixed freights and concentrating on single-product block trains, something that British Rail was to home in on a decade or more later apart from Dr Beeching's merry-go-round coal trains, liner trains (for ISO containers) and a few block oil trains. So, the Irish decision to stick with the vacuum brake made sense at the time. The A class even used the vacuum brake system for the locomotive brakes.

In early service, the A class proved their ability to haul trains well and to run them at the speeds required. However, the Crossley engines were prone to vibrations that in time shook body-mounted equipment and pipes severely, to the point where breakages and leakages were problematic.

I recall joining an A class-hauled train at Dromod in 1956; I stepped into the fourth carriage, which was visibly bouncing on its springs in time with the revolutions of the diesel engine! During a visit to Inchicore Works I saw a heap of bent connecting rods and damaged pistons piled in a corner of the works yard. The exhaust from these locomotives was always visible.[12]

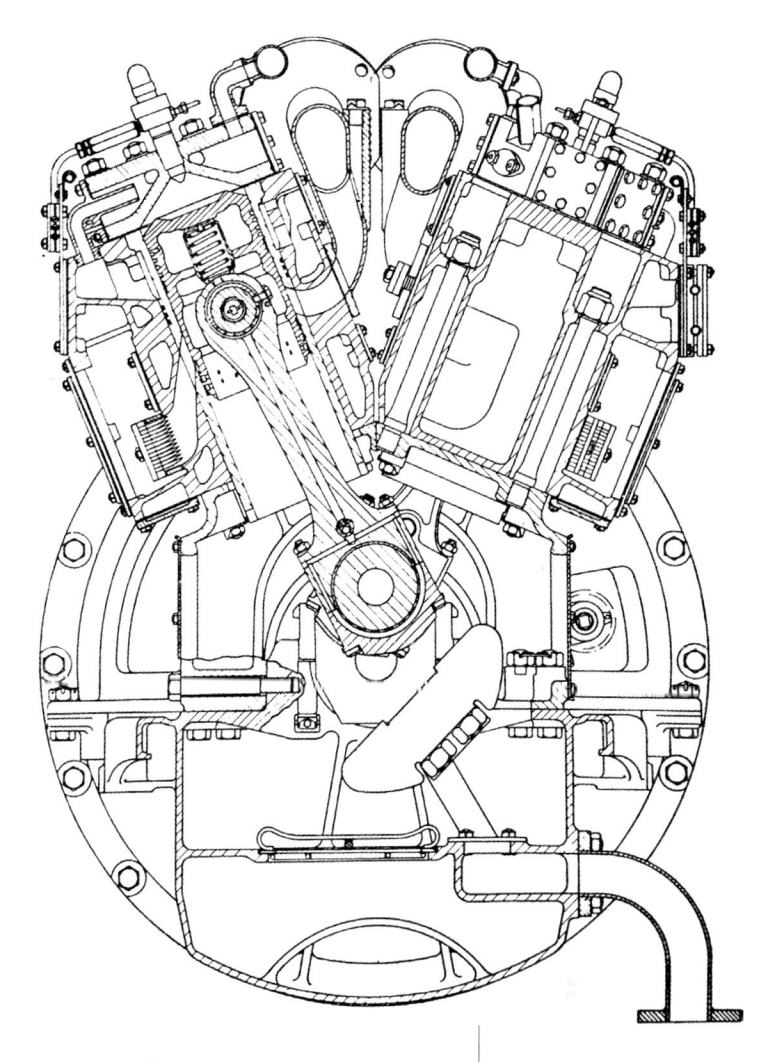

In the early 1960s, the A class fleet was at a low ebb. Availability

This cross-section of a Crossley two-stroke diesel engine shows (for the left hand cylinder) the inlet and exhaust ports and passages. By an ingenious means of linking the inlet and exhaust air flows, a level of air intake charging was achieved using the exhaust pulse from one cylinder to pressurise the intake air for another.
Metropolitan-Vickers

---

12 In 1963, when a friend and I arrived at Inchicore Works, I remarked that we had been hauled by an A class locomotive on the boat train from Dun Laoghaire to Dublin Kingsbridge via the Phoenix Park tunnel. The engineer who greeted us commented: 'How did you know it was an A class? You wouldn't have seen it for the smoke!'

At Westland Row station, Dublin, in July 1956, A39 has arrived with an express from Sligo. Meanwhile, an old MGWR 0-6-0T has just placed the stock of a southbound train in the bay, probably stock for a Dun Laoghaire boat train.

At Athenry, A37 stands with a heavy freight bound for Galway, waiting for a passenger train from Limerick to Galway that has reversed in the adjacent platform track to clear the section ahead.

A25 shows what a Crossley two-stroke engine can do as it starts a Gaelic football special out of Cork Glanmire Road station on a Sunday morning in July 1957. It wasn't just steam locomotives that could create impressive smoke effects!

On a summer Sunday in 1956, Co-Co A28 has run round its stock in the sidings alongside Rosslare Harbour station after a journey from Dublin via Wexford. These were the days when passengers arriving on a ferry from Fishguard would disembark alongside the station, show their luggage to customs officials at a table alongside the boat, and then walk the short distance to the waiting train.

for traffic was never much more than 80 per cent and was sometimes worse. Chapter 24 explains the actions CIÉ took that transformed this fleet into reliable workhorses, but that was beyond Mr Bulleid's time there.

When introduced, the A class locomotives were painted overall in metallic silver paint, including the bodies, bogies, and external equipment. External lettering, numerals and logos were in mid-green. This was part of a scheme, attributed to Oliver Bulleid, to make CIÉ's passenger trains look modern with new, shiny, unpainted aluminium-clad carriages being hauled by silver locomotives. Even the four-wheeled heating vans that OVB had built at Inchicore were clad in aluminium panels. Indeed, a full formation of silver locomotive and train was posed for a 1955 publicity picture, though real life train formations were usually mixed in different shades of green and silver.

The silver paint on diesel locomotives did not wear well. After several years, it became streaked with oil and exhaust residues as well as the effects of cast-iron brake block dust. The standard CIÉ mid-green was a more serviceable colour, and this became the norm at the first repaint. After Bulleid's time, the early 1960s

The A Class Co-Co Diesel Electrics • 151

saw a change to black as the main colour, lined out in white and tan, later in just white. In later decades, this morphed into tan becoming the main colour, with a black band across the sides and ends. The last version was when the CIÉ railways were separated into a wholly-owned company, Irish Rail/Iarnród Éireann; this body added white edging and new logos to the black band. By this time the class had been renumbered into the 001 series and had been re-engined. That story is pursued in in a later chapter.

Class	A Co-Co as built*
Builder	Metropolitan-Vickers
Number in class	60
Introduced	1955
Diesel engine	Crossley HSTV8 2-stroke
Engine power	1,200bhp
Electric traction equipt.	Metropolitan-Vickers
Traction motors (6 dc)	MV137CW
Maximum tractive effort	46,000lbf
Maximum speed	75mph
Weight in w.o.	85tons 6cwt
Number series	A1-A60

* Details of the class after rebuilding with GM engines in the 1960s/1970s are in a table in Chapter 24.

In 1963, after seven or eight years of operation, this A class Co-Co demonstrates how badly the silver paint lasted in normal running conditions. The locomotive running numbers are not sufficiently visible to identify the locomotive! The train is a working from Dublin to Galway via the former MGWR main line and is seen turning on to the Athlone line at the approach to Mullingar station.

152 • OLIVER BULLEID'S LOCOMOTIVES

The first A class version of the black, white and tan livery looks smart on locomotive A52 as it stands stabled at Limerick in summer 1963.

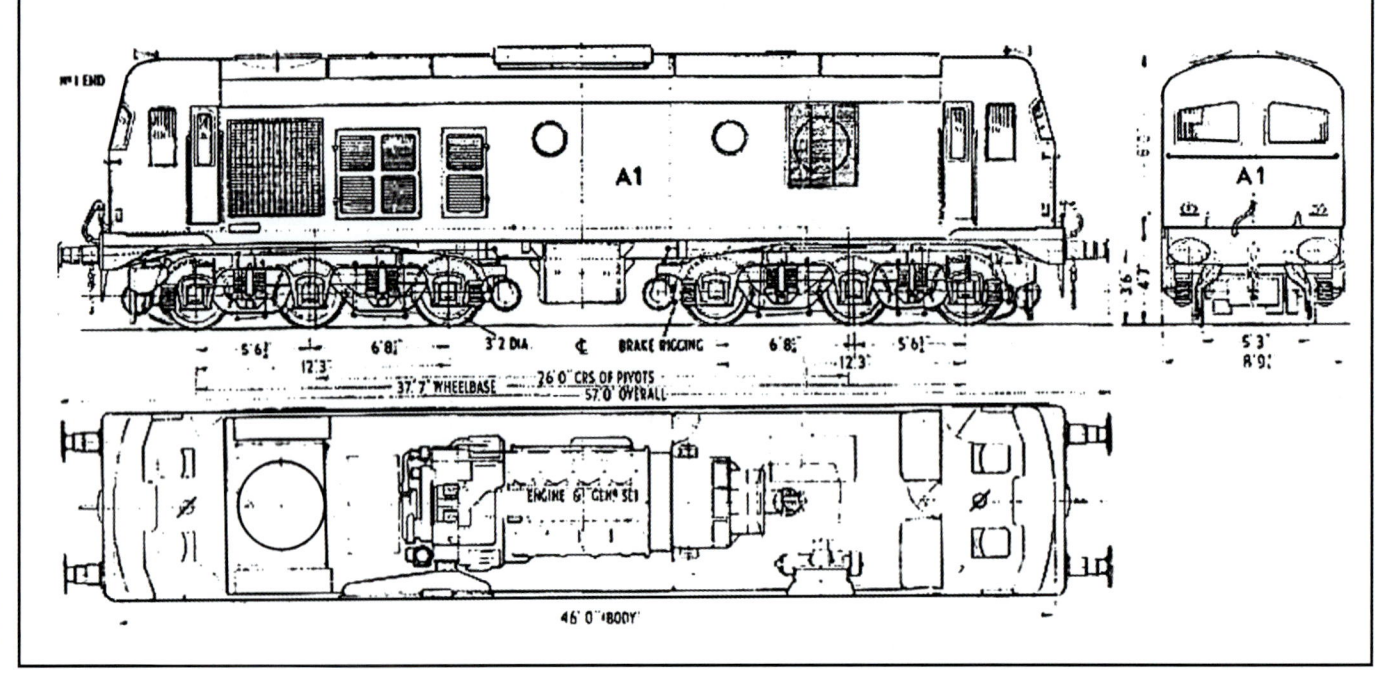

A class locomotive diagram.

Chapter 18
THE B CLASS A1A-A1A DIESEL ELECTRICS

When CIÉ was considering the number of locomotives to be included in the future diesel locomotive fleet, thought was given to what should be done with the twelve Sulzer/M-V power units and eighteen traction motors stored at Dalkey. An intelligent use of these would be to include, among the orders for the new diesel fleet, one for twelve medium-powered locomotives to which they could be fitted. This order went to the Birmingham Railway Carriage & Wagon Company at Smethwick, Birmingham, only the third order the company had received for diesel locomotives. Intended for use on main and secondary routes the axle-load had to be kept down to only 14½ tons; recognising that the power output only needed four traction motors, BRC&W selected the wheel arrangement A1A-A1A to spread the load on the track, a first in the British Isles.[13] A neat

---

13. The only other locomotive type of this wheel arrangement known to the author to have run on main line railways in the British Isles is the British Rail Class 31, the former Brush Type 2.

On one of its first revenue-earning trips, on the August bank holiday Sunday of 1956, A1A-A1A B102 pauses at Mallow with the midday Cork to Dublin Kingsbridge service. When new, the silver-painted livery looked quite smart on these well-designed, lightweight locomotives. Cabside recesses for tablet-catching equipment are evident, though the equipment has not been installed.

Any livery on a plain-shaped diesel locomotive looks shabby if unkempt or allowed to remain in place too long without repainting. The CIÉ mid-green with no lining is not a happy fit on B101, seen stabled at Limerick Junction in summer 1963.

locomotive design resulted which, like the A class, used swing bolster bogies with compensated primary suspension. There were two cabs, again at the ends of a full-width body. The locomotive weighed just 75 tons, an excellent example of applied mechanical engineering. Credit must be given jointly to BRC&W and to CIÉ because two of the railway's engineers were seconded to BRC&W to support the design work.

As with the A class, the 960bhp Sulzer six-cylinder four-stroke engine and Metro-Vick dc generator were centrally located on the underframe, with the cooler group at one end and sundry equipment at the other. There was a reciprocating compressor for locomotive braking, and a reciprocating exhauster for the train brakes. The traction motors were blower cooled. Locomotive braking was by direct air, but train braking was vacuum only.[14]

The BRC&W B class locomotives proved to be reliable mixed traffic locomotives. The two routes they were most used on were Waterford-Limerick and Mallow-Tralee, but they appeared at times all over the CIÉ system.

As new, they were delivered in 1956 painted the then standard all-over silver-grey. This was replaced later by mid-green, and later still with versions of black, white and tan.

The class remained in service until the late 1970s. Partly due to reducing levels of freight traffic, the class was selected for withdrawal. At that time, they were the only class powered by what by then was regarded as non-standard

---

14. On my only journey behind a B class, in summer 1956, No B102 was hauling the Sunday midday train from Cork to Dublin Kingsbridge. At the Mallow stop, the driver was worried that he had a good train brake but the locomotive brakes were ineffective. Presumably this was a result of incorrect adjustment, a teething error on a brand new machine. The train did reach Dublin as planned.

The B Class A1A-A1A Diesel Electrics • 155

B109 in black-and-tan colour waits for the signal at Mallow when working a Cork- or Tralee-bound freight on 8 June 1964. On main line work, no tablet catcher has been fitted.
Colour-Rail FIE04527

B110 stands at Cork Glanmire Road depot in summer 1963 in cleaned black, white and tan livery. This class used the stored Sulzer/Metro-Vick power units (engine plus generator) and traction motors that had been put aside after the project for prototype 1,830bhp Co-Co main line diesels had been abandoned under O.V. Bulleid's influence.

diesel equipment, namely the Sulzer engine. All other classes by then were General Motors-powered. CIÉ gave thought to fitting the B class with the GM 8-645 diesel engine and modifying the traction motors for 85mph top speed, and fitting equipment for multiple working. The decision to buy the General Motors 071 class locomotives stopped this course of action. The last B class locomotive was withdrawn in 1978. B103 is preserved and is held by the Irish Traction Group at Carrick-on-Suir.

B class locomotive diagram.

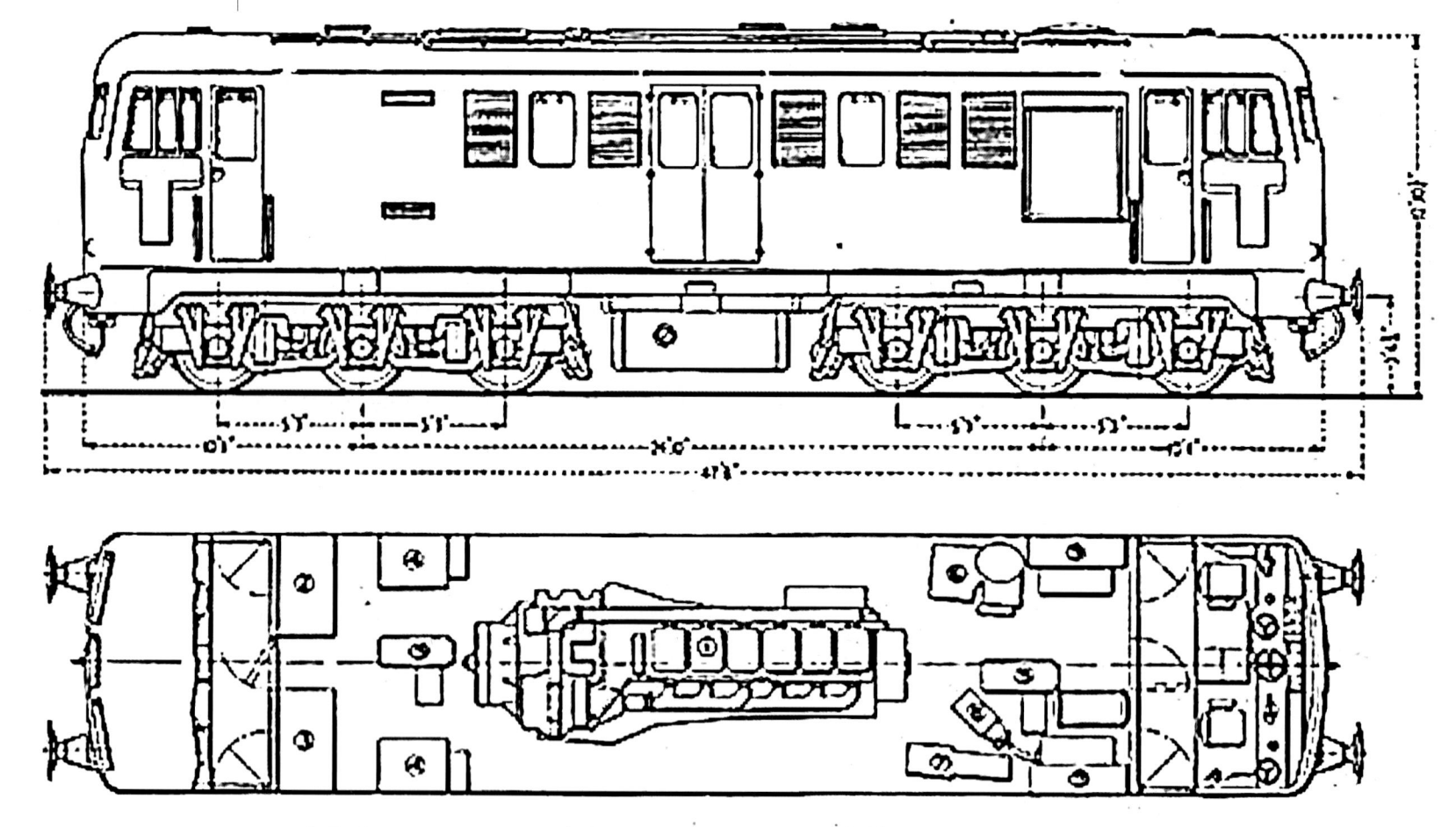

Class	B A1A-A1A
Builder	BRC&W
CIÉ revised class	101
Number in class	12
Introduced	1956
Diesel engine	Sulzer 8LDA28
Engine power	960bhp
Electric traction equipt.	Metropolitan-Vickers
Traction motors (4 dc)	MV137CW
Maximum tractive effort	41,800lbf
Maximum speed	75mph
Weight in w.o.	75tons 9cwt
Original number series	B101-B112
Post-1972 number series	101-112

1. Engine-generator set
2. H.T. control cubicle
3. L.T. control cubicle
4. Battery compartments
5. Traction motor blowers
6. Compressor
7. Vacuum exhauster
8. Cooling water circulating pump
9. Radiator for engine water and oil

Chapter 19
THE C CLASS BO-BO DIESEL ELECTRICS

How much influence OVB applied to the purchase specification for the C class diesel locomotives one can only conjecture at this distance in time. My guess is – not a lot. Oliver Bulleid's reputation in his designs for the Southern Railway was not one for timidly specifying low power outputs. Indeed, the opposite was true of his Pacifics and the Q1s, and indeed for his SR main line diesels.

Yet the C class, as the Metro-Vick Bo-Bos were officially classified, were intended to be just 550bhp, a mere 50bhp higher than the Southern Region of British Railways was installing in each power car of its new diesel electric multiple units. The C class were intended for branch line services, some of which were mixed trains made up with ancient six-

The author's first journey behind a C class Bo-Bo was inauspicious in that the 550bhp locomotive was clearly overloaded by its eight-coach return excursion from Youghal. It is pictured after arrival at Cork Glanmire Road station on a sunny evening in July 1957. This was not really what the class was designed for, however, which was for lightly-loaded branch line trains and secondary goods and ballast workings.

C202 at Drimoleague on the main line of the West Cork system illustrates one of the types of traffic for which the C class was procured. It has arrived in summer 1957 with a train from the Baltimore branch composed of three six-wheeled coaches. Ireland was the only place in the British Isles using rigid-wheelbase carriages on the national railway system by this date.

wheeled carriages and a few goods wagons in tow. The first deliveries were allocated to the Valentia and West Cork branches. They were also allocated to station pilot duties.

The C class was in effect a smaller and shorter version of the A class from the same manufacturer. The same double-cab layout with full-width body was used, riding on compensated two-axle bogies. The traction motors were the same as used on the A class, but just four in number. The traction generator was similar to that used in the B class. The engine was a smaller sized version of the A class engine, still with 'exhaust pulse pressure charging'. The C class was naturally doomed to significant levels of vibration and mechanical failure by dint of the Crossley engine within. Unlike the A class, but in line with the B class, the C class used air for the locomotive brakes and vacuum for the train brakes.

I came across the C class on several journeys. The first was, to me, very significant. No C217 was brand new when I found it at Youghal in summer 1957 at the head of quite a long excursion train returning to Cork. This Bo-Bo had eight coaches in tow, some of which were bogie vehicles. Five hundred and fifty brake horse power is not a lot when hauling a train of this length that stops at all stations. As might be expected, progress was pedestrian, particularly the observed slow accelerations from stops and the limited maximum speeds, perhaps around 30mph, between stations. This was not what the class had been purchased for, was it? The train on which I had previously travelled to Youghal had fourteen six-wheelers and two vans, and ran sparklingly with an A class at the head. The C was weak by comparison.[15]

---

15. When, in 1963, my friend and I asked at Dundalk depot for some stored steam locomotives to be hauled into the open so that we could photograph them, the only CIÉ locomotive available to do it was a C class diesel. The driver who was detailed to carry out the shunt told us, 'We won't use that – it couldn't pull the skin off a rice pudding!' He climbed aboard a nearby WT class 2-6-4T from the Ulster Transport Authority without authorisation and used that to make the shunt; the UTA crew arrived during the proceedings and stood by looking most bemused!

My second trip was with C202 doing what it had been designed to do. It arrived at Skibbereen on the single track branch line from Baltimore with two six-wheelers and a van, and reached the junction at Drimoleague with time to spare. Replacing a steam 2-4-2T on this branch line duty was well within the C class capability.

CIÉ was soon experiencing mechanical difficulties with the C class. As the nature of the railway changed, due to the rise in affordable road transport and the railway line closures arising from the 1958 Transport Act, minor branch lines were being closed all round the system during the 1950s and 1960s. In time, the C class locomotives began to be seen as inadequate for the needs of the more modern railway that was emerging, with its block freight trains, faster passenger train speeds and loads, and heavier peak-hour suburban workings around Dublin.

Like the A and B classes, all except two of the C class (C231 and C234) entered service in the all-over silver livery. The two exceptions were turned out in green, which looked better if not startling, and this was gradually applied to other members of the class. In the 1960s, they went into black with few white embellishments, before the major rebuild that occurred well beyond Bulleid's time at Inchicore.

The later stages of the C class story are taken up in Chapter 24.

Class	C Bo-Bo as built*
Builder	Metropolitan-Vickers
Number in class	34
Introduced	1956
Diesel engine	Crossley ESTV8 2-stroke
Engine power	550bhp
Electric traction equipt.	Metropolitan-Vickers
Traction motors (4 dc)	MV137CW
Maximum tractive effort	34,445lbf
Maximum speed	75mph
Weight in w.o.	57tons 0cwt
Original number series	C201-C234

* Details of the class after rebuilding with GM engines in the 1960s/1970s are in a table in Chapter 24.

By May 1959, C231 had received a coat of green paint lined out in white, which improved its appearance when compared with silver-painted members of the class. It was photographed at Bray with a Dublin city-bound train of mixed carriages, the third and fourth being Park Royal-supplied vehicles that had been delivered during Mr Bulleid's time at Inchicore. These coaches were just over 10feet wide and made full use of the larger Irish loading gauge compared to the more restrictive one in Britain. *Colour-Rail IR505*

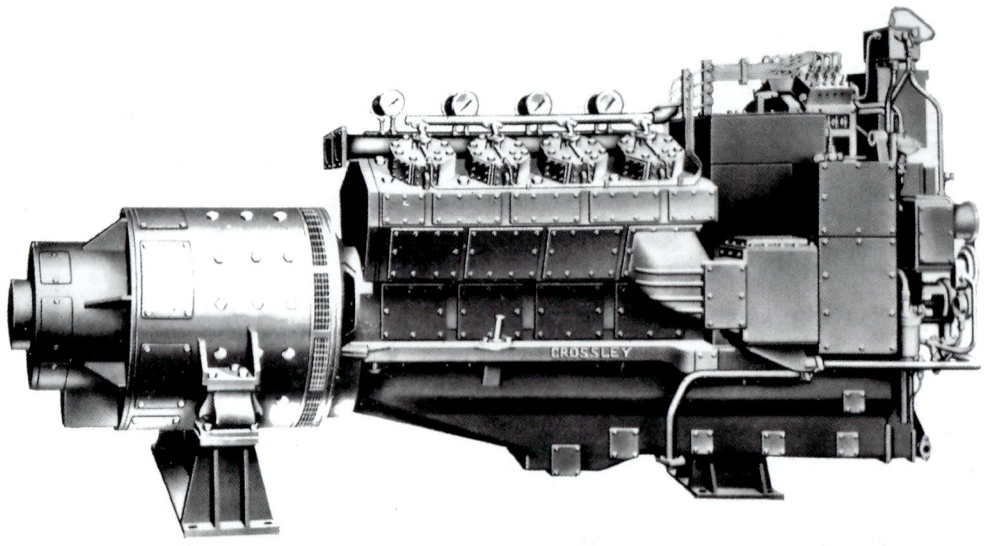

Possibly the nadir when it comes to C class liveries was this overall black colour with minimal decoration as seen on C208 at Inchicore. *Alan Watts/ Colour-Rail IR334*

The Crossley ESTV8 two-stroke diesel engine with Metro-Vick generator attached. *Metropolitan-Vickers*

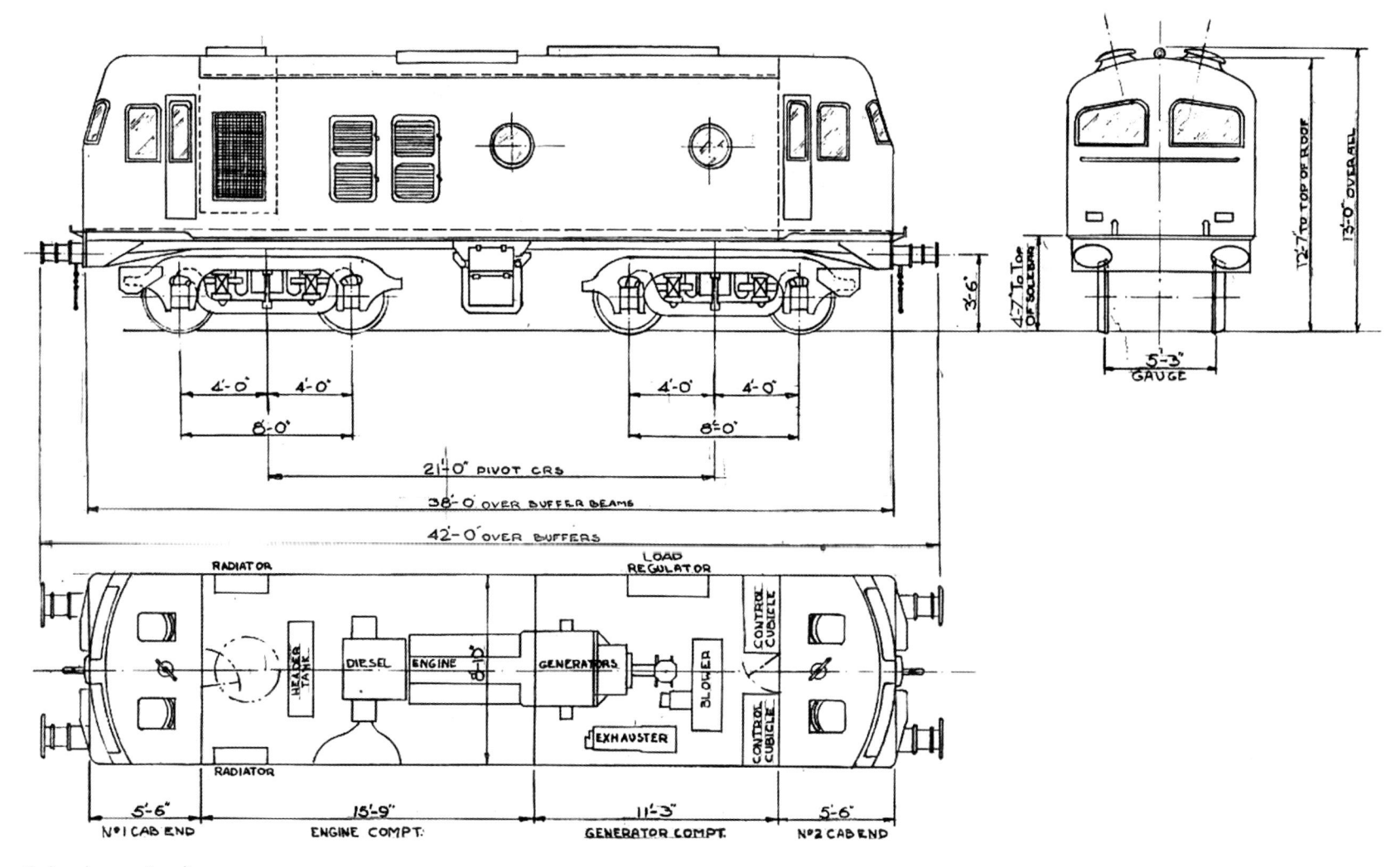

C class locomotive diagram. *Metropolitan-Vickers*

Chapter 20
THE G CLASS 0-4-0 DIESEL HYDRAULICS

Rather adventurously, CIÉ wanted to try a minimalist approach to its most lightly-trafficked branch lines, those for which even a C class Bo-Bo would be deemed too big and expensive to operate. Such branch lines included those between Banteer and Newmarket, and Gortatlea and Castleisland which had been closed and were reopened experimentally with one G class locomotive each to see if this method of working could be economic. The third locomotive took over the Banagher branch.

The G class four-wheeled diesel locomotives were ordered from Deutz in Germany and the three locomotives of the initial order arrived in 1956. They were effectively standard Deutz diesel hydraulic shunting locomotives, gauged for 5ft 3in, and driven by 130bhp diesel engines through Voith hydraulic torque converters and chains to the axles. The idea

In the back of Tralee shed sits G class four-wheeled diesel locomotive G602 in its original condition. This class was used for shunting in tight locations or where light loads had to be moved. The first three were 130bhp machines. They did not have through braking equipment and so were not suitable for moving passenger stock.

was that a small locomotive such as this could haul short goods trains. The train would be single manned; indeed, apart from occupation crossings, the potential was there for the branch lines each to be worked by one man, though this extreme was perhaps not fully realised.

That the locomotives also had potential as depot and yard shunting machines must have been one prompt behind a second order being placed for a further seven locomotives, delivered from 1961, after OVB had retired. These had a raised horsepower rating of 160 and were fitted with vacuum train braking. One was allocated to work passenger and freight on the Loughrea branch line. I did not see many of these locomotives working during my visits to Ireland. One was certainly present as Limerick wagon works shunter in 1963. By 1978, they had all been withdrawn, the branch line experiment having reached finality as traffic continued to switch to road. The railway's established policy of running mainly block, single-product freights and letting the train engines shunt them as required did away with the need for separate shunting locomotives.

The G class locomotives that survive at the time of writing are one from the first batch and four from the second, shared between the Irish Traction Group and the Downpatrick & County Down Railway.

Class	G 0-4-0	G 0-4-0
Builder	Deutz	Deutz
CIÉ revised class	601	611
Number in class	3	7
Introduced	1956	1961
Diesel engine	Deutz F/A8L 714	Deutz F/A8L 714
Engine power	130bhp	160bhp
Hydraulic transmission	Voith with chain drive	Voith with chain drive
Maximum speed	20mph	20mph
Weight in w.o.	18tons 0cwt	22tons 0cwt
Original number series	E601-E603	E611-E617
Post-1972 number series	601-603	611-617

These small locomotives were used in an attempt to put new life in otherwise uneconomic branch lines. In the 1950s, 0-4-0 diesel hydraulic G601 was working a short goods train when seen at Kanturk on the Banteer - Newmarket branch in County Cork. The lack of a continuous train brake prevented these early G class locomotives from working passenger trains. The Newmarket branch kept going until February 1963. *George Mahon/Irish Railway Record Society*

A further seven G class locomotives were delivered in 1962. These had 160bhp engines, were equipped with vacuum brake control for handling fitted stock, and some were experimentally tried as a means of running short branch lines more economically. G616 was stabled in Inchicore Works yard in summer 1963.

On 4 August 1967, G612 was working a mixed train that included a passenger coach and heating van on the Attymon Junction to Loughrea branch, which left the Dublin – Galway main line a little over half way between Athlone and Galway. The photographer clearly drew a small crowd during the stop at the one intermediate station, Dunsandle, perhaps being a rare sight on that patch! This method of working helped the branch to survive until its closure in 1975; it was Ireland's last minor branch line. *Tony Price/Irish Railway Record Society*

Chapter 21
THE E CLASS 0-6-0 DIESEL HYDRAULICS

Rather than perpetuate the heavy style of 0-6-0 diesel electric shunting locomotives, such as the D class, CIÉ ventured to design its own six-wheeled diesel hydraulic shunting locomotive using a Maybach engine and Mekydro transmission. This produced a 420bhp locomotive of lighter weight and with a high top speed of 100km/hr, 62mph. The idea was that this type could also be used for transfer freight work, for which a limit of 40mph was imposed, and keeping the possibility to use them for light passenger trains in the future. The first batch of nineteen locomotives emerged in 1957. In summer 1963, E414 was employed moving redundant steam locomotives around in the sidings at the back of Inchicore Works and placing them for cutting up.

As CIÉ became well acquainted with diesel traction in general as well as in detail, it became bolder in its approach. A need had arisen for a heavier shunting locomotive that could also act as a small train locomotive when required.

Design work was undertaken at Inchicore. The locomotives carried a Maybach higher-speed diesel engine, type MD220 of 420bhp, driving through a Mekydro transmission. The three axles were driven and coupled together by cardan shafts and thus were of the 0-6-0 wheel arrangement (or C in modern notation). Weighing 39 tons, they were lighter than the D class shunters that Inchicore had produced in 1947-48, an advantage of the use of faster engine speed and hydraulic transmission, though perhaps of lesser advantage for undertaking heavy shunting work when wheelslip was an observed

The E Class 0-6-0 Diesel Hydraulics • 167

problem. They rode on leaf primary springs with no secondary suspension. As designed, they had a top speed of 62mph. The first batch delivered nineteen locomotives for general use around CIÉ.

The Mekydro transmission was a patented system by Maybach which used an hydraulic torque converter driving through a four-speed automatic mechanical gearbox. Some observers describe this as a hydro-mechanical transmission.

It enables a locomotive to exert full torque at each gear step, a traction advantage over the Voith transmission which uses a torque converter up to a low running speed and then switches to direct drive for higher-speed running.

In service, the locomotives gained a reputation for rough riding. This batch was used mainly for station and yard shunting, though their higher speed range enabled them also to work yard transfers.

Four years after Bulleid had finally retired, a second batch of fourteen E class locomotives to a modified design appeared from 1962. These were of a more conventional outline, and were fitted for operation in multiple. The intention was, in addition to shunting, to use this type on secondary passenger workings that were lighter than those that needed a heavier Bo-Bo or Co-Co locomotive. In September 1962, the first of the batch, E421, was returning

The later batch of fourteen locomotives that was delivered from 1962 had a tidied-up aesthetic appearance. E430 was usefully shunting stock in the station at Dublin Amiens Street in June 1963. The wagon labelled UT with an 'N' prefix to its number 5480 indicates a vehicle of GNR(I) origin that was allocated to the Ulster Transport Authority in 1958 when the GNRB's assets were split between UTA and CIÉ. One of this batch of E class locomotives, E421, derailed at speed, following which the speed limit for all the E class was reduced to 25mph.

from Kildare to Inchicore with a test train of five bogie coaches when it derailed at Newbridge, causing much track damage but fortunately no human casualties. Evidence suggested that the locomotive's instability at speed was the cause of the derailment, about 200 yards of track being rendered unusable. (If he was ever told about this derailment in his retirement, Mr Bulleid's memory must have harked back to the Southern Railway's accident at Sevenoaks in 1927 in which the circumstances were in many ways similar, though with much worse consequences.)

Suffice it to say that the E class speed limit of 62mph was summarily reduced to 25mph later that year, substantially reducing the locomotives' usefulness. They eked out the rest of their service lives as station and yard shunting locomotives.

The 401 series was withdrawn between 1968 and 1977, and the 421 series between 1979 and 1983. Three exist in preservation. 421 and 432 are on the Downpatrick & County Down Railway, and 428 is an exhibit at Dunsandle station, on the Loughrea branch that was closed in 1975.[16]

Historically, the E class was the last locomotive type to be designed and built in Ireland.

Class	E 0-6-0	E 0-6-0
Builder	CIÉ Inchicore Works	CIÉ Inchicore Works
CIÉ revised class	401	421
Number in class	19	14
Introduced	1957	1962
Diesel engine	Maybach MD220	Maybach MD220
Engine power	420bhp	420bhp
Hydraulic transmission	Mekydro KL64 torque converter/ 4-speed gearbox	Mekydro KL64U torque converter/ 4-speed gearbox
Maximum tractive effort	21,730lbf	23,940lbf
Maximum speed	25mph*	25mph*
Weight in w.o.	38tons 16cwt	42tons 16cwt
Original number series	E401-E419	E421-E434
Post-1972 number series	401-419	421-434

* Originally designed for 62mph, this speed proved to be impractical due to unstable riding, and was reduced in late 1962 to 25mph.

---

16. Locomotive E428 had its moment of glory in 1986 when it hauled a charter train on CIÉ tracks between Tuam and Claremorris, claiming to be the very first preserved diesel locomotive to work on a main line anywhere in the British Isles (unless any reader knows different).

Chapter 22
THE TURF-BURNING LOCOMOTIVES

At this point in the narrative, it is useful to recall that CIÉ had included in its traction and rolling stock modernisation strategy a requirement to obtain some new steam locomotives for seasonal traffic work, such as sugar beet trains and holiday workings, and for infrastructure trains and shunting, for which the purchase of new diesel locomotives or railcars would be uneconomic. The locomotives would, in effect, form a traction reserve that the railway could also fall back on in the half-expected event of a shortage of diesel fuel or foreign currency (Ireland had no indigenous oil). This in turn led to a wish to rely on the potential of Irish turf as a fuel for these new steam locomotives, the sort of challenge that would delight a fertile engineering mind, such as Oliver Bulleid had.

Since turf ('peat' in British English) has very different volatility characteristics from coal, the volume of turf that would need to be burned in a steam locomotive firebox to produce a given amount of work would be approximately two to three times the amount of coal that a conventional engine would need. This fact had been confirmed decisively during the 1939-45 'Emergency' when coal supplies to railways in Éire were seriously reduced due to the UK's own export restrictions. Valiant attempts had been made in Ireland to use turf on what were normally coal-burning steam locomotives to keep freight trains running, but the larger amount of peat needing to be carried in tenders and fired into fireboxes, and the significant problem of ash disposal, led to several incidents of freight train locomotives going cold before reaching their destinations.

K3 2-6-0 356

OVB was apparently undeterred by all this, and set about firstly converting an existing locomotive to burn turf as a test bed for the future new build project. The selected locomotive was one of the K3 class of inside-cylinder 2-6-0s that had been bequeathed to CIÉ when it took over the Great Southern Railways at nationalisation in 1945. No 356 had originally been built as a 0-6-0 for the Great Southern & Western Railway in 1903. The class had proved too heavy for the then permanent way and had been rebuilt after four or five years with a radial truck ahead of the coupled wheels; a later development was a bigger boiler, enabling the class to perform as competent main line freight locomotives for about forty years.

Among requirements for a conversion to burn turf would have been a desire to improve the efficiency of the steam circuit so that the steam produced could do more work, thus reducing the amount of additional fuel-handling capacity needed for the change from coal to turf. OVB consulted the Italian firm of Locomotive a Vapor Franco, who sent a diagram showing a K3 with Crosti pre-heating drums each side of the boiler; these fed the heated feed water to the boiler clack valves with an additional feed rearwards into a long bogie tender to warm the water held in it. Apart from the bogie tender, the first set of modifications to No 356 did indeed incorporate such a scheme, though Bulleid insisted it was different from the

170 • OLIVER BULLEID'S LOCOMOTIVES

The locomotive chosen for Mr Bulleid to modify experimentally to prove the concept of turf-burning was class K3 2-6-0 No 356. The example illustrated here is 361, seen at Mallow depot in July 1956. Built as a 0-6-0 for the Great Southern & Western Railway, the class was modified into a 2-6-0 type by the addition of a radial truck at the front, and then later with a bigger boiler, thus becoming a class of useful freight locomotives.

OVB consulted the Italian firm of Crosti, which had considerable experience of fitting pre-heating drums to the boilers of old Italian locomotives to improve their steaming efficiency. Crosti submitted this outline scheme, which was not vastly different in appearance from how 356 originally emerged, apart from the use of a six-wheeled tender on the latter. *Crosti*

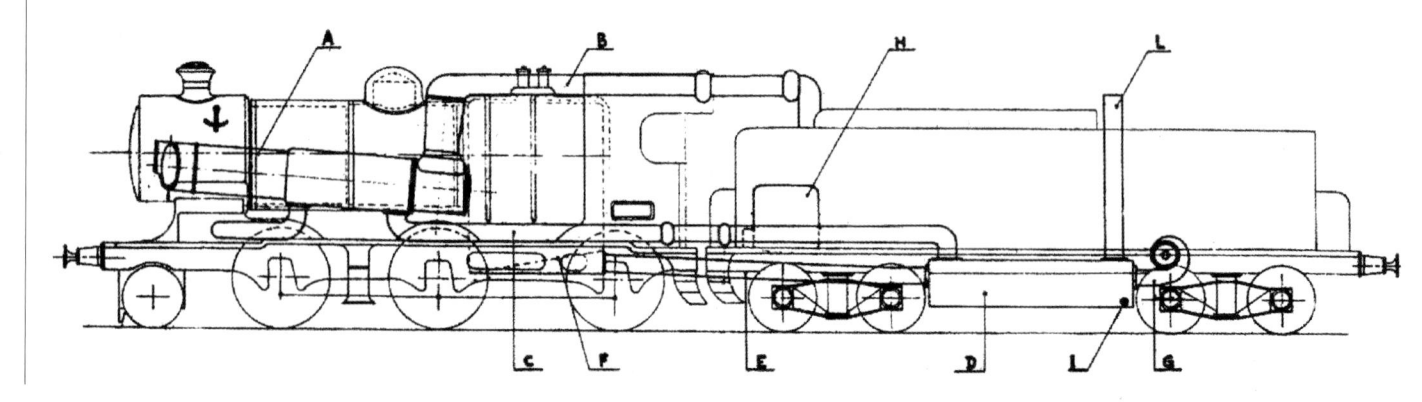

SCHEMA DELL'INSTALLAZIONE DI PRERISCALDATORI D'ACQUA DI ALIMENTAZIONE "CROSTI" E DELL'IMPIANTO PER LA COMBUSTIONE DI TORBA SU LOCOMOTIVE G.S.R. CLASS 355

Italian patented system because his engine was designed to burn turf! The six-wheeled tender attached to 356 was rebuilt to have a considerably enlarged fuel capacity, and to contain steam heating coils to warm the water in the tank. Turf was fed into 356's firebox by an augur which ran at a fixed speed and thus throughput. The firebox was replaced with one in which combustion air entered the box through *tuyères* incorporated in the firebars; these forced the air in at pressure from a pump. The issue of increased ash accumulation in the smokebox was dealt with by fitting an ash disposal chute below the smokebox door, prominent in all but the earliest photographs of this machine. The later pictures of 356 show much larger pre-heating drums (at least at the exterior).

Increasing the flow of combustion air was a priority. With there being little extra room on the locomotive and tender for the size of pump needed, a small wagon was attached to the rear of the tender; this carried an air draughting fan to increase the air flow into the firebox to assist turf combustion; this fan unit was powered by a Leyland diesel bus engine. There is clear evidence that the boiler produced at least enough steam to lift the safety valves.

2-6-0 356 was modified at Inchicore Works in 1952 with two pre-heating drums and much additional pipework and trunking to assist in the transfer of heat to the feed water and to the tender tank. It is seen with its enlarged six-wheeled tender attached.
W.H.C. Kelland collection, courtesy Bournemouth Railway Club Trust

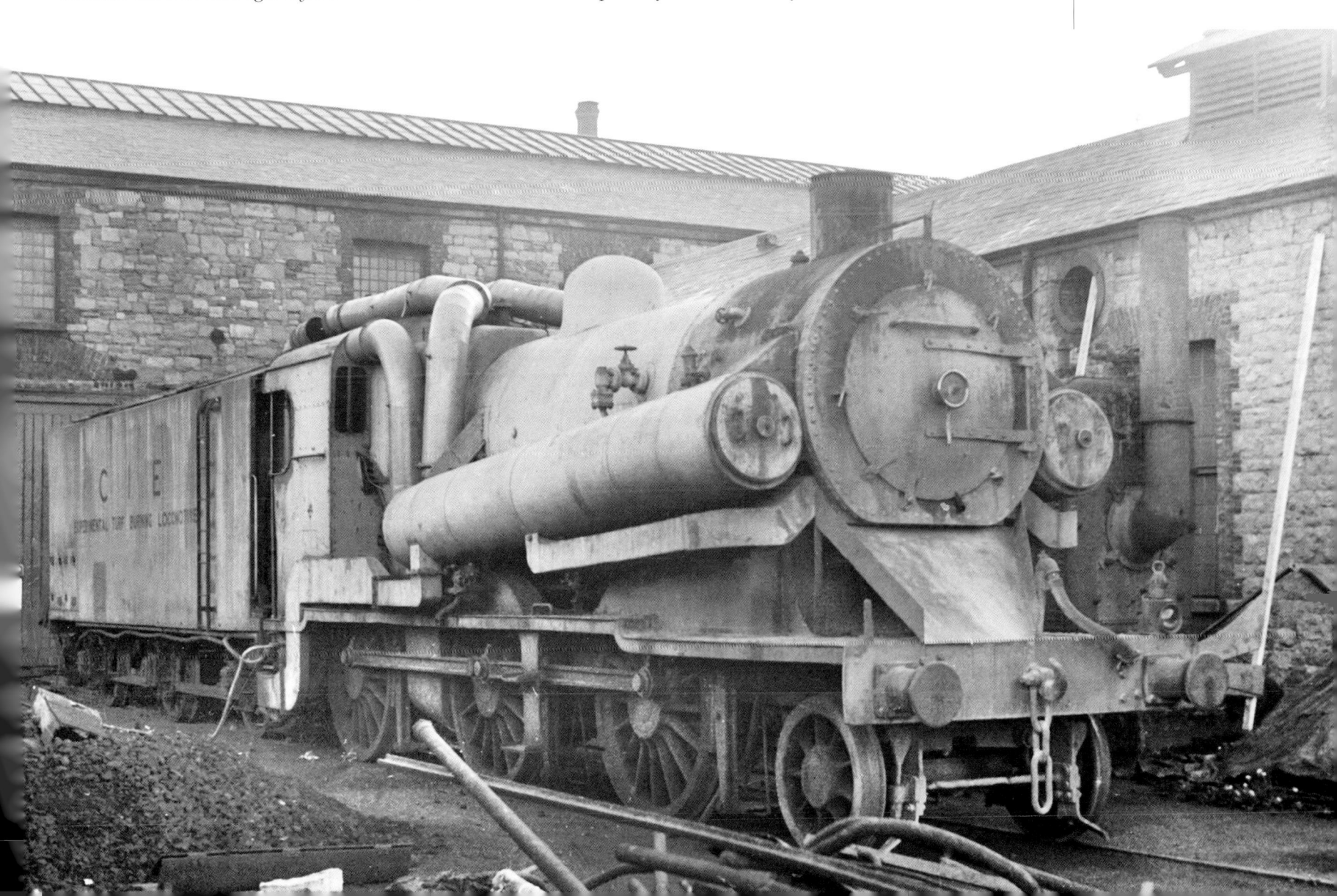

By 1954, 356 had gained a trolley behind the tender that carried a more powerful diesel engine blower to provide the draught necessary to force enough combustion air through the *tuyéres* into the firebox.
F.A. Wycherley

Looking into the smokebox of 356, one can see the three-row superheater and the lack of a conventional blastpipe. On the left the exhaust gas tubes within one of the two preheater drums are visible. *Anthony O'Toole, courtesy E. Shepherd*

The fuel was milled peat, as used in some Irish power stations. The turf was milled fine enough to be fed from the tender bunker to the firebox via a series of screws. *Anthony O'Toole, courtesy E. Shepherd*

The Turf-Burning Locomotives • 173

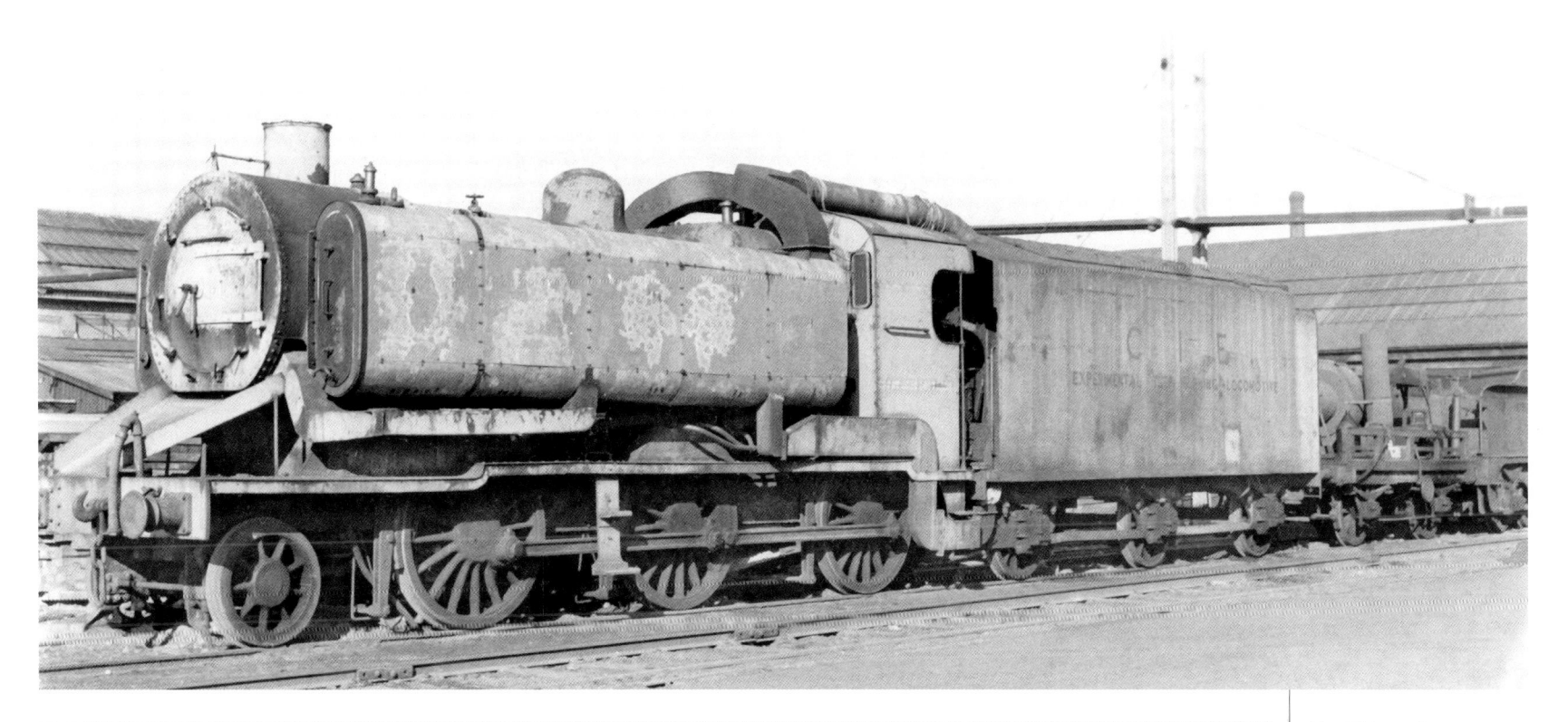

No 356 was later modified further with much larger casings for the pre-heaters which gave it a somewhat neater appearance. This change may have helped to convince Crosti's that the firm's patented system was not being used on 356! *IRRS*

For most of its trials, behind the tender of 356 was coupled this wagon carrying a Leyland bus diesel engine that drove a blower for enhancing the flow of combustion air. *IRRS*

356 was photographed in steam at Inchicore around 1955 making enough steam to lift a safety valve. The simultaneous release of steam from other places in its system would suggest questionable overall energy efficiency, however. *Probably John Click*

No 356 carried out a number of trials in steam on the main line, mainly between Dublin and Kildare. Confidence in the 2-6-0's performance must have been reasonably high because on 9 June 1953 it was driven on a loaded trial run from Dublin to Cork with 521 tons behind the tender wagon, this presumably being a freight train. The train was banked up the gradient to Clondalkin and 356 was then on its own for the rest of the trip, for most of which it steamed sufficiently well. A table from the test report shows that 356 kept or bettered the section timings in eight out of the eleven sections listed, included blowing off excess pressure through the safety valves on the climb to Ballybrophy. Only on one section, Mallow to Blarney, did 356's own performance cause any time loss. This was caused by a small air leak on the induction fan pipework on the wagon attached to the tender, but all lost time was regained before arriving in Cork. The return journey the next day terminated at Mallow when a turbine rotor ring became loose. The trials were temporarily suspended for two weeks until repairs could be completed on site.

The rebuilding of 356 had demonstrated that turf had potential as a locomotive fuel but, had there been any thoughts of modifying a fleet of existing locomotives to burn turf, they had by then been quietly forgotten. Before 1957, progress on the main line prototype locomotive was sufficiently advanced for work on 356 to cease. It was scrapped late that year.

0-6-6-0T prototype No CC 1

It is clear that the project to build a main line turf-burning steam prototype locomotive was geared towards two different bodies' agendas. CIÉ's requirement was for the first of a series of up to fifty locomotives for seasonal and back-up use, locomotives that could be fired either by oil or by turf, and which could replace diesel locomotives when emergencies dictated. OVB had his own agenda, namely to continue to prove that a total-adhesion steam locomotive could match a main line diesel for performance, a bee in his bonnet that had driven him through the 'Leader' project on the Southern Railway. The Irish prototype cleverly combined the two aims in one machine.

Early sketches went through much the same thought lines as did the 'Leader' development, including ideas for four-axle locomotives versus six axles. As on the Southern, the weight of equipment to be included within the locomotive quickly precluded a 0-4-4-0T (or B-B) configuration and a six-axle locomotive emerged as the ideal.

Development was slow. OVB commented that the 'total' dieselisation programme that had been initiated by the CIÉ Board 'above my head' had to take priority over steam locomotive experiments, both in time and money available. As the CME, he had to be involved in fleshing out the dieselisation programme, in preparing the works and depots around the country to handle the new fleets, and in the challenges faced during introduction of this new form of traction; again he was fortunate in the availability of competent local engineers to whom this work could be delegated. It is doubtful whether Mr Bulleid took more than a cursory interest in any of this.

For the turf-burner, many different configurations of engines and drives, and essays up blind alleys such as the potential for using sleeve valves, were researched. He had secured the experience of Ricardo again as consultant in the project. This time, his friend was seen to have written, 'My dear Bulleid, after all these years, have you not learnt?' in a clear sign of frustration that yet again there was a risk of OVB heading along roads of additional complication when such was not necessary.

Conscious that the technical staff at Inchicore were so immersed in the diesel programme that there was not enough available talent to support him on the steam locomotive design, Bulleid persuaded Roland Bond at BR headquarters to release two young but experienced engineers who were well acquainted with steam locomotive design and testing. John Click and Ron Pocklington duly arrived in Dublin and began inputting common sense into the prototype as its design progressed.

No CC 1 was shorter and lighter than the 'Leader'. There were similarities, of course. The bogies were again plate-framed with primary leaf spring suspension and were each supporting the underframe on segment bearers. This arrangement had served under the SR Co-Co electrics before the 'Leader' and turf-burner and was a simple, straightforward design, albeit perhaps on the heavy side. As on the 'Leader, the wheelsets were coupled with Morse chains encased on the outside of the bogie

One of CC 1's bogies rests over a pit in the erecting shop at Inchicore. The three curved sector plates on which the underframe rode are visible at the top of the frame, as are the axle end sprockets for the coupling chains. Suspension, as with all Bulleid's bogie locomotives, is through straightforward primary leaf springs, in this case with compressed rubber shock-absorbent blocks at the ends of the spring hangers. *Hugh Davies*

frames. Wheelsets were smaller than on 36001-5 at 3ft 7in and were to the B-F-B patent as on all his previous steam locomotives.

The body and equipment were carried on a strong girder underframe. The crew cabs were centrally placed, either side of the boiler with driving positions just ahead of the boiler compartment. This ensured that communication within the crew was good though, as the firehole door was on only one side of the firebox, in one direction the driver and fireman were necessarily separated. The more central cabs were at the expense of a more restricted forward view, but the drivers of large steam locomotives were already used to that. At the outer ends of the locomotive were the turf hoppers, front and rear, and the water tanks.

The boiler was quite unlike any locomotive boiler known to me, being of approximately rectangular section, of welded steel construction, with two short rectangular barrels flanking a deep central firebox. It is likely to have been based on power station practice, something of which the Irish had unique experience; at that time about a third of electric energy in the republic was generated in power stations fuelled by turf. Pre-heated feed water was supplied through Weir pumps. On CC 1, turf was fed mechanically by screws from the turf hoppers, and distributed into the firebox by high pressure steam jets. This gave a measure of control by the fireman in the cab. The principle followed was of independent control of firing and air supply (this was in contrast to a coal burning steam locomotive in which the variable exhaust outlet pressure pulls greater or lesser quantities of air through the fire grate as required to match the rate of working). The gases were drawn through the firebox and water heating circuits by a steam turbine at each end of the locomotive, and exhausted through the locomotive roof via spark arrestors. The steam generated in the boiler passed through rudimentary superheaters in the smokeboxes before reaching the engines and then exhausting to atmosphere, again through a chimney pipe in the roof.

Thankfully, it was political pressure to get the prototype running that led to a change of heart in OVB about the form the engines in the bogies should take,

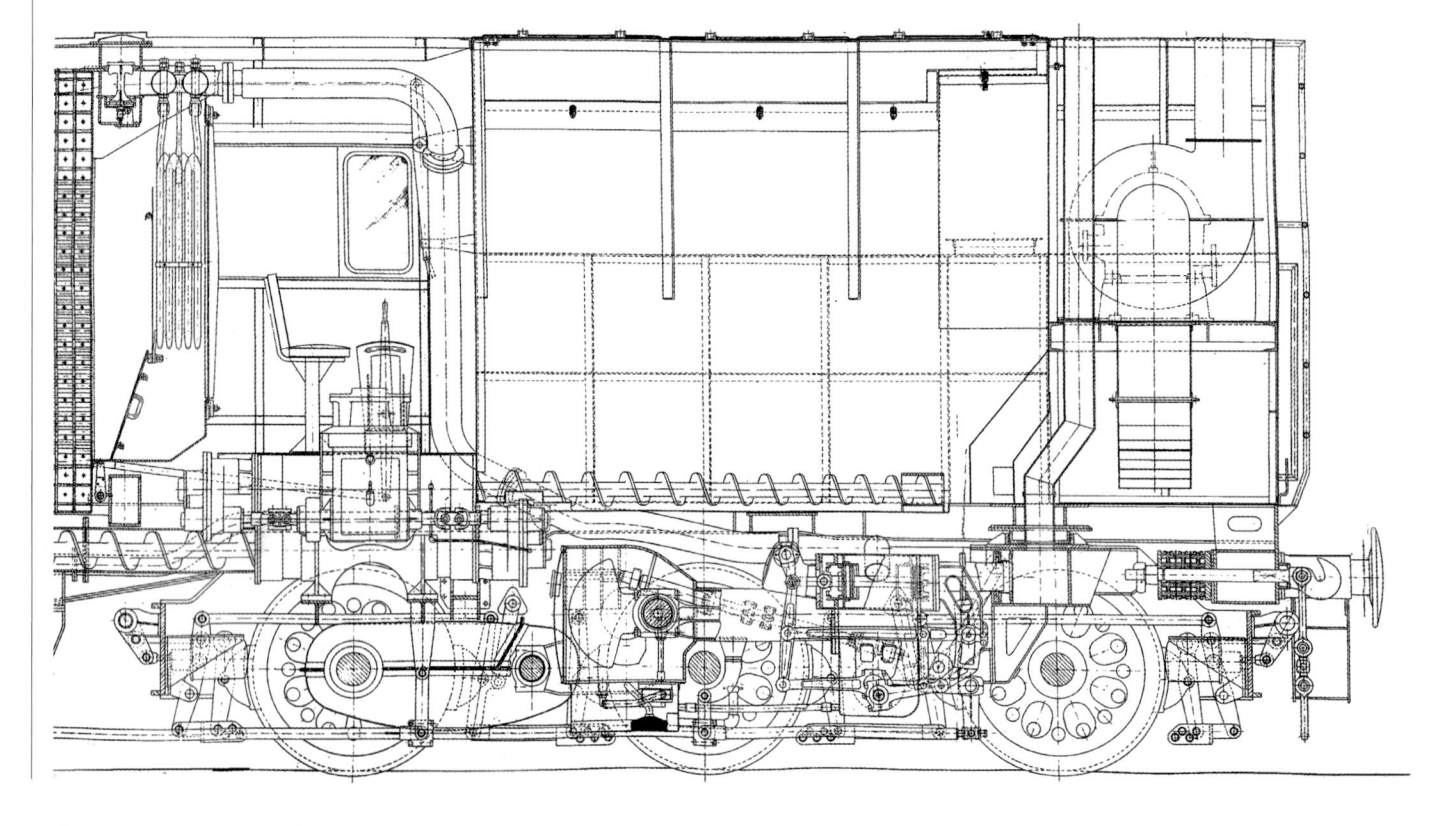

This part of a general arrangement drawing shows one end of the turf-burner 0-6-6-0T and includes the turf bunker, the screw that carried milled peat from the bunker to the firebox, and the large air fan or blower. In the bogie one can pick out the B-F-B wheelsets and the compact engine and valve gear. A driving cab is shown together with one of the main steam pipes that took steam to the engines.
G. Beesley collection

The Turf-Burning Locomotives • 177

probably also influenced by the two British engineers on loan to Inchicore. Each engine was a simple two-cylinder fabricated machine with piston valves giving inside steam admission. The fabrication was welded steel, with cast iron cylinder liners. The cylinders were 12inches diameter and 14inches stroke, with 7in diameter piston valves, and drove a crankshaft that was chain coupled to one axle. The engine parts were grease lubricated. The engine unit was designed to be lifted out of the bogie complete with valve gear if the need arose for a replacement to be fitted. The valve gear was an ingenious and compact version of Bulleid valve gear, driven by geared shaft from a helical gear on the crankshaft. All these features showed willingness to learn from experience of both the valve gear on the Bulleid Pacifics and that on the 'Leader'.[17]

Locomotive braking was by an Oerlikon air brake, though the locomotive also needed a vacuum exhauster to control the train brakes. The brake actuators applied clasp brakes to the wheels, two brake blocks on opposing sides of the tyre treads.

---

17. At Inchicore the design of CC 1 was shrouded in secrecy. I realised this in the summer of 1956 when a friend and I were being shown round Inchicore Works by a fellow engineering apprentice from CIÉ. He took us to where CC 1 was being assembled, and we enjoyed a couple of minutes in the pit looking up at the bogies and engines within them. Suddenly he called us out of the pit with urgency. He had been tongue-lashed by an engineer, and we had to leave in a hurry. 'He's an Englishman,' he explained. My guess is that the Englishman was John Click.

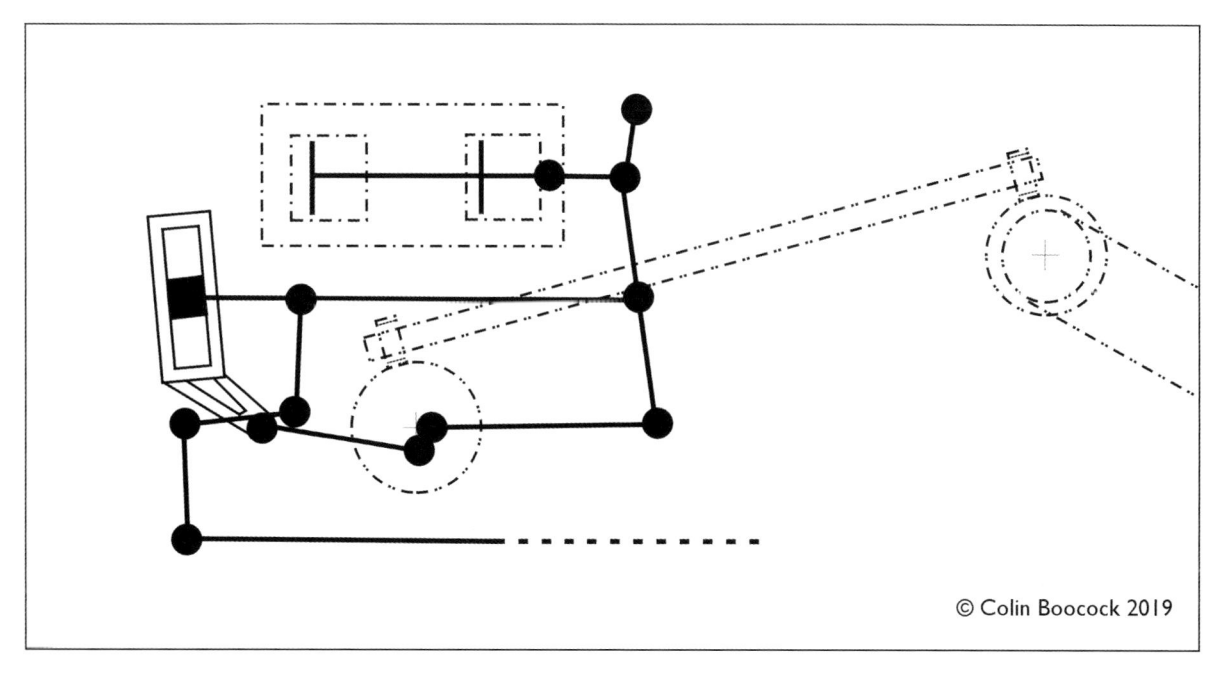

© Colin Boocock 2019

The compact valve gear for CC 1 was fitted as an integral part of the engine unit. In this diagram, the drive from the crank axle is the chain on the extreme right, which drives a worm and pinion at the upper end of the geared shaft. The lower end (left) drives through another worm and pinion a second lay shaft to which are attached the eccentrics that drive the miniaturised valve gear. The whole engine unit could be lifted out from the bogie and replaced by a repaired one if needed.

On 15 August 1957, CC 1 was engaged in load starting trials in Inchicore Works yard. On this occasion it had at least twelve coaches of varying antiquity in tow. *Courtesy E. Shepherd*

CC 1 underwent many trial runs on the main line, some running light engine as on this day, and others with useful loads. This view shows the locomotive after fitting with smoke deflectors which can be seen at the outer ends of the locomotive. These are the larger deflectors which were fitted after trials with a smaller version. *C.L. Fry*

Trial running began in September 1957. An early difficulty was exhaust steam blocking the driver's view. This was resolved by fitting smoke deflectors, one on each front corner of the bunkers. Once the size of the deflectors had been optimised the system worked – shades of experience with the SR Bulleid Pacifics here. During movements in Inchicore Works yard, an accident occurred when CC 1 collided with diesel Bo-Bo 1100. The reports from the people driving the locomotives claimed that both locomotives were stationary at the time of impact, causing OVB considerable amusement.

The subsequent road trials of CC 1 were deemed to be satisfactory in that a steaming rate of 14,000lbs per hour could be reliably attained by an experienced crew, and speeds up to 60mph were achieved in main line running. Turf consumption on loaded runs was between 84 and 99lbs per train mile including turf used in lighting up from 100lb/sq in and stabling. A major issue against continuing with the turf-burner design was its weight. At 118 tons on six axles, CC 1 averaged just under 20 tons axleload. That restricted it to main lines only. For it to have been of general-purpose use across the

The Turf-Burning Locomotives • 179

majority of CIÉ's tracks it would have needed an axleload of less than 15 tons to be within reach of achieving real usefulness.

In early 1958, a formal visit by the UK's Institution of Locomotive Engineers took place to Inchicore Works, and OVB acted as host there. No CC 1 was painted up for the occasion and gave footplate rides to the senior visitors, some of whom were impressed and others who were frankly bemused. Oliver Bulleid retired later that spring at the age of 75, having reached a number of successful milestones in his technical career. By then it was already clear that total dieselisation was intended by the CIÉ Board to be the way forward. With oil supplies reasonably assured, there was no need for a standby fleet of steam locomotives. CC 1 was quietly put to one side, to remain outside the back of Inchicore Works until its final scrapping which took place late in 1963.

Class	CC 1 0-6-6-0T
Engineer	O.V.S. Bulleid
Number in class	1
Introduced	1957*
Cylinders (4)	12in x 14in
Coupled wheels	3ft 7in
Boiler pressure	250lbf/sq in
Grate area	22.75sq ft
Tractive effort	20,000lbf
Weight in w.o.	118tons 0cwt
Number series	CC1

* This locomotive was experimental and was not taken into operating stock.

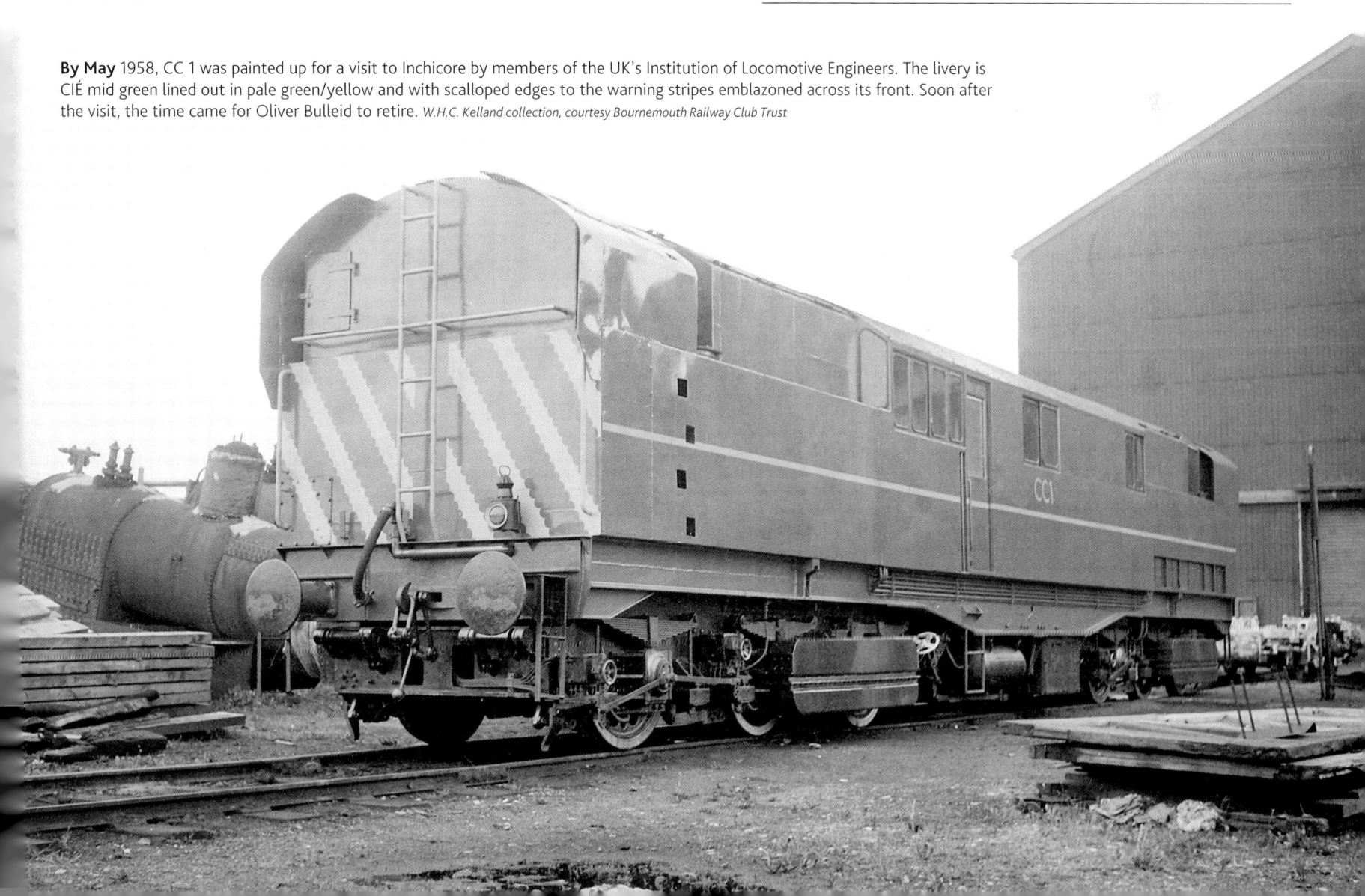

By May 1958, CC 1 was painted up for a visit to Inchicore by members of the UK's Institution of Locomotive Engineers. The livery is CIÉ mid green lined out in pale green/yellow and with scalloped edges to the warning stripes emblazoned across its front. Soon after the visit, the time came for Oliver Bulleid to retire. *W.H.C. Kelland collection, courtesy Bournemouth Railway Club Trust*

180 • OLIVER BULLEID'S LOCOMOTIVES

The boiler of CC 1 was a double-ended unit with central firebox and two barrels and truncated smokeboxes. Its rectangular section was reminiscent of power station practice but drew some gasps of disbelief from visiting UK railway engineers! It was stabled on a wagon at Inchicore in 1966, some time after removal from CC 1.
Kevin A. Murray/Irish Railway Record Society

This is an early official CIÉ weight diagram for CC 1, except that weights had not been entered when this version was published. Interestingly, the machine is shown as a 'turf/oil loco'. *CIÉ*

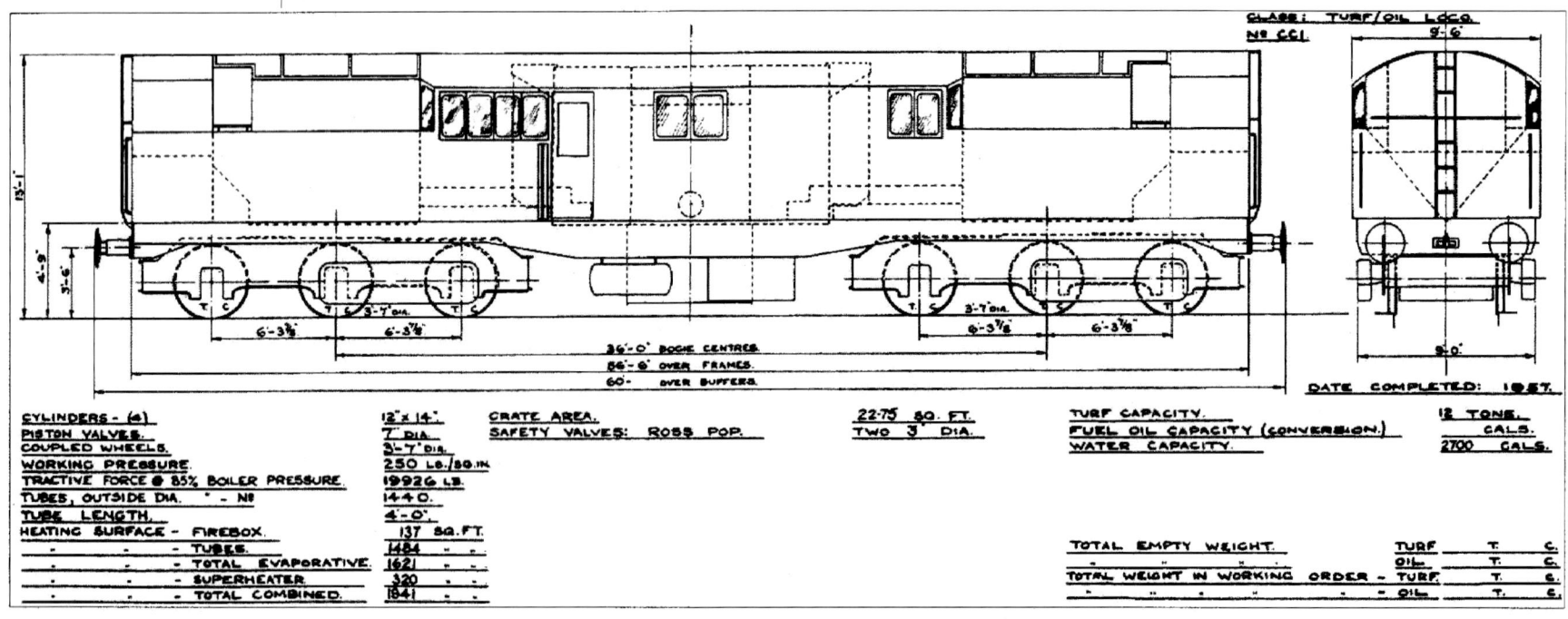

Chapter 23
THE REBUILT BULLEID PACIFICS

In Chapters 5 and 8, I laid bare the difficulties that the Bulleid Pacific locomotives experienced in terms of high fuel and oil consumption and difficulties in maintenance. Coal and water consumption were higher than with other similarly-sized locomotives because of the valve events which were not always as accurate as they seemed from the driving cab. Maintenance within the air-smoothed casing, and particularly inside the oil bath, was difficult, leading to missed opportunities and occasional mechanical failures.

Oil getting onto boiler lagging from the oil bath gave a readily inflammable surface for braking sparks to reach, with consequential fires. Oil leaching over onto wheel treads did nothing for adhesion at starting on a locomotive type that was at least ten tons lighter than other railways' equivalents; wheelslip was indeed prevalent when working heavy trains. The rather crude regulator valves contributed to drivers' difficulties in starting without wheelslip. The fluted coupling rods had a tendency to bend during high speed wheelslip. The gunmetal (brass) axleboxes with their white-metalled horn surfaces were wearing by around 55,000 miles, a lower distance than modern Pacifics such as the Peppercorn A1s were achieving.

Despite all this, the Bulleid Pacifics were well-loved by their crews and operators alike who had machines that would keep time during most circumstances. They had a cab environment that was the envy of drivers from other Regions who drove them, notably of the Western Region. And with their well-judged name series and beautifully-designed nameplates they were immensely popular with the public and the railway fraternity, enthusiasts included.

The Southern Region Board wanted to keep down unnecessary costs; the expense of running the 140 Bulleid Pacifics was an obvious focus for a study. This showed that savings were possible with a payback period of around five to six years (hindsight showed that to be close, but on the optimistic side). The Southern's Mechanical & Electrical Engineering department had the task of producing a scheme, and engineer Ron Jarvis was given overall charge of the project.

The rebuilding
Ron's approach was a practical one. The aim was to get running costs down, and it was logical also to keep the cost of rebuilding down to a sensible minimum. The 'Merchant Navy' class would be the first to be tackled. Rebuilding would take place when each locomotive was due for a full general overhaul, so only the cost of modification would be additional. Ron Jarvis's scheme kept every part of the locomotive that was good, almost without alteration. Thus the boiler with its thermic syphons and steel firebox, the main frames, bogie, pony truck and all wheels, the outside cylinders, cab and tender were all kept, with little modification. The Lemaître exhaust system was kept, as was the electric lighting system. The key changes tackled the main difficulties and excess cost generators.

Items discarded included:

- The Bulleid valve gear and its oil sump.
- The air-smoothed casing.
- The odd-shaped smokebox with its corrugated steam pipes.
- The gunmetal coupled axleboxes.

- The steam operating gear for the firehole door.
- The crudely fabricated chimney and petticoat.
- The outside-admission inside cylinder.
- The steam reverser.
- The fluted coupling rods.
- The regulator.

New features included:

- Three sets of Walschaerts valve gear, one for each cylinder.
- A standard screw reverser.
- A new design inside cylinder (an enlarged 'Schools' class cylinder according to two sources) that had inside admission; a new cylinder was necessary because the original inside cylinder piston valve rod could not be driven directly by a Walschaerts gear without a rocking shaft, and rocking shafts were 'out'.
- In front of the new inside cylinder was a strong fabricated box stretcher carrying part of the smoke box saddle.
- A new, cylindrical smokebox that was proportioned to current scientific experience.
- New smooth steam pipes replaced the former corrugated 'flexible' ones.
- A cast petticoat leading up to a cast chimney of smoother proportions. Like all BR standard engines, the chimney had a 'Horwich' style outside lip.
- The boiler was lagged with fibreglass mattresses contained within standard lagging plates held by bands as was BR standard practice.
- The safety valves were moved back to the second barrel ring to avoid priming when stopping sharply.
- A more sensitive regulator was fitted to improve finesse of starting control.
- Balance weights were added to the crank axle and to all coupled wheels.
- A rocking grate with drop section.
- The light Pacifics also received ashpan dampers (the MNs already had these).
- Rectangular section coupling rods were fitted.
- A full set of side brackets, running boards and valances was added, to the BR standard format but set slightly lower down, and a pair of smoke deflectors of the LNER type as used on the BR standard Pacifics and 9Fs.
- New steel axleboxes with manganese steel liners were fitted, matched with manganese steel horn guides.

Some of these details could quite readily have been added to existing Bulleid Pacifics without the extra cost of rebuilding, and indeed some were. But the key issues of fuel consumption and shorter-than-ideal intervals between lifting could only be tackled with the major parts of the scheme. An interesting by-product of the rebuilding was that all 'Merchant Navy' locomotives emerged identical (apart from an external pipe run on 35018), there being no difference between the appearance of the first, second and third batch engines as there had been before.

The 'Merchant Navy' locomotives were the first to begin the process. Locomotive 35018 *British India Line* entered Eastleigh Locomotive Works for its general overhaul and rebuilding late in 1955.

When they emerged from the works after rebuilding, the 'Merchant Navy' locomotives were three tons heavier, due largely to the extra balance weights, the heavier front stretcher and the full boiler cladding, running plates and valances with their associated brackets. The Walschaerts valve gear also added some mass. This was not a problem, as the SR's main line track was by then adequate to take this extra weight.

Not all the Bulleid Pacific tenders were in good condition, and seven needed new tanks. The new tanks that were fabricated for these were of 5,250 gallons water capacity. In appearance, their tank tops were designed to appear straight from front to back, with no changes of level as had been the pattern when the previous tenders were cut down for better rear visibility. With the new tender tanks, rearwards visibility was maintained, and a better-looking tender resulted. At least five of the new tanks ended up behind 'Merchant Navy' engines, and one behind 'West Country' Pacific 34039 *Boscastle*. Another new tank was, I understand, built to fit on a former 6,000 gallon three-axle tender frame. This new tank was reportedly of 7,000 gallons capacity, and as such would be the biggest on the Region, if not on BR. (That is the tender I subsequently learned was coupled to 34046 *Braunton*.)

When 35018 emerged from the erecting shop in February 1956, it excited many comments, mostly complimentary as regards its appearance. The rebuilding showed how well-proportioned Mr Bulleid's locomotives actually

The Rebuilt Bulleid Pacifics • 183

On the morning of 9 February 1956, the first 'Merchant Navy' to be rebuilt, 35018 *British India Line*, sees daylight for the first time as it is steamed outside the erecting shop at Eastleigh Locomotive Works. It is being prepared for its light trial run to and from Botley, the intermediate station on the Eastleigh to Fareham line, a trial that all express engines received after overhaul at Eastleigh. The smoke deflector handrails are yet to be fitted.

A close up of the valve gear on 35018 shows the standard outside Walschaerts gear, similar in its components to BR standard practice but arranged for outside admission cylinders; the return crank is set back, and the radius rod drives the vertical combination lever below instead of above the piston valve rod. Non-fluted coupling rods add strength, but Bulleid's neat crank pin fixings are used, as are the original three-part slide bars. A visible addition is balance weights on the coupled wheels.

were when their natural shape was revealed, that is without the all-embracing air-smoothed casing. The nameplates were affixed to the mid-point of the boiler barrel, similarly to the position of a 'Duchess' nameplate on the LMS, and looked fine. The rebuilt 35018 was first steamed outside the erecting shop, then it went on the normal light engine trip out to Botley on the Fareham line and back to check that nothing extraordinary, such as a hot bearing, was afoot.

Early runs

35018 was later put to haul a stopping train from Eastleigh to Southampton Central. There the diagram had the locomotive recess for a couple of hours in the Down bay platform, giving the driver plenty of time to check on bearings, valve gear, slide bars, indeed anything that might get warm. The next part of the duty was a stopping train to Bournemouth. On this first run, 35018 disgraced itself, as one of the outside cylinder piston valve rods ran hot from the pressure of the high-pressure gland that kept the input steam from leaking out of the steam chest. The valve rod seized and bent the radius rod. The seizure was assumed to be

The Rebuilt Bulleid Pacifics • 185

On 17 February 1956, 35018 was rostered for its first loaded run, one used by all rebuilds before being sent back to their owning depots. It is seen leaving Eastleigh with a stopping train for Southampton Central, where the locomotive was diagrammed to recess and then take on another stopping service to Bournemouth. In this photograph, the fireman is leaning out of the cab peering at the valve gear, suspecting a problem, which indeed did occur because later that afternoon the engine's right hand piston rod seized in its high-pressure gland, bending the radius rod and bringing the service to an untimely halt near Lyndhurst Road.

The third attempt, on 19 February, was successful after the offending glands had been given greater clearance with the piston valve rods, and no more seizures were recorded. Here 35018 sits at Southampton Central between its two stopping train duties. The vacuum ejector exhaust pipe run that bends downwards in front of the nameplate on the driver's side of the locomotive is unique to this engine. All other rebuilt Bulleid Pacifics have the pipe run straight, the downward bend being just behind the smoke deflector.

A comparison of front ends is seen at Southampton Central on 30 March 1956 as 35018 calls with the Up Bournemouth Belle, overtaking 34101 *Hartland* on a stopping service. Both locomotives are now active in preservation, both in their rebuilt state.

due to heat expansion. The gland was eased somewhat on Works and a new radius rod fitted. The engine was rostered on the same train the next day. The same thing happened. Further easing proved to be successful, and 35018 ran its third trip to Bournemouth with no problems. It then went to its allocated depot, Nine Elms, which soon rostered 35018 to its heaviest duty, the Pullman train the Bournemouth Belle.

35018 worked the 'Belle' right through the summer of 1956 (apart from boiler washout days and scheduled maintenance days) and indeed it was frequently on the train in the following years, having obviously become Nine Elms' favourite engine. The Bournemouth Belle in the summer was made up of twelve twelve-wheeled Pullman cars, with a total tare weight of around 525 tons, so it was no sinecure.

The rebuilt 35020 *Bibby Line* was to be tested, using the Swindon dynamometer car to take measurements, running in controlled road test conditions. For this work, it was outshopped with one of the very few tenders that had

The Rebuilt Bulleid Pacifics • 187

35018 settled down to being the regular engine on the Bournemouth Belle, as seen on 21 April 1956 at Bournemouth West, where it is starting its heavy Pullman train and facing the 1 in 90 incline up towards the Branksome triangle where the train will then swing north and east to gain the Weymouth – Bournemouth Central - London route. As it leaves the terminus, the train is getting a helpful push by the M7 0-4-4T that brought the empty stock into the platform.

A month later, *British India Line* was seen approaching Boscombe station, the last it would pass before Bournemouth Central, with the Down Bournemouth Belle. Its clean condition shows the respect that Nine Elms depot had for this engine, the class in general, and the prestigious train it was rostered to pull.

On 8 June 1956, 35020 *Bibby Line* had been set up with a high-sided tender and coupled to the Western Region dynamometer car for controlled road tests on the West of England Main Line between Salisbury and Exeter. The use of one of the very last unmodified tenders was practical in that the many pipes and wires needed to connect the engine to the dynamometer car could be contained behind the high side raves. It is seen ready to leave Eastleigh depot en route for Salisbury so these trials could begin.

not been modified with low side raves. This enabled the test crew more easily to stow the plethora of pipes and wires that were needed to pass between the locomotive and the dynamometer car to drive the instrumentation. No 35020 actually looked most appealing with the high-sided tender, temporary though it was.

The engine was tested on the fast and demanding West of England main line between Salisbury and Exeter, a route that abounded with long, steep gradients and many opportunities for high speed running. 35020 acquitted itself well. The BR Board published a test report that showed that the performance objectives of the rebuilding, namely good valve events and economic use of fuel and water, had been met. A real compliment was paid when one of the test crew said that this was 'the most predictable locomotive we have ever tested'. 35020 did the same work at the same speeds at the same control settings day after day.

Several drivers took some time to get used to the control settings needed to reach the performances they wanted. Because the valve gear did not overrun, and because the reverser did not creep forward unnoticed as speed built up, the rebuilt engines had to be driven with a wider regulator opening to get the same performance at the cut-off indications that drivers were used to setting on the original locomotives. In reality, the engines were therefore being worked more efficiently by default – higher steam chest pressures and more expansive working being the order of the day. Once a driver had adjusted to the new way of working, the rebuilds produced much the same sparkling performances as they had before rebuilding. 35022's unofficial record of 104mph through Axminster before rebuilding was matched more than once in the run-up to the Bournemouth electrification in 1966 and 1967 after BR had raised the main line speed limit from 85 to 100mph.

There is however one feature of the rebuilds that I still hold to be less fortunate. From the works manager's office at Eastleigh, one could witness Up expresses passing by with various hard-working locomotive types from 'Lord Nelsons' (always quiet and smooth running), air-smoothed Pacifics (much the same though more boisterous) and rebuilds.

A feature of the rebuilding was Ron Jarvis's conviction that the locomotives had to be 'properly' balanced. The coupled wheels had balance weight pockets welded to them, and these were filled with the appropriate amount of lead, this amount being confirmed or adjusted by rotating the wheels at speed in this balancing machine in Eastleigh Locomotive Works.

The cut-down side raves on a 5,000 gallon tender as fitted to 35013 when rebuilt enabled a better rearwards view from the cab as well as prevented coal droppings from lodging and blocking the view. The yellow plate at the back marked TIA indicates the type of water treatment on this locomotive.

The rebuilt locomotives produced a hammer blow that could be felt through the office floor. I always believed that OVB was correct in his analysis of the self-balancing nature of a three-cylinder locomotive and that the Brighton team were wrong to add so much additional balance weighting to the rebuilds. This testimony bears that out.

Rebuilding the 'lightweights'

Later in 1957, work started at Eastleigh on rebuilding the 'West Country' and 'Battle of Britain' 4-6-2s. The pattern was exactly the same as with the 'heavyweights', and all significant variations within the two lighter classes were eliminated. Once again, the weight increased by about three tons, this time with a significant restriction: the rebuilds were not normally permitted west of Exeter St David's, at least until any future civil engineering strengthening work was done. In reality, this probably never happened. The Southern's secondary routes in Devon and Cornwall took a heavy toll during the so-called 'Beeching cuts' and this restriction quickly ceased to be an embarrassment.

A feature of the 'West Country' class was the splendid nameplates that adorned these locomotives. The original grouping of the main nameplate above an enamel badge with the 'West Country class' scroll beneath was not appropriate for the shape of the rebuilt locomotives. Instead, the plates were grouped with the badge (where there was one) above the nameplate, with the class scroll underneath, all fixed to a bracket atop the running board and sited over the centre couple axle. The effect was excellent. Similarly, the 'Battle of Britain' badges were fixed above their nameplates instead of below and looked very professional.

As with the heavier 'Merchant Navy' class, the 'lightweights' were noticeably more sure-footed in starting, and soon showed themselves to be masters of their duties as before.

Allocations of rebuilt locomotives were not specifically concentrated at any particular depots, being generally put to where the original locomotives were habitually employed. The rebuilds appeared in equal measure in the west of the Region as well as on the South Eastern Division, with a few at Brighton on the Central Division.

Was it worth it?

All thirty 'Merchant Navy' class engines were rebuilt. BR called a halt to the rebuilding programme when the sixtieth 'lightweight' rebuild had been ordered. This left fifty of the 'WC' and 'BB' classes in air-smoothed condition. The last rebuild emerged from Eastleigh Locomotive Works in 1962. By this time, all SR routes west of Salisbury had been transferred to the Western Region, in my view a subtle way of getting the Southern into line with official policy to remove steam by 1967 or 1968. Until then, the SR had expected to replace steam by electrification to Salisbury and to dieselise west of there, steam disappearing in the early 1970s. The WR, having vigorously pursued a heavy rationalisation of routes and tracks, had a surplus of diesel locomotive capacity and was well able to plan the early elimination of steam traction on its lines. Indeed, diesel hydraulic locomotives were soon to be seen regularly at London Waterloo on Exeter expresses.

By 1963, a few air-smoothed 'West Country' locomotives had been withdrawn as surplus to needs, all of which were due for heavy overhaul. This was to become the regular pattern. The best condition locomotives remained in service as long as they had work to do, and that included 'unrebuilt' locomotives as well as the rebuilds.

Early in 1963, I was delegated the task of carrying out on behalf of the SR and the BR Board a financial back-check of the rebuilding process to determine whether the project had been value for money. I was working in the M&EE headquarters offshoot at Brighton at the time, and was delighted to find that the accountant there had amassed a mountain of records of expenditure at the depots and works. These costs were sufficiently sub-divided into locomotive classes that I could add up the costs that each depot had attributed separately to original and to rebuilt locomotives. I doubt if the depot people entering that data had any idea that it would be used in the way I intended, so it was an unbiased exercise.

I can't remember all the figures now, but these facts I do recall, when related to the rebuilds:

- The average rebuilding cost per locomotive was £8,500 above the cost of the general repair. After rebuilding:
  - Coal costs were at least 10 per cent lower than before.
  - Lift intervals at works for axlebox repairs were extended from about 55,000 to 90,000 miles.
  - Depot maintenance costs were lower.
  - Oil consumption was cut from about one gallon per 100miles to almost negligible.
  - The pay-back period was about 6½ years.

The average life of the rebuilt locomotives after rebuilding was around 6½ to 7 years, so British Railways had got its money back, but only just. Apparently, the BR Board meeting minute that congratulated the SR on a well-run project was the only minute for some years that even mentioned steam locomotives!

A late heyday

In 1966 and early 1967, reports were rife about drivers of SR Pacifics making good use of the raising of the main line speed limit to 100mph. A number of societies have retained records made by enthusiasts at that time. Suffice it to write here that records were indeed broken. The maximum speed authenticated by a known competent train timer was 106 mph with a rebuilt 'Merchant Navy'. An interesting secondary record was that of 34102 *Lapford* which was said to have been the only 'lightweight' ever to have been reliably timed at 100mph, and that quite late in its life having never been rebuilt!

Steam ended on the Southern in July 1967, and most of the surviving SR Pacifics went to Woodham's yard at Barry Island for scrapping. That is one reason why thirty-one of these iconic machines still survive in preservation today. The other reason must be that Bulleid's Pacifics are in any case extremely popular and well-regarded locomotives!

Class	MNX* 4-6-2
Engineer	R.G. Jarvis
Rebuilt by	BR Eastleigh
BR power class	8P
Number in class	30
Introduced	1956
Cylinders (3)	18in x 24in
Coupled wheels	6ft 2in
Boiler pressure	250lbf/sq in
Grate area	49.5sq ft
Tractive effort	33,480lbf
Weight in w.o.	97tons 18cwt
BR number series	35001-35030

* The Class designation reverted from MNX to MN as soon as all the class had been rebuilt.

Class	WCX and BBX 4-6-2
Engineer	R.G. Jarvis
Rebuilt by	BR Eastleigh
BR power class	7P 5FA
Number in class	60
Introduced	1957
Cylinders (3)	16⅜in x 24in
Coupled wheels	6ft 2in
Boiler pressure	250lbf/sq in
Grate area	38.25sq ft
Tractive effort	27,715lbf
Weight in w.o.	90tons 1cwt
BR number series	34001, 34003-5, 34008-10, 34012-14, 34016-18, 34021, 34022, 34024-29, 34031, 34032, 34034, 34036, 34037, 34039, 34040, 34042, 34044-48, 34050, 34052, 34053, 34056, 34058-60, 34062, 34071, 34077, 34082, 34085, 34087-90, 34093, 34095-98, 34100, 34101, 34104, 34108, 34109.

35005 *Canadian Pacific*, rebuilt in 1957, was one of seven that received new tender tanks to replace heavily corroded ones. These were of 5,250 gallons capacity and were distinctive with their straight line along the top of the tender tank. The yellow painted solid disc under the locomotive number indicates the tender is fitted for briquette water treatment; this simpler system replaced the TIA.

35012 *United States Lines* was heading the Up Bournemouth Belle Pullman train at Bournemouth Central on 24 May 1959. The sharp curve here, like the one at Salisbury, was a hindrance to easy starts with heavy trains, but the rebuilds were distinctly more sure-footed.

The Rebuilt Bulleid Pacifics • 193

35013 *Blue Funnel* starts away from Eastleigh with no fuss on an evening semi-fast from Bournemouth West to London Waterloo in summer 1956.

On the approach to Christchurch heading west, 35014 *Nederland Line* faces a couple of miles uphill at 1 in 99 with the Bournemouth Belle. The author believes that these locomotives are handsome from any angle.

The Rebuilt Bulleid Pacifics • 195

35014 *Nederland Line* rolls into Templecombe with an Exeter to London Waterloo service. Nowadays almost all the surrounding railway activity has gone. There is now just a loop line and two platforms here. Back in the 1950s, the yards were busy with S15-hauled freights and ex-LMS engines off the Somerset & Dorset line.

The self-weighing tender got moved around among 'MNs'. 35024 *East Asiatic Company* received it after rebuilding, seen here at Eastleigh depot before returning to its home depot.

196 • OLIVER BULLEID'S LOCOMOTIVES

A 'Merchant Navy' rebuild specially cleaned for Royal Train duty was a splendid sight, even if some of the carriages it was hauling were distinctly from another era! 35027 *Port Line* brings Her Majesty the Queen and the Duke of Edinburgh past Eastleigh on 24 April 1959 after they had attended an naval event at Portland, near Weymouth.

In 1957, 35027 *Port Line* restarts from Southampton Central with a Waterloo to Weymouth fast train. These trains were soon to be accelerated to a two-hours timing between London and Bournemouth, a timing that the electric trains of today only just manage to beat, though they do have a few additional stops to make!

The Rebuilt Bulleid Pacifics • 197

The light Pacifics were rebuilt to the same theme as the 'MNs'. 34010 *Sidmouth* is seen leaving Bournemouth Central bound for Weymouth while unrebuilt classmate 34020 *Seaton* stands in the depot yard. The red push-pull set, a former L&SWR set, on the right carries the set number 1. The SR inherited the practice of marshalling coaches in semi-permanently coupled fixed sets, finding it an operating and maintenance convenience.

On 25 July 1959, 34021 *Dartmoor* rolls through Tonbridge with the Down Man of Kent.

The light Pacifics could go where their heavier sisters could not. During diversions away from the main line for engineering work at New Milton, 34031 *Torrington* takes the curve through Wimborne with a morning express from Bournemouth West to London Waterloo. This route was the original L&SWR main line to Dorchester that completely missed Bournemouth, which in the nineteenth century was just a fishing village. Locomotives with high axleloads such as the 'Merchant Navy' class, the 'Lord Nelsons' and the 'Schools' were normally banned from this route. (Wimborne signal box really did lean back like that!)

When on the main lines, the rebuilt light Pacifics could perform very well indeed. Beginning the sixteen miles of 1 in 252 up from Allbrook Junction is 34037 *Clovelly* with an Up express in 1961. This shows that even when rebuilt into a 'conventional' shape, the Bulleid Pacific drivers sometimes had their view ahead marred by drifting steam, particularly with a side wind as here.

The Rebuilt Bulleid Pacifics • 199

Towards the end of steam working of the Golden Arrow, Stewart Lane depot's favoured motive power for this prestige train was rebuilt 'West Country' 34100 *Appledore* (a name that probably meant nothing to inhabitants of Kent!). The train is approaching Beckenham Junction in 1961 with the author's boss, John Click, on board this locomotive. The poor guard had to ride in the four-wheeled BY van at the back of the train.

Other boat trains worked by rebuilt Pacifics included those for Southampton Western and Eastern Docks. Many were given titles that reflected the shipping line for which the passengers were heading. Passing Eastleigh Airport southbound on 16 September 1959 is 34010 *Sidmouth* carrying the Holland American headboard. The train includes a former Pullman car in Southern stock green that is acting as a catering vehicle.

Even after Bath Green Park depot had managed to discard its own allocation of light Pacifics for regular workings, Bournemouth shed had to provide extra power at summer weekends to work expresses over the very hilly Somerset & Dorset route. This relief to the Pines Express on the last Saturday of such workings over the S&D in September 1962 has 34047 *Callington* (I believe) as the train engine, being piloted by BR class 4 4-6-0 75023. The load over this route for light Pacifics as well as for LMS and BR class 5 4-6-0s was eight coaches; anything heavier, like here, needed a pilot locomotive.

Some 'Merchant Navy' rebuilds had extended rosters that kept them out of depots during the times when cleaners were on shift, and so became very dirty, even though they were fine mechanically. Such is 35023 *Holland-Afrika Line* which is seen passing Millbrook station near Southampton's Western Docks with the 1.30pm London Waterloo to Bournemouth on 18 February 1961.

The Rebuilt Bulleid Pacifics • 201

In the last year of steam operation on the Southern Region, 1966-1967, the speed limit on the Bournemouth main line was lifted from 85 to 100mph and many drivers took advantage of this to stretch their Pacifics' performances; there was competition to join the 'ton club'. Most engines at this time were looking unkempt from lack of cleaning, but the SR had made special arrangements for the locomotives to receive extra valves-and-pistons overhauls, particularly at Guildford depot which was used as a 'centre of excellence' for this work in the run-up to electrification. Thus the Bulleid Pacific fleet was able to perform sufficiently well right up to the end of steam in July 1967. Earlier that year, 35023 *Holland-Afrika Line* was photographed calling at Pokesdown with a Waterloo to Bournemouth semi-fast service. The engine was commendably clean for that period, but like the rest of the fleet its nameplates had been removed for safe keeping.

It is understandable that Bulleid Pacific nameplates were seen as potentially excellent collectors' pieces. The 'Merchant Navy' class plates, shaped like the Plimsoll line marking on a ship, included the shipping lines' official flags in their vitreous enamel centres. 35005 *Canadian Pacific*'s plate illustrates the official BR stance with black-painted backing.

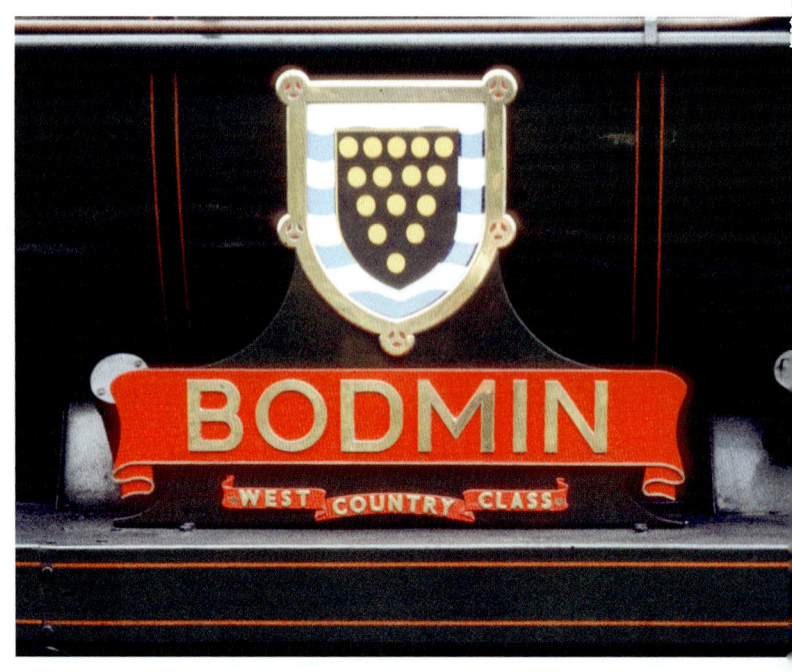

By the early 1960s, Eastleigh Works went back to painting nameplates with their original backing colours, red generally and blue for the 'Battle of Britain' class. 34016's plates look superb in this condition.

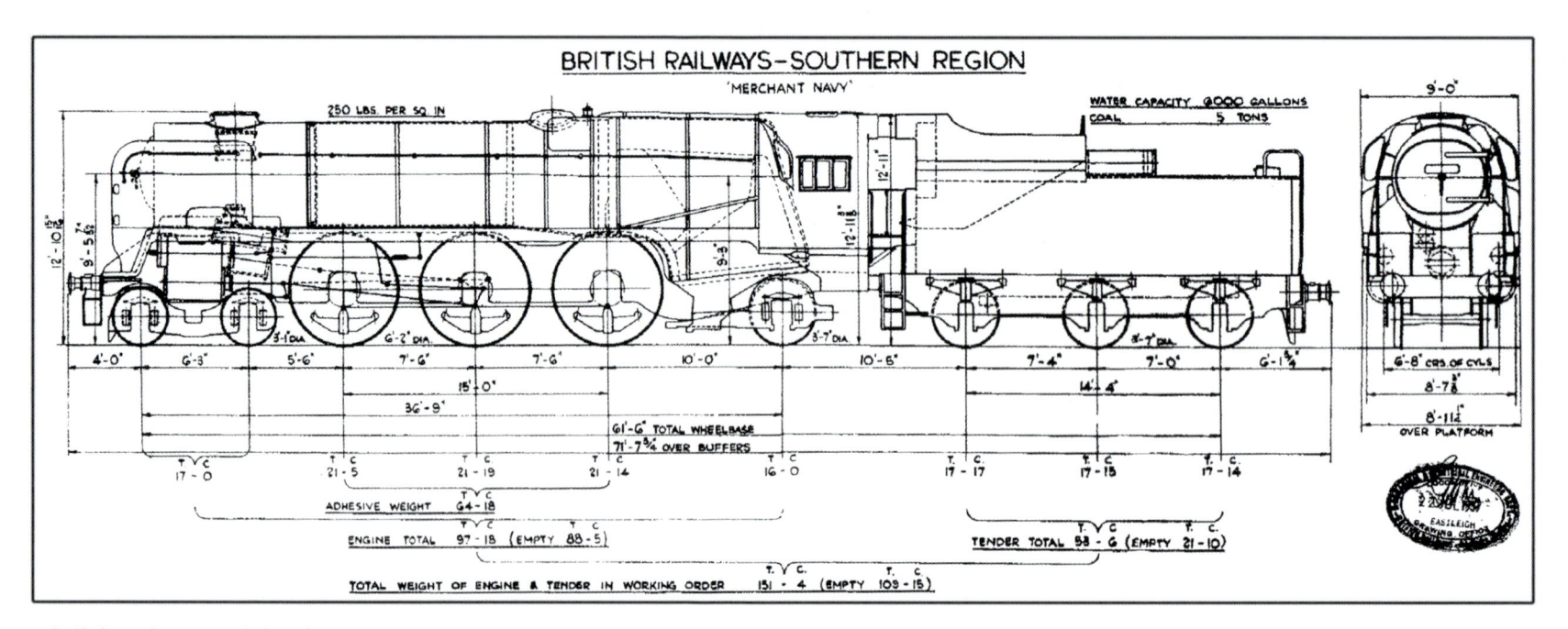

Rebuilt 'Merchant Navy' class diagram. *BR*

Chapter 24
RE-ENGINING THE A AND C CLASS DIESEL ELECTRICS

In Chapters 17 and 19 I chronicled the beginnings of the A class Co-Cos and C class Bo-Bos in Ireland, and emphasised that, while the locomotives could successfully haul the trains intended for them, their Crossley diesel engines were unreliable and caused vibrations that damaged interior pipework and equipment. By the early 1960s, CIÉ was becoming desperate to solve the problems permanently. The railway had taken delivery in 1961 of fifteen American single-cab diesel electric locomotives of Bo-Bo configuration and with two-stroke General Motors engines of the EMD 8-567 type. These locomotives performed so well and so reliably that CIÉ engineers developed a scheme to replace the Crossley diesel engines in the A and C classes with EMD engines.

General Motors initially resisted this idea because GM had a clear policy of supplying complete locomotives, not power units, and certainly not engines to couple to other manufacturers' generators. Quite remarkably, and after noting that CIÉ was also exploring using Maybach diesel engines as possible replacements for the Crossleys (CIÉ already had experience of this make in its E class shunters and had just fitted two of the C class with Maybach engines in a rather provocative gesture), GM agreed to supply two 12-645 diesel engines for prototype fitting to two A class locomotives. This was to be the first time that General Motors was to accept that a foreign railway was sufficiently competent to undertake this work. The prototypes proved to be very successful.

So it was that in 1968 Inchicore Works began the task of re-engining all the A class. GM's EMD division supplied the 12-645E engines for the Works to fit. Each new GM engine was coupled to an existing

The fitting of General Motors engines to the A class Co-Cos resolved their inherent unreliability. In this photograph, 029S makes a smoke-free departure from Dublin Heuston (the former Kingsbridge) with an express for Galway via Portalington. The train is formed of Mark 2d air-conditioned stock to a British Railways design but equipped with vacuum brake; the leading vehicle is for train electric supply and carries a diesel generator set. The 'S' suffix to the locomotive number indicates that it is modified to work in the area signalled for DART electric suburban trains; once all the fleet was so branded the suffix was dropped.

204 • OLIVER BULLEID'S LOCOMOTIVES

023 runs through the centre road at Kildare with the daily train of anhydrous ammonia tanks from Mallow to Arklow on 12 May 1988.

Also in 1988, 057 manoeuvres at Waterford after arriving with a train from Dublin Heuston.

main generator and placed on a purpose-designed bedframe within the A class engine room. The rebuilding included fitting of General Motors' own systems for fluids – oil, water and coolant – which added to the future reliability of these locomotives. The new engines were rated at 1,325bhp, a rating below the engine's own potential but within the capacity of the locomotive's Metro-Vick dc generator at its designed rotation speed of 800rpm. For a time, eight engines were rated at 1,650bhp at 900rpm in locomotives intended for heavier express passenger workings such as the Cork and Galway expresses. The traction motor armature fields were rewound to enable faster running at speeds up to 85mph.

Re-engining the A and C Class Diesel Electrics • 205

The re-engining programme was entirely successful. The A class became reliable, relatively smoke-free and smooth-running locomotives. Their roughly 40-years total life span was a credit to the work that Inchicore did on the programme, and to the performance of their EMD engines and the Metro-Vick electric traction equipment. From 1972, the A prefix to their numbers was dropped. The locomotives were then numbered in the 001 series to 060.

Work began in 1970 on a similar exercise to replace the 550bhp Crossley engines in the thirty-four C class Bo-Bos. This time, CIÉ took advantage of the robustness of these locomotives' Metro-Vick electric traction equipment and bought EMD 8-645E diesel engines of 1,100bhp output. At a stroke this action doubled the power that a C class locomotive had at its disposal, yet it proved to be within the capacity of the generator and traction motors. All this was possible because the 550bhp Crossley engines had run at 1,000rpm and the maximum speed of the 8-645 EMD engine was 900rpm. Additional cooling elements were added to cope with the higher heat output of the new engines. The C class locomotives were reclassified B201 as this work proceeded; they were later to become simply the 201 class.[18]

With their new power rating, the B201s were drafted to work outer suburban trains around Dublin, some in push-pull mode using de-engined diesel railcar vehicles. They also proved more useful than before on freight services. It was the introduction of the DART electric suburban scheme in 1984 that sounded the end for the class, the last being withdrawn in 1986. Six redundant locomotives were bought by Northern Ireland Railways for infrastructure workings and for a potential lignite traffic from a proposed mine near Lough Neagh. The latter did not materialise, and the locomotives' age proved a problem, the last being withdrawn in 1994.

Four 001 class are preserved, and three of the 201s.

Four years later, at Drogheda in October 1992, 056 comes off the Navan branch with one of the Tara Mines block trains of lead and zinc ore, and prepares for its run up the main line to the capital. CIÉ utilised its diesel locomotives on an all-line basis. Any locomotive could turn up anywhere between Cork and Belfast!

---

18. After the C class locomotives had been withdrawn, in 1995 CIÉ took delivery of new 3,200bhp Co-Cos which it classified 201. These locomotives also (coincidentally?) totalled 34 locomotives. Nos 206 to 210 carried the names of the same rivers as the GNR(I) VS class 4-4-0s with the same running numbers.

Outside Inchicore Works are two former C class locomotives that have been re-engined with 1,100bhp GM engines and renumbered B210 and B227. *Gerald Beesley*

Coming off the Howth branch at Howth Junction is B214 propelling a push-pull suburban train to Dublin. *Gerald Beesley*

Re-engining the A and C Class Diesel Electrics

Class	001 Co-Co
Re-engined	CIÉ Inchicore
CIÉ original class	A
Number in class	60
Introduced	1968
Diesel engine	GM EMD 12-645E 2-stroke
Engine power	1,325bhp*
Electric traction equipt.	Metropolitan-Vickers
Traction motors (6 dc)	MV137CW
Maximum tractive effort	46,000lbf
Maximum speed	85mph
Weight in w.o.	82tons 0cwt
Original number series	A1-A60
Number series when re-engined	A1R-A60R
Post-1972 number series	001-060

* Nos 002, 027, 035, 036, 046, 054, 056 and 059 received 1,650bhp engines and had 80mph maximum speed.

Class	201 Bo-Bo
Re-engined	CIÉ Inchicore
CIÉ original class	C
Number in class	34
Introduced	1970
Diesel engine	GM EMD 8-645E 2-stroke*
Engine power	1,100bhp
Electric traction equipt.	Metropolitan-Vickers
Traction motors (4 dc)	MV137CW
Maximum tractive effort	34,445lbf
Maximum speed	85mph
Weight in w.o.	61tons 10cwt
Original number series	C201-C234
Number series when re-engined	B201-B234
Post-1972 number series	201-234

* Nos C233 and C234 were experimentally re-engined in 1965-1966 with Maybach MD650 engines at 980bhp at 1,200rpm, until re-engined with GM engines in 1979-1980.

Re-engining the C class locomotives boosted their performance with double their original horsepower, thanks to the robustness of their original Metro-Vick electric traction equipment. 232 calls at Dublin Conolly, the former Amiens Street station, with a Drogheda to Wicklow outer suburban train formed of Park Royal stock. Loaded to up to six coaches, these locomotives would have struggled with such loads in their original condition.

No 208, the former C208 then B208, sits in the bay platform at Bray in 1984 with a short push-pull train for Greystones. The train is formed of two former diesel railcars with their traction equipment stripped out and 'vandal-proof' plastic seating installed. One ex-railcar acted as a driving trailer.

Chapter 25
MR BULLEID'S LEGACIES

Because of the edict from the UK's Curator of Historical Relics that locomotives for the national collection should be as near as possible to their original condition, no 'Merchant Navy' was proposed for the collection. Fortunately, private finance came from various quarters that in time enabled thirty-one Bulleid Pacifics to be purchased for preservation including eleven rebuilt 'Merchant Navy' locomotives. The first, bought direct from British Railways, was 35028 *Clan Line* whose support group maintain it in sparkling condition. It is depicted climbing the north ramp of Ais Gill near Newbiggin with the Lord Bishop commemorative train on 30 September 1978 when Bishop Treacy's memorial at Appleby station was unveiled.

Happily, 35029 *Ellerman Lines* was sectioned to become an educational exhibit at the National Railway Museum at York. For a couple of decades at least it stood upon motored rollers that enabled visitors to see the action of the Walschaerts valve gear in detail. At the time of writing in late 2019, 35029 stands over a normal inspection pit, while GWR 4-6-0 4003 *Lode Star* is on the rollers.

What is a legacy?

A fitting epitaph for any engineer is to acknowledge what remains of his work in real terms many years after his working life is over. Most engineers can quote a structure or design that they initiated that survived their retirement; or maybe a learned paper propounding a new management philosophy. Any author can quote some of his or her books or articles that are still in demand.[19]

Oliver Bulleid's legacies

OVB's obvious legacies in the UK are the thirty-two preserved steam locomotives of his designs that exist in the twenty-first century. There are eleven 'Merchant Navy' class locomotives still in existence, all rebuilds of course, of which 35028 *Clan Line* has been performing the longest in preservation. That engine and 35018 *British India Line* are not the only ones to have gained reputations as sparkling main line performers in their preservation years. We must not forget that 35029 *Ellerman Lines* was specially cut open for exhibiting in the National Railway Museum at York where it sometimes stands on rollers that allow its coupled wheels to rotate slowly so that new generations of visitors can see how a steam locomotive works.

The twenty preserved light Pacifics include ten originals and ten rebuilds. 34067 *Tangmere* and

---

19. A recent legacy from my own retirement years stands for all to see in Markeaton Park, Derby, namely the Famous Trains model railway building. The charity I set up opened this in April 2014. The building contains the East Midlands' largest OO-scale model railway and several others. It's open to the public every weekend and Monday throughout the year from 11am to 4pm, and will have received its 40,000th visitor by the time this book is published. I'm happy to quote that as a legacy.

34092 *City of Wells* (with a Giesl ejector) among others have put out some remarkable performances in recent decades.

33001, the preserved Q1 0-6-0, spent some years working on the Bluebell Railway in Sussex, for a time running as Southern Railway C 1. I was delighted to be hauled by it when Mary and I visited that railway on 6 September 1994 when we celebrated the fortieth anniversary of my starting work on British Railways. 33001 now sits in the great hall of the National Railway Museum. Perhaps its austere appearance looks a little out of place alongside such older gems as the Stirling single No 1 and GWR *Lode Star*, but it is good that this example of a successful Bulleid design should be on show there.

In fact, only three of the thirty-two preserved Bulleid locomotives are part of the national collection. In addition to the Q1 0-6-0, 'Battle of Britain' 4-6-2 34051 *Winston Churchill* is a static exhibit at York. It is there because BR's Curator of Historical Relics insisted that locomotives for the national collection had, wherever possible, to be in their technical 'as built' form, and 34051 fitted that ideal closely as well as bearing the famous name; and it was the engine that had hauled the great man's funeral train. The 'as built' rule is why there is no 'Merchant Navy' in the collection apart from 35029 despite the popularity of that class with the public. (Indeed, 850 *Lord Nelson* with its Lemâitre exhaust and self-trimming tender, both Bulleid modifications, only just crept in to become part of the collection!) All the other preserved Bulleid engines were rescued by privately-inspired funding.

I have already commented on a few of the technical advances that transferred successfully from the Bulleid locomotives into some of the BR standard locomotive designs. The biggest was the boiler of the 7MT 'Britannia' class. While it is not an exact copy, its overall dimensions are close to the Bulleid light Pacific boiler. Regrettably, the BR design avoided the benefits of the steel firebox and thermic syphons, lost on the anvil of conventionality. OVB's simple method of fixing steel tyres to steel wheels was used on the BR standards, as was the narrower-than-standard spacing of the main frames on those classes with wide

One of the twenty light Pacifics now in preservation is 34092 *City of Wells* which is looked after by a team at Howarth on the Keighley & Worth Valley Railway. On its home ground in 1985 34092 climbs away from Keighley with a train for Oxenhope. This engine has been a popular performer on main line work in recent decades.

Another light Pacific that has gained a good reputation for sparkling main line running is 'Battle of Britain' 4-6-2 34067 *Tangmere*. Several preserved locomotives earn money for their sponsors by appearing at gala days on heritage railways. 34067 spent a long weekend on the West Somerset Railway early in 2006 during that railway's 'Somerset & Dorset' gala. Here the clean machine leaves Blue Anchor station heading for the seaside resort of Minehead and carrying the correct headcode for an S&D service between Bath and Bournemouth West.

In the early 1990s, the Bluebell Railway was looking after the preserved Q1 on behalf of the National Railway Museum. On 6 September 1994 C 1 (known as 'Charlie One' on the Southern) had arrived at Kingscote with a train from Sheffield Park.

Once its active life on the Bluebell Railway was over, the preserved Q1 took up its place in the Great Hall of the National Railway Museum at York where it stands looking 'different' among classic steam locomotives such as a GWR 'King'. 34051 *Winston Churchill* is out of sight at the other end of the Hall.

fireboxes (7MT and 6MT Pacifics, and the 9F 2-10-0s). The Bulleid steam locomotives had tubular steel welded footsteps, as did the standard locomotives, and tender-back ladders, too.

On BR's diesel fleet, the earlier locomotives all used the Bulleid design of folding headcode discs that covered the marker lamps when closed. The first Type 4 designs copied the Bulleid 1Co bogies shamelessly. Indeed the English Electric Type 4 design, the erstwhile Class 40 in later years, was essentially the Southern's 10203 with a different body shape.

My main concern is the number of Bulleid features that were *not* used on the BR standard steam classes that perhaps ought to have been. For example, why did the entire BR standard fleet of 999 locomotives not use electric lighting in their cabs, over the injector overflow pipes and as marker lamps? Southern drivers were critical of the BR Class 5 4-6-0s because of this omission, as they also were of the wide tenders on the SR batches of Class 5s when compared with the modified tenders of the Bulleid Pacifics which had a much better rearwards view.

Also, the well-thought-out clasp brakes used on his Pacifics' coupled wheels were ignored in the BR standard range.

Keeping the idea of copper inner fireboxes alive was also strange in an age where the SR had proved the advantages of steel fireboxes with proper water treatment.

In Ireland one looks hard for any obvious Bulleid legacies today, apart from some of the preserved diesel locomotives and rolling stock. I think I am correct in saying that the first diesel locomotive servicing facility at Inchicore, known as 'The Ramps' in Diesel

2 Shop, was built during OVB's time there and survives today, but probably not much else. A few A class diesel locomotives, a B, and some Cs, Es and Gs carry the name forward, though in Ireland they regard them totally as either Metro-Vick or BRCW/Sulzer or Inchicore or Deutz products; OVB's name doesn't enter into the discussion there in the context of diesels, whereas the names of Lucas Collins, Jack Johnson and Matt Devereux (Assistant Running Superintendent, then from 25 January 1956 Assistant CME Maintenance) are often mentioned. The turf-burner 0-6-6-0T, like the 'Leader' before it, was withdrawn and scrapped once its author had left that particular railway for good.

However, it is often overlooked that, with the turf-burner 0-6-6-0T in particular, Bulleid had proved that a steam locomotive on two bogies could run well with similar characteristics of diesel locomotives. CC 1 was not economically better than a diesel. It was too heavy, and in history there are other types of total-adhesion, double-bogie steam locomotives that worked well, notably some types of Mallet and Fairlie locomotives that were also of moderate weight.

Of the locomotive classes that were taken into stock during OVB's tenure of the CME posts but were not his original designs, there is the Q class 0-6-0 30541 on the Bluebell Railway, at least four USA 0-6-0Ts, one Ashford-built 0-6-0 diesel electric shunter and in Ireland one of the two Bo-Bo diesel prototypes.

Oliver Bulleid will however be remembered for many years yet, even by people who never met him in person. His reputation as an original and adventurous engineer will continue to provoke discussion among railway enthusiasts and engineers for as long as people discuss steam locomotives. And that can't be a bad legacy to have, can it?

Apart from 1100 in the museum at Cultra, there are several preserved diesel locomotives from the Bulleid era in Ireland. Soon after being restored to something like its original silver livery, former CIÉ Co-Co A39 stands at Inchicore Works on 30 October 1998. The outer colours belie the fact that it is a re-engined locomotive.

Mr Bulleid's Legacies • 215

Visible in this group of restored Irish locomotives, nearest the camera, are Metro-Vick Co-Cos A3 (right) and A13. They are seen on 19 May 2018 standing on tracks laid in a field at Moyasta in County Clare having been evicted from storage, mainly in Dublin. The three-feet gauge track on the left is part of the heritage West Clare Railway's nascent future route to Kilkee, an aspiration that is slowly moving forward. The broad gauge collection here is isolated from the main line railways of Ireland. Other locomotives have fared better, being cared for by the Irish Traction Group at Carrick-on-Suir near Waterford or on heritage railways such as the Downpatrick & Country Down Railway.

After withdrawal, five of the ten CIÉ G class locomotives entered preservation. G611 was photographed during a visit to what is now called the Downpatrick & Country Down Railway near Newtownards in Northern Ireland.

Controversy is never very far away when Mr Bulleid's creations are discussed. For example, on the platform at Bishop's Lydeard on the West Somerset Railway, 34067 *Tangmere* waits patiently as a passenger harangues the engine crew about his pet theory, while a small crowd looks on. The driver and fireman look suitably bemused!

APPENDIX 1: CIÉ INVITATIONS TO TENDER FOR DIESEL LOCOMOTIVES, 1952

Alsthom, Paris, France.
Montreal Locomotive Works, Ltd., New York, USA.
Société Anonyme John Cockerill, Seraing, Belgium.
Baume et Marpent, Haine Saint Pierre, Belgium.
Birmingham Railway Carriage & Wagon Co. Ltd., Smethwick, UK.
Brissoneau et Lotz, Paris, France.
Brush Traction Ltd., Loughborough, UK.
Crossley Brothers Ltd., Manchester, UK.
Daimler-Benz Aktiengesellschaft, Stuttgart, Germany.
Davey, Paxman & Co., Ltd., Colchester, UK.
De Dietrich & Cie., Reichshoffen, France.
Deutsche Bundesbahn Hauptverwaltung, Offenbach (Main), Germany.
English Electric Co. Ltd., Marconi House, London, UK.
George Fischer Limited, Schaffhausen, Switzerland.
Batignolles-Chatillon, Paris, France.
General Electric Co., Dublin, Ireland.
General Motors Corporation, La Grange, Illinois.
International General Electric C. of New York, Ltd., London, UK.
Arn. Jung Lokomotivfabrik G.m.b.H., Jungenthal bei Kirchen an der Sieg, Germany.
Klockner-Humboldt-Deutz, Köln, Germany.
The Hunslet Engine Works, Leeds, UK.
M.a.K., Kiel, Germany.
M.a.N., Nürnberg, Germany.
Metropolitan-Vickers Electrical Co. Ltd., Manchester, UK.
North British Locomotive Co. Ltd., Glasgow, UK.

Nuove Reggiane, Reggio Emelia, Italy.
Nydqvist & Holm Aktiebolag, Nohab, Trollhattan, Sweden.
Oerlikon Engineering Co., Zurich, Switzerland.
C. Wykeham & Co., Ltd., London, UK.
Renault, Billancourt, France.
Sulzer Bros. (London) Ltd., London, UK.
Clayton Equipment Co. Ltd., London, UK.
Drewry Car Co. Ltd., London, UK.
Hudswell Clarke & Co. Ltd., Leeds, UK.
Fiat, Societa Anonima, Torino, Italy.
Metropolitan Cammell Carriage & Wagon Co. Ltd., Birmingham, UK.
Yorkshire Engine Co. Ltd., Sheffield, UK.
Fairbanks, Morse & Co., Chicago, USA.
Compagnie de Fives-Lille, Paris, France.
Breda Elettromeccanica, Milano, Italy.
Simmering-Graz-Pauker, Wien, Austria.

Twenty-two of the above forty-one invitees responded to the invitation to tender.

APPENDIX 2: AVAILABILITY AND RELIABILITY OF CIÉ DIESEL TRACTION

Availability for 20 weeks ending 25 October 1958

Class/Type	Fleet size	Average No. in traffic	Availability %	Total miles run	Miles per unit per week
A	60	48.0	80	79,113	1,648
B	14*	11.2	80	17,559	1,568
C	34	23.8	70	15,527	652
AEC railcars	60	47.4	79	67,759	1,430

* Including the two prototypes.

Reliability of diesel traction to 25 October 1958

Class/Type	Fleet miles to 25-10-1958	Total failures	Miles per failure	Engine failures	Miles per engine failure	Ratio of engine to total failures	Engine make
A	10,086,492 from 18-9-1955	1,025	9,840	440	22,924	43%	Crossley
B	1,531,472 from 1-5-1956	195	7,854	73	20,979	37%	Sulzer
C	945,196 from 18-3-1957	143	6,610	75	12,602	52%	Crossley
AEC railcars	5,717,132 from 18-3-1957	128	44,605	12	476,428	9%	AEC

These statistics were extracted from a report by D. Herlihy titled *Review of the change from steam to diesel traction on Córas Iompair Éireann*, dated November 1958, and adjusted to UK convention.

BIBLIOGRAPHY

Rebuilt 35017 *Belgian Marine* storms up the 1 in 99 of Pokesdown bank near Bournemouth with the Down Bournemouth Belle Pullman train on 1 February 1959.

Allen, Cecil J. and Townroe, S.C., *The Bulleid Pacifics of the Southern*, Ian Allan, 1951 and 1976. *The first useful publication outlining the development, design and performance of the original Bulleid Pacifics.*

Allen, Cecil J., *The Locomotive Exchanges*, Ian Allan, 1949. *An essential summary of a most interesting if not always scientifically-managed set of comparative locomotive trials.*

Boocock, Colin, *Locomotive Compendium – Ireland*, Ian Allan Publishing, 2009. *Probably the only book that illustrates and describes every locomotive type to operate on the national railways in Ireland from 1949 to 2009.*

Boocock, Colin, *Locomotive Compendium – Southern*, Ian Allan Publishing, 2010. *My attempt to summarise and detail all Southern Railway-originated locomotives operating on the Southern Railway and Region from 1948.*

Bulleid, H.A.V., *Bulleid of the Southern*, Ian Allan, 1977. *A valuable biography by OVB's son expanding on Sean Day-Lewis's work.*

Burridge, Frank, *Nameplates of the Big Four including British Railways*, Oxford Publishing Co., 1975. *Certainly the definitive publication that covers nameplates of steam and non-steam locomotives from 1923 to 1975, including inherited designs from earlier times. In addition to name lists, the book illustrates each type of plate with dimensioned drawings as well as good photographs.*

Chacksfield, J.E., *Ron Jarvis – From Midland Compound to the HST*, The Oakwood Press, 2004. *A well-researched biography of the right man in the right place at the right time.*

Day-Lewis, Sean, *Bulleid – Last Giant of Steam*, George Allen & Unwin, 1964 and 1968. *The first objective, definitive biography of O.V.S. Bulleid and his locomotives.*

Robertson, Kevin, *The Leader Project – Fiasco or Triumph?* Ian Allan Publishing under its OPC imprint, 2017. *Packed with probably the most complete collection ever published of drawings, diagrams and photographs of these unusual locomotives, and a most comprehensive text, full of useful facts supported by the author's own conclusions.*

Scott-Morgan, John, *The Original Bulleid Pacifics*, Haynes Publishing, 2012. *A wide-ranging discussion of the Pacifics before rebuilding, including some personal reminiscences by people intimately involved in their operation; profusely illustrated.*

Shepherd, Ernie, *Bulleid and the Turf Burner and other experiments with Irish Steam Traction*, KRB Publications, 2004. *An excellent analysis of the efforts in Ireland that went into proving how steam locomotives could burn peat ('turf' in Ireland). The book describes and illustrates in detail the trials with 2-6-0 356 and the development and construction of the Bulleid 0-6-6-0T CC 1, and summarises trial running with useful appendices.*

http://www.railfaneurope.net/, *the web site of the European Railfan Server that lists useful data of all locomotive types currently and recently operating on the national railways of all countries in Europe.*

http://www.semgonline.com/, *the web site of the Southern Railway E-Group that contains a mine of information and listings about almost anything you can think of covering the Southern Railway and its successors.*

INDEX

100mph, 98, 189, 191, 201

AEC, 14, 134, 135, 219

B-F-B wheels/Boxpok, 49, 73, 75, 107, 108, 111, 176
Branch lines, 39, 133, 157, 159, 163, 165
BRC&W, 14, 153, 155, 156
Bredin E.C., 11, 130
Brighton drawing office, 15, 19, 20, 99, 114
Brighton Works, 14, 70, 118, 119, 121, 122, 126, 184, 195, 200
Brush, 131, 135, 138, 153
Bulleid valve gear, 47, 48, 80, 115, 118, 177, 181

Click J.G., 8, 18-22, 175, 177, 199
Collins L., 136, 137, 214
Crossley, 14, 19, 146, 147, 149, 151, 158-160, 203, 205, 217, 219

Deutz, 162, 163, 214, 217
Devereux M., 214
Downpatrick & County Down Railway, 163, 168, 215

Eastleigh Works, 54, 55, 62, 70, 71, 86, 100, 202
Ellson G., 23, 42, 43

Financial back-check, 190

General Motors/GM/EMD, 14, 15, 136, 137, 140, 141, 145, 147, 151, 156, 159, 203-207

GNR, 17, 19, 43
GNR(I)/GNRB, 137, 144, 167, 205
Gresley H.N., 16, 17, 42, 43, 45, 46, 60, 87
Giesl exhaust, 22, 87, 211

Herlihy D., 14, 136, 219

Inchicore, 15, 16, 19, 22, 131, 135-141, 143, 144, 147, 150, 159, 160, 164, 166, 168, 171, 174, 175, 177-180, 203, 205-207, 214
Irish Traction Group, 156, 163, 215
Ivatt H.A., 16, 19

Jarvis R.G., 15, 19-21, 121, 181, 189, 191, 221
Johnson J.J., 214

Lemaître, 23-31, 36, 39, 46, 60, 74, 87, 181, 211
LMS, 14, 19, 20, 35, 36, 39, 43, 45, 64, 70, 73, 108, 122, 124, 126, 184, 195, 200
LNER, 16, 17, 39, 43, 64, 99, 119, 182

Maunsell R.E.L., 19, 23, 26, 27, 29, 31, 35-42, 66, 80, 81, 83, 102-104, 119, 127
Maybach, 166-168, 203, 207
Mekydro, 166-168
Metro-Vick, 14, 131, 137, 139, 145, 146, 154-160, 204-207, 214, 215
Milne Commission, 14, 19, 131, 134
Mirrlees, 131, 135, 138
Morse chain, 48, 175

National Railway Museum, 22, 76, 210, 211-213
Newbridge accident, 168

Oil bath, 47, 58, 82, 181

Park Royal, 14, 134, 135, 139, 159, 207
Prototype, 14, 15, 19, 34, 99, 121, 124-127, 136-141, 146, 155, 174-176, 203, 214, 219

Raworth S., 66-71
Ricardo, 16, 115, 175, 182
Riddles R.A., 19, 20, 121, 182
Rocker shaft, 18, 47, 48, 58, 182

Second World War, 14, 79, 108, 136
Sevenoaks accident, 23, 168
Stephenson's valve gear, 36, 37, 74, 75, 218
Sulzer, 14, 131, 136, 139, 141, 146, 153-156, 214, 218

The Emergency, 136
Thermic syphons, 44, 45, 117, 181, 211

Ulster Folk & Transport Museum, 141, 214

Walker Brothers of Wigan, 142, 143
Walschaerts valve gear, 36, 46-48, 100, 182, 184, 210
West Clare Railway, 136, 142-144, 215